Tales of the State

Tales of the State

Narrative in Contemporary U.S. Politics and Public Policy

Edited By

Sanford F. Schram and Philip T. Neisser

ROWMAN & LITTLEFIELD PUBLISHERS, INC.

Lanham • Boulder • New York • Oxford

ROWMAN & LITTLEFIELD PUBLISHERS, INC.

Published in the United States of America
by Rowman & Littlefield Publishers, Inc.
4720 Boston Way, Lanham, Maryland 20706

12 Hid's Copse Road
Cummor Hill, Oxford OX2 9JJ, England

British Library Cataloguing in Publication Information Available

Library of Congress Cataloging-in-Publication Data

Tales of the state : narrative in contemporary U.S. politics and
public policy / edited by Sanford F. Schram and Philip T. Neisser.
p. cm.
Includes bibiographical references and index.
ISBN 0–8476–8502–0 (cloth : alk. paper). — ISBN 0–8476–8503–9
(pbk. : alk. paper)
1. Political planning—United States—Case studies. 2. United States
—Social policy—Case studies. 3. United States—Foreign relations—
Case studies. 4. Discourse analysis, Narrative.
I. Schram, Sanford. II. Neisser, Philip T., 1957– .
JK468.P64T35 1997
320.973—dc21 97-9879
CIP

ISBN 0–8476–8502–0 (cloth : alk. paper)
ISBN 0–8476–8503–9 (pbk. : alk. paper)

Printed in the United States of America

™ The paper used in this publication meets the minimum requirements of American National Standard for Information Sciences—Permanence of Paper for Printed Library Materials, ANSI Z39.48–1984.

Contents

Acknowledgments

Many people helped bring this collection together. The editors want to thank all the contributors for agreeing to participate and cooperating in ways that made even the most mundane aspects of editing an enjoyable exercise. The editors also thank Scott Daniels at the University of Hawai'i and Jackie Rush at the State University of New York at Potsdam for extremely capable assistance in preparing the manuscript for publication, and Jennifer Knerr and Julie Kuzneski at Rowman & Littlefield for wise editorial guidance. Sanford Schram thanks all his colleagues at the University of Hawaii and elsewhere who commented on the contributions to this volume and Joan, Jack, and Ryan who provided support throughout this project. Phil Neisser offers his thanks to northern New York, to SUNY Potsdam—students, staff, and faculty—to his friends, to Zoo, Groove, to the trio, and to his family, especially Andrea.

Introduction

Sanford F. Schram and Philip T. Neisser

The essays collected in this volume are organized around the theme that just as narrative is central to people in their everyday private lives, so it is to the public affairs of the state. For instance, just as there are "folktales" that lend coherence to the lives of "common folk," "policy-tales" do the same for policy elites. Both elites and masses rely on unsubstantiated stories for making sense of what they do, and for both, these tales can at times take extreme forms. For example, it is debatable which is more questionable: (1) stories of right-wing militia groups that refer to the U.S. government as ZOG—Zionist Occupation Government tied to a conspiracy of Jewish-British bankers (i.e., the Illuminati) who are dedicated to forging a One World Government (MacDonald, 1980); or (2) stories by presidents and their minions about how the liberalism of the 1960s created an irresponsible welfare class (Magnet, 1993).

What about the differences between (1) government-sanctioned research that locates the origins of AIDS in monkeys in Africa, and (2) rumors among some African Americans that suggest AIDS was invented by the government to eliminate African-American males? The "research results" might seem more factual than the "rumor," but in either case tale-telling is at work. The respective stories make sense of events according to a less than factually documented storyline (Fiske, 1993).

As the essays in this volume demonstrate, stories, some more controversial than others, as well as narrative practices in general, play a pervasive role not only in popular culture but also in politics and public policy making. So much so, that at times the narratives prevalent in one realm become indistinguishable from those in another realm (see Scott, 1990). For instance, elite and mass stories regarding the Vietnam War have often merged to make the democratic aspirations of the then-North Vietnamese seem unbelievable while their hoarding of American prisoners of war (POWs) and those missing-in-action (MIAs) seem entirely believable (Franklin, 1993). The essays in this book therefore not only share a focus of how narrative is as important for politics as it is for anything else; they also help demonstrate how politics is often about the same stories that influence other spheres of life.

The Plan of the Book

The essays that follow illustrate the many forms of politically powerful narrative, from origin stories about the Founding of the United States as a "New Promised Land" to contemporary bureaucratic legends about those who receive public assistance. Tales of the state range from rumors, gossip, and folktales to the use of stereotypes and icons, to the implied stories buried in the seemingly neutral analytical models of "political science," "economics," and "sociology."

Initial chapters stress the role of stories of history and identity that tap the prevailing mythology of "America." Other early chapters emphasize how stories help provide identity for key political actors, whether it is the president or a Supreme Court justice. Several authors emphasize how selective narrative practices, especially unsubstantiated rumors regarding policy problems, are used episodically to construct politically-biased depictions of public problems. Some essays emphasize narrative practices that bolster prevailing but questionable assumptions about the political economy. Finally, several chapters emphasize narrative practices that are embedded in all discourse, making the unavoidable political selectivity of narrative—sometimes called "bias"—an ineliminable part of all representational practices, including even those of the state.

In addition to this diversity, these chapters have common themes. They help show, for example, how policy narrative is a particularly effective medium for reinscribing race, gender, or class identities in ways that have profound political consequences affecting how people both get to influence and are influenced by politics. Stories of welfare queens, black criminals, foreign terrorists, or even free-traders and other policy characters are seen not just as another dimension to the politics of making public policy. They also comprise a critically constitutive medium that shapes the identities of both those who enact policy and those who are acted upon by it.

Another common theme is the pervasiveness of narrative. Recognizing the constitutive role of stories in practicing politics and making public policy lets us consider how such practices and policies are themselves narratives. The term "public policy" already masks its own subject matter, making it a matter of policy (within the discipline, if not the state) that public policy is assumed to be some sort of entity that does not need to be interrogated for its own narrativity. Yet what are public policies but stories narrating our relations (between citizens, between the citizen and the state, between states, etc.) in politically selective ways? Whether the stories are about foreign enemies in a brave new world order, global environmental change, postindustrialism, illegal immigration, welfare dependency, or the state of race relations, the politics of public policy-making is played out in terms of stories that mediate how public problems are comprehended.

Part I is entitled "Origin Stories." Michael J. Shapiro examines the role, past and present, of anti-immigrant narratives in the process of constituting that never finally formed entity called "America." Carl Swidorski looks at another foundational tale when he critically examines the story of U.S. history as a "march of liberty." Finally, Miriam B. Rosenthal and Sanford F. Schram examine how the ever-popular "American Dream" continues to operate as a pervasive, if tacit, narrative that has profound implications for how policy discourse is framed.

Part II, "Institutions, Actors, and Narratives," examines tale-telling as it unfolds in the most obviously political realm of governmental institutions and electoral campaigns. John Kenneth White notes the centrality of performance and storytelling to the office of the president of the United States. Sanford F. Schram argues that the political power of the Contract with America lies largely in its power as representational practice: a text/image that reinscribes the basis for disciplining the citizenry under a retrenched social welfare state. Leslie J. Vaughan ends with an examination of the strategic tale-telling of Clarence Thomas. As is well-known, he successfully battled to win confirmation as a Supreme Court justice. Vaughan, however, tells a relatively unknown tale about how Thomas won confirmation in part by telling tales about himself. These were stories of personal uplift that Thomas unwittingly claimed reflected how he emulated his hero Bigger Thomas—the self-hating, misogynist African-American male in Richard Wright's *Native Son.*

Part III is called "Identity Stories in Public Policy." Here Jonathan Goldberg-Hiller examines how gay rights opponents in Colorado and elsewhere in recent years have tried to resist the successes of the gay rights movement. Goldberg-Hiller highlights the strategy of "disidentification" that identifies gays and lesbians with those in power and disidentifies them with other oppressed groups. Next, R. Scott Daniels looks at the battle over "freedom of expression" on the Internet. It may be that what some find so threatening is not exactly "pornography" but the cyberworld's apparent allowance for different narrative practices that allow for the construction of different and transgressive identities. Barbara Cruikshank also looks at identity, inverting the sometimes expected relation of narrative to practice when she stresses how the material practices of the state give rise to stereotype-reinforcing narratives about welfare queens. Finally, Gerard Fergerson examines how a new place-based discourse reinscribes racial inferiority by embedding it in coded language of "the inner-city underclass."

In part IV, "Tales of Domestic Policy," Sanford F. Schram, Lawrence Nitz, and Gary Krueger examine how welfare migration is a persistent, if factually unsupported, rumor in both popular culture and policy deliberations. Joseph Kling dissects the idea of "devolution," the turning of more governmental authority over to the states. Kling demonstrates how devolution is itself premised on a questionable, and latently discriminatory, implied narrative that Republicans, and to a lesser extent Democrats, accepted about who are the people to whom government should be accountable. Phillip H. Sandro highlights the factual misrepresentations and ideological selectivity of the common policy assumption that small business is the engine of job growth. Joel Best provides an example of how advocates often use undocumented statistics without checking their sources in order to build support for their claims. The example is of the unsubstantiated rumor about the declining numbers of white male workers. Best shows how it grew out of a statistic in a government report that then took on a life of its own as a policy-tale independent of its original context. Ruthanne Kurth-Schai and Charles R. Green examine the dominant stories used in education policy debates and offer the case for one particularly nuanced version that can serve as the basis for more enlightened policy.

Part V is entitled "Tales of Global Policy." Donald R. Culverson examines how racist stereotypes were embedded in the policy narratives of government officials charged with framing U.S. policy toward South Africa. Joseph Peschek looks at how exaggerated stories about the Soviet Union were used to induce "threat inflation" and drive up the human, social, cultural and economic cost of fighting the Cold War. Philip T. Neisser examines how the narratives associated with the North American Free Trade Agreement (NAFTA) were premised on exploiting the almost-sacred story of how a nation's wealth is tied to its commitment to free trade with other countries. The particular version of "free trade" that was used to support NAFTA was derived from a set of stories about postindustrialism, technology, and progress—stories that were themselves tied to tales that helped constitute the industrial age. Frances Fox Piven ends the book with a meditation on whether globalization is inevitable or even necessary, or whether it is only being narrated as such in order to facilitate political reorganization on terms favorable to elites.

Some Terms For Narrative Analysis

Some terminological distinctions might help the reader follow how these essays examine the role of narrative in contemporary U.S. politics. "Stories" are discrete narratives focused on describing or explaining a particular phenomenon, such as apartheid or welfare dependency. Stories can be called "narrative practices" or even "representational practices" but so can other forms of textual representation including literary tropes, stereotypes, or even popular icons. These practices sometimes help build "imaginaries," fabulous ways of seeing that become more than fable as they enter into and constitute communities and individuals.

Narrative therefore helps constitute the world as we know it. It is in this sense that some say even human identities are "written." Thus, in the terminology of inscription used by many, stories are said to "inscribe," or "reinscribe," realities upon the individual body or even the collective body politic. In fact, "the body," whether individual or collective, from this perspective can be denaturalized. It can be seen not as a preexisting natural phenomenon but a textual representation that people, individually and collectively, embody. And when we embody a narrative practice, we help to reinscribe it in our individual and collective selves.

Such narrative practices then can also be said to "mediate" reality: not only to filter, but to produce, as when perceptions are mediated by attitudes or when behavior emulates a model or approximates a norm. Mediated realities, like "the global economy" or "the underclass," are shaped by that which is apparently outside the "thing itself." Yet, we can never know the "thing itself" independent of how it is mediated in narrative and other representational practices. As such, state stories, like all narratives, are "already there." They are "already there" in the sense that they are not so much an artifact of a preexisting factual reality as they are constitutive of it and even written into it. It is this "already there-ness" that makes such stories so potent—i.e., they are not as dependent upon fact as perhaps we often would like to assume. Stories therefore are arguably "foundational," preexisting facts and living beyond them, often surviving empirical refutation, in not just popular culture but everything else including politics and public policy-making. That is why "counterstories" that offer alternative narratives as to why things are the way they are can be an important political resource. Therefore, the analysis of narrative in politics becomes a critical practice as well as a theoretical activity.

The Value of Narrative Analysis

One could argue that beyond specifying terms it is important to make certain analytical distinctions. For instance, it might be important to distinguish implicit narrative structure from consciously told tales, and to distinguish among stories, gossip, and rumor. It might be important as well to go on to suggest which types of tales operate most frequently and effectively where and when. It might be even worthwhile to revisit the distinction between folktales told by the common folk and the types of stories traded by policy elites. Or to highlight how narrative works in policy-making as opposed to policy analysis. Yet such distinctions are not the concern of this volume and perhaps they ought not to be. The point is that stories, wherever told, whether unconsciously articulated through the invocation of prevailing discourse or consciously fashioned by participating in the rumor mill, are critical constitutive forces in politics and public policymaking.

This emphasis on narrative grows out of the emerging literature that provides an alternative to the dominant positivist understanding of the public policy-making process and public policy analysis. A growing number of policy analysts have emphasized how representational practices (whether they are rhetorical, discursive, or symbolic) contextualize, frame, or narrate policy problems and their solutions (see Stone, 1997; Rein and Schon, 1994; Roe, 1994; Forester, 1990; Hawkesworth, 1988). Policy analysis and policy-making, necessarily, whether intentionally or not, are activities that are critically dependent upon these representational practices, and the study and evaluation of public policy must correspondingly of necessity attend to how these representational practices mediate what policy-makers, analysts, and citizens take to be the reality and objects of concern of the political process (Norton, 1993; Dolan and Dumm, 1993).

According to our particular offshoot of this emerging literature, the analyst's primary goal should not be to distinguish reasoned deliberation from instances of rumormongering, but to interrogate all policy-making activity for its narrativity and assess the consequences given the persuasiveness of particular tales (Stone, 1997). One major advantage of this sort of approach to policy analysis is that it creates an opening for a variety of types of analysis that traditionally have been excluded from the field, such as psychoanalysis, Marxism, social constructionism, structuralism, poststructuralism, cultural studies, etc.

Yet what some proponents of narrative policy analysis fail to emphasize is that stories and such do not so much misread political reality as construct political space itself, letting us know where it begins and where it ends, who populates it and who does not, which of their concerns are to be included and which are to be excluded. Stories in particular create a narrative coherence that not only defines but helps realize political spaces, and they necessarily do so in politically biased ways. Stories map space and keep time in ways that impose coherence on identities, interests, and institutionalized groupings. As Michael Shapiro (1988) has suggested, political space is literally materialized through the enactment of narratives when political actors use these stories as scripts for engaging in political performances, from lobbying to policy formulation, from mass mobilization to posturing by political leadership. And since it is almost always the case that more than one story can be told to make sense of any particular area of concern or issue, stories are necessarily not innocuous and disinterested but instead are potentially dangerous and interested. They are critically constitutive elements in shaping political practice and making public policy, as a growing group of political scientists (see Dolan and Dumm, 1993) and policy analysts (see Rein and Schon, 1994) have come to emphasize.

We do not intend the term "story" to denigrate any "knowledges" on the grounds that they are narrative in form and/or fail to meet objective standards, as all such beliefs contain important "social truths." Tale-telling is an important way in which people, coalitions, and groups let others know who they are, what their interests are, and how those interests can be served, whether it is in terms of fulfilling "the American Dream," the "social contract," the intentions of the "Founding Fathers," the "global political economy," the "brave new world," etc. Those in privileged positions need to learn to "listen" to the knowing voices of the weak, the marginalized, the homeless, the poor, etc. John Fiske (1993), for instance, has suggested how subjugated knowledges, often taking the form of "counterhistories" or "alternative narratives," constitute a form of popular resistance to what passes for knowledge among the dominant "power-bloc" and cannot be fairly assessed according to hegemonic standards of rational empiricism. Fiske offers the example of what he calls "blackstream knowledge" about racial genocide as a counternarrative that offers an alternative understanding of the history of treatment of African Americans in the United States—an understanding that is not directly interpretable according to the prevailing "mainstream" standards of rational empirical evidence (Delgado, 1989). By staging an encounter between blackstream and mainstream knowledges as competing narratives with competing standards for evaluating their own evidence, Fiske provides a way of seeing how all, even statistical, knowledge is narrative and therefore political (also see Gusfield, 1984). Once the pervasiveness of narrative is recognized, it becomes easier to see why counterstories of a government conspiracy to eliminate African-American males are too easily dismissed while hegemonic, often scientific, stories of self-induced violence among African-American males are too easily accepted.

This then is not a question of factual versus narrative knowledge, as Hayden White (1980) would have it. It is not a question of fiction versus nonfiction or of the facts of true stories versus the pulp of other stories. Even true stories are still stories. Facts, along with everything else, are constructed through what we are calling stories. As Jean-François Lyotard (1980) suggests, all is narrative. For Lyotard, to use language, to communicate, to promote common understanding, whether through scientific study, investigative journalism, or political argument, is to build narrative structure and to tell a story.

While some of the contributions to this volume are grounded in the not-so-Lyotardian distinction between factual versus narrative knowledge, all the contributions provide opportunities for examining the power of storytelling in influencing politics and policy-making. Taken together, these examinations reveal politics and policy-making as always about "reinventing government," if not in the terms of the 1990s policymaking fad (Osborne and Gaebler, 1992). To argue for "reinventing government" is unremarkable in the sense that political discourse is always reinventing "government" so that it can be said that there is some better way to fashion the state and make public policy, even if that better way is really a recycling of old concerns in new narratives designed to make more appealing the interests to be served in those approaches. The 1990s version of reinventing government is a case in point—a highly selective, partial reconstruction of what government is and how it can be executed more efficiently through privatization and the adoption of private sector management techniques.

While narratives construct facts and we must accept their ineliminable political character, none of this is to say that one story is as good as another, or as it is often complained: "Well, then, it's all relative." Although it might not be possible to get entirely beyond narratives to a purely factual basis of the world, some tales are tall tales, not only in that they do not accord with established facts, but also because such stories constitute a form of denial, or a construction of reality that erases alternative knowledges, perhaps covering up what would otherwise be obvious facts.

Every narrative simultaneously builds what Mieke Bal (1988) calls "structures of attention" and "structures of inattention." Narratives that structure inattention to profound instances of violence, subordination, or even just plain neglect can be said to be, if not tall tales, then tales of less than full disclosure that need to be read according to a counternarrative that builds in attention to these instances of wrongdoing. Thus, the typical stories of welfare recipients as fraudulent render invisible the strength, hard work, sacrifice, caring, and survival skills of those who have almost no resources. To highlight this silence implicit in the narrative voice of welfare stories is to suggest a different narrative. One can "unread" stories, highlight "remainders" of narratives, and read again for what they have left out (Shapiro, 1995). Highlighting narrative exclusions opens the door to a politics of inclusion and alters the political situation.

Some narratives then are better than others. It just might be, however, that the grounds for saying so are not to be ultimately found in some free-standing ready reserve of objective facts we can point to for assessing any policy-tale. In fact, emphasizing how policy struggle is a textual problem of competing narratives enables us to question the distinction between indeterminate symbolic dimensions and determinate material dimensions of social life. Stuart Hall (1986) has written: "we need to think of material conditions in their determinate discursive form, not as a fixed absolute." Indeed, the grounds for assessing narratives are politics itself—i.e., the narratives of politics suggest the politics of narratives. While lies and unsubstantiated rumors in policy discourse can be challenged on one level by an appeal to facts and documentation (as, say, in the rumors about Anita Hill in her charges of sexual harassment against Clarence Thomas; see Mayer and Abramson, 1994), at another level all narratives, including all tales of the state, must be examined for the political implications of their narrativity. Those interested in revising existing imbalances in power assess state narratives for their structures of inattention and promote those stories that structure attention to what has previously been left out.

Politics and public policy-making are in good part a critical struggle over which tales the state will tell (Stone, 1997). Our approach holds that political and policy analysis necessarily must account for this struggle by examining the role of narrative in state practices and highlighting why it is that some tales tend to have more currency than others. The idea is to engage in critical thinking about the relationship of politics, narrative, and policy analysis. In the process, policy analysis becomes part of politics and politics becomes part of policy analysis.

The chapters that follow are of course themselves differing narratives about the role of narratives in politics and public policy-making and therefore what they have to say about the politics of narratives applies to them as well. This might be unsettling if we are looking for political or policy analysis to serve as some safe, stabilized site for the articulation of objective and rational analysis of politics or public policy. Yet political and policy analytical texts, as much as any other texts, ignore their textuality only at their own peril. Much of their politics lies in their narrativity. Proponents of institutional, behavioral, rational choice, and other approaches ascendent among political scientists and policy analysts often dismiss the narrative dimension of not only politics and public policy-making but also of their own texts. In fact, what are institutions, individuals, and rational interests, if they are not understandings in narrative form about established practices, persons, and principles for making optimal decisions? Study of the politics and policy-making from institutional, individual, and rational choice perspectives needs in each case to be revised to take account of the storied nature of what is referred to as the literal institution, the real self, and the objectively rational choice. Each of these is a narrative artifact of analytical stories.

Therefore, this book has several goals. One is to highlight the role of narrative in politics and policy-making. Another is to promote a more politicized policy analysis. Building on both of these is still another goal, which is to undermine the validity of the elite/folk distinction that supports some of our society's most pivotal fables about who is authorized to act on behalf of whom. Once we recognize that elites tell tales too, then it becomes more possible to challenge ascendent tales and offer alternatives by including the common folk in the process of constructing tales of the state. The point is to suggest a more democratic view of policy knowledge and in the process enter into efforts to democratize ongoing political and policy struggles.

Why These Tales for This State?

One important initial question is: What are the most influential narratives of the contemporary U.S. political system? Can we identify those stories of origins, institutions, or practices that are the most critical for exercising power in U.S. politics and public policy today? Some stories, for instance, can be said to be integral to U.S. political practice, whereas others build on these "constitutive" narratives. Some stories of elections, for example, are constitutive of the very practice of elections, as in accounts that imply that people are rational agents who can choose freely in voting or other activities. Without this idea present, an "election" would not be an election. On the other hand, there are tales that, while nonconstitutive in relation to elections as elections, are nonetheless fundamental in that they help constitute U.S. political reality. One such tale that informs U.S. elections is that of the country's alleged democratic roots, Founding Fathers and all. By this tale, a hard-won revolution in the name of individual freedom and the rights of the majority triumphed over tyranny; thus citizens should be thankful of the very chance to cast a ballot. Like so many tales, this story has life independent of the historical facts because of the ways it makes people feel, and the interests it serves, in the present. Should this tale be transformed, elections in the United States—their meaning and functions, even their form—would probably be substantially altered; arguably that is what is happening to electoral politics today as the United States confronts rampant voter absenteeism.

Such fundamental tales of the state, whether constitutive of institutions or not, specify a special kind of meaning that is common, and thereby help construct disparate individuals as "citizens of a state." They take individuals and make them into "a people" (Connolly, 1991). They help engender a process of identification that mobilizes the citizenry on behalf of the state and legitimates the state acting on behalf of its citizenry (Edelman, 1988). "America" comes to be materialized through discourse, embodied in its citizenry, and represented in the state, whether it is in times of war or at tax time, whether it is to promote the sacrifice of lives or money on behalf of the state.

In other words, both mundane stories of daily life and dramatic accounts from the frontlines of battle execute a sort of narrative statecraft by reinforcing the banal truths by which political institutions operate, thereby serving to buttress the processes by which identities and practices are or are not affirmed. For Richard Ashley (1989), on the grand stage of international relations statehood is constructed out of manhood by way of narratives that enable the sovereign state to be seen as standing in for the sovereign selves who constitute the polity even when the populace has not had the opportunity to authorize state action. Yet the storied construction of sovereignty is matched by stories of everyday living, including the contemporary "urban legend." These stories are often founded on beliefs that arise as a product of the social strain of contemporary urban life. Urban legends "express fears that the complexities of modern society threaten the traditional social order." Joel Best (1990) explains a variety of stories, from rumors about carjackings to Halloween sadism and product tampering, in this way. Best, for instance, shows that with scant empirical evidence Halloween sadism has become taken-for-granted; the story lives on because of a variety of functions it performs and interests it serves. It gives a name to people's anxiety, thus transforming it into a more manageable fear, while at the same time deflecting attention from threats to children that are more difficult to confront but are much more important. Like stories of international terrorism, urban legends give voice to anxiety about personal control that in turn legitimates increased forms of state action and surveillance.

The circulation of contemporary legends, urban or international, is, then, not limited to ordinary citizens; policy elites are also prone to tell themselves tales about their shared anxieties (Rogin, 1987). There is, for instance, the story of how the United States lost the war in Vietnam because of the press and the protests back at home. Such "lessons of Vietnam" are generated by policy elites. Like the other tales, they serve as common meanings, yet in this case also provide a critically powerful basis for state practices.

Among the commonly told tales are some that come up over and over and that find their way into myriad other tales. These might be called political "metastories," the fables that come before, or that lie behind, so much of what is said in political life. Metastories constitute the institutional context that often is invoked to produce more local and specific stories. They give urban legends their legendary quality by tying the ephemeral to what is enduring—e.g., linking stolen cars to violations of personal safety previously thought to be inviolable. If the tale of a decline in safety is a ubiquitous metatale, so is it hard to live in America without accepting some version of "the American way" or "the American Dream." This would be to live at odds with the beliefs expressed in the shared way of life, and this is to be alienated. In the face of living with such contradiction it is to stories that people turn, to make the incoherences of their lives coherent. To highlight the role of metastories in politics and elsewhere is then to illuminate our insistence on coherences and our efforts to rationalize away incoherences as aberration, deviance, and anomaly.

Metastories include that which passes for the common sense regarding the public sphere; thus in the United States they constitute what Anne Norton (1993) calls "liberalism." By this she means the "hegemonic" (dominating and governing) philosophy of social contract and market individualism, including both its current "liberal" and "conservative" variants. The metastories of this liberalism are often stories of democracy and freedom that end up encouraging a self-defeating brand of resistance to state action. We want to emphasize one such ironic metastory that today has particular currency. It legitimates the existing political economy by delegitimating the state. One of the metastories of U.S. politics is the old American tale of the evil bureaucratic state. This tale narrates a story of an ever-expanding, yet arbitrary and incompetent, national state. Today it serves to rationalize efforts to retrench an already limited state, as, for example, through its incarnation in the Republican Party's 1994 Contract with America. It paints the U.S. state as evil, while preserving the belief that the political system is nonetheless glorious. The power of this set of tales can be said to hang on the efforts of many to see themselves as "free" even in the face of the binds faced by them and the state under the conditions imposed by contemporary capitalism. It is at this moment that the "healthy" cynicism of liberal suspicion of the state collapses into an unreflective cynicism that reinforces nonstate centers of power (multinational corporations, for example).

Other narratives circulate in U.S. politics today; some to an extent compete with the liberal metatale of the incompetent but glorious state. Competition among narratives, and even an almost instrumental interchangeability among apparently competing narratives, is all the more likely in our arguably postmodern age, where Lyotard (1984) says there is an "incredulity of metanarratives." The generalized suspicion of discourse, an idea for example that culture is "all brainwashing," is, however, no guarantee against its power. In a way the opposite is the case, as incredulity by itself fails to provide any sort of alternative metastory. Indeed, counterliberal tales seem to have less resonance in the current period, dominated as it is by conservative attacks on the welfare state in a post-Cold War era of an increasingly global political economy that makes the state appear decreasingly effective (Connolly, 1982).

This context deserves a little elaboration. Capitalism posits autonomous markets; in practice however, markets require state support, from the enforcement of contracts to interventionist foreign policies. At the same time, the state (and, in a sense, everybody in the society) in a capitalist society necessarily depends on the successful pursuit of profit by private investors. This means that the state generally will find itself unable to adequately address certain problems, such as unemployment and poverty. Yet the state must appear to be at least trying to manage problems. As a result, it will often be the locus of blame for society's ills. Arguably, capitalism has developed so as to require more and more state subsidy of investment (because of monopolizing tendencies and the globalization of markets). Certainly, the level of subsidy has increased over the past century, while at the same time many people face new levels of uncertainty with regard to health care, future employment for themselves and their children, retirement, personal safety, and environmental integrity. The state's inefficacy in addressing these issues, however, is likely only to intensify in an increasingly deterritorialized, global political economy. Therefore, conditions are ripe for a particular legitimation story that seeks to delegitimate the state.

On the one hand, this means the state not only runs a big budget deficit, but suffers as well from a "legitimacy deficit" (Habermas, 1973). Yet the portrayal, in story after story, of the state as the province of the incompetent and corrupt, as the locus of sound democracy poisoned by personal greed and bureaucratic mindlessness, serves the purpose of preserving the idea that the state is indeed the place where power exists. This in turn supports the idea that Americans live in a democracy and that individual freedom is not an illusion. People are encouraged to believe they participate in a democracy even as they are discouraged from using popular power for public purposes through the state (Morone, 1990). Such is a critical incoherence embedded in the alleged coherence of this ascendent story of the U.S. political system. All the while, the contradictions of the state and the market are backgrounded: "free markets" subsidized by the state are seen as "free" and a state that is constrained in its ability to attack the problems is seen as incompetent.

This perhaps postmodern cynical metastory is ironically often reinforced by stories of the triumph of goodwill, and even the victory of the system itself, once it is seen as allowing for such acts of goodwill. This upbeat side of the American antistate metastory is frequently found in popular culture, particularly television culture that permeates contemporary society writ large, with its preference for protagonists who rise above the constraints of institutionalized daily life. "Hawkeye" Pierce (Alan Alda) of *M*A*S*H*, the popular television series, provides an enduring example. The corrupt and bumbling, rule-bound army is made better by the humane mavericks, like Hawkeye, who break the rules and do it right. Thus the metastory of the incompetent but power-hungry state has roots not only in the structural situation of late capitalism but also in the realities and traditions more unique to the United States.

In general, the focus on the state as at fault for today's problems serves to prop up the order as it is. Such a tale undermines the power of the government to address problems because it deflects attention from structures that could be altered. The same vilification of the state can, however, play in other directions, especially if harnessed to an agenda for transformation. The instrumental cynicism encouraged by this tale can be converted to a more healthy cynicism that challenges the "official stories" it no longer believes. Even without such an agenda, those who take pleasure in hating government may help keep alive the idea that there is knowledge that differs from official knowledge, and this itself could play a part in an unpredictable politics of the future. Yet even as the ineffective state metastory can serve a variety of programs, it needs to be questioned for the way it maps political space and charts the course for contemporary policy struggle.

State tales are then often antistate tales in the cynical U.S. "Republic of Signs" (Norton, 1993), where stories are deployed even where they are no longer earnestly believed. They are arguably important tales, even if they do not by themselves legitimate anything in particular, let alone a positive state. The state itself is a storied site constructed through narrative that builds in structures of inattention to the illegitimate ways in which if not its legitimacy, then its political affectivity, has been achieved (Zizek, 1989). For a time, the less-than-virgin birth of the immaculate state could be erased in the origin stories that serve to legitimate the state. Erased were the acts of violence and exclusion that enabled the peaceable kingdom to come into being. State origin stories did not just sanction the state; they lent their legitimizing power to narratives about the various phenomena that fall within the purview of the state. Today, the power of stories may lay beyond the conventional idea of legitimation. From stories about what is foreign and alien to stories about who is an enemy, to stories about who is deserving and entitled, state-sanctioned stories carry a special potency associated with the ability of the state to act even when its legitimacy is subject to cynical suspensions of disbelief.

In other words the stories told by those acting in the name of the state still carry weight and are in need of examination, even in a postmodern age that questions the very metanarratives that continue to be used to reinforce ascendent identities, relationships, and practices, and even if they end up more often than not being state tales that undermine the state.

Part I
Origin Stories

1

Winning the West, Unwelcoming the Immigrant: Alternative Stories of "America"

Michael J. Shapiro

In 1994, as part of an intensifying war on immigrants, "House Republicans pledged, in their Contract with America, to cut off virtually all welfare benefits for legal immigrants who are under 75 years old" (Rosen, 1995: 22). Then recently, the war was extended to foreign tongues; a House committee approved a bill "making English the official language of the United States" (Schmitt, 1996: All). Throughout "American" history, "strangers in the land" (Higham, 1955) have been subjected to a variety of anxiety-driven forms of hostile scrutiny and policy initiative. During the period of the passage of the Alien and Sedition Acts at the end of the eighteenth century, for example, the Federalists whipped up an anti-alien hysteria, arguing that "the root of all evil in the United States was the large foreign-born population," which, among other things, would "contaminate the purity and simplicity of the American character" (Miller, 1951: 41).

The contemporary political climate, which encourages attacks from various segments of the social and political order—right-wing journalists, nativist groups, regional labor organizations, state governors, national leaders, and legislative bodies—is part of a venerable American tradition. If there is a consistent impetus to the various episodes of anti-alien initiative in the history of U.S. politics, it is to be found in the cultural anxieties that these actions and articulations reflect. Alien-others, who, in various periods, have been "Indians," French speakers, Irish, southern Europeans, eastern Europeans, Asians, and third world immigrants, and most recently, "illegal aliens" crossing the U.S. border with Mexico, have been constructed as threats to valued models of personhood and to images of a unified national society and culture.

These images, moreover, have historical and ontological depth; they are continuously recycled in the narratives that constitute the "American" nation. Although immigrants are seen from a rationalistic standpoint as competitors for jobs, more significantly they constitute an ontological disturbance in the American stories that people seek to appropriate. Immigrants both disrupt national stories and attract warranting attention from an authority (the state) that many want to appropriate for purposes of individual and collective identity affirmation.

We can achieve some historical distance and thereby effectively situate the predicates and modalities of expression of current anxieties by examining an earlier articulation. In a much-read academic and tradebook treatment of the threat of immigration to America's national culture, the then eminent sociologist E. A. Ross equated policies that allowed a rapid influx of immigrant aliens into the United States with "race suicide" (1914: 299). Certainly the "race" expression is jarring in the context of what is now acceptable academic and journalistic discourse about the effects of immigration—today's "metaracists" explicitly deny that they are racists (Balibar, 1991a) and refer instead to "national suicide" (Auster, 1990) or "cultural suicide" (Brimelow, 1995). But I want to focus first on the remarkable evidence of the senses that Ross invokes for his argument. He seems to have felt that he required no epistemic authority for his views beyond what he (as a trained sociologist) could see:

> To the practised eye, the physiognomy of certain groups unmistakably proclaims inferiority of type. I have seen gatherings of the foreign-born in which narrow and sloping foreheads were the rule. There were so many sugar-loaf heads, moon-faces, lantern jaws, and goose-bill noses that one might imagine a malicious jinn had amused himself by casting human beings in a set of skew-moulds discarded by the Creator. (Ross, 1914: 286)

And Ross got around; he performed his eye witness ethnography in a variety of venues:

> That the new immigrants are inferior in looks to the old immigrants may be seen by comparing, in a labor day parade, the faces of the cigar-makers and the garment workers with those of the teamsters, piano-movers and steam-fitters. (1914: 288).

Doubtless, Ross saw himself and his "practised eye" as self-made. But however Ross might have wanted to imagine himself as a "self-made man," reliant only on systematic methods rather than a traditional form of bigotry, his "practised eye" represents a historically produced assemblage of perspectives: epistemological models of the subject, geographic imaginaries, ethnographic "knowledges," spatial and economic histories, and national narratives, among others. A summoning here of the various ideational contexts within which Ross's gaze was trained will help frame a historically sensitive approach to the political/cultural construction of the threat of the alien-other.

Ross's confidence in his gaze owes much to a historical transition that took place in the nineteenth century. Whereas subjective vision was suspect during the prior two centuries, the situation of the observer during the nineteenth "depended on the priority of models of subjective vision" (Crary, 1991: 9). And, most significantly, the observer that had been created in that century was thoroughly implicated in the variety of social and economic forces. As an "ambulatory observer" taking in the sights within the "new urban spaces" (Crary, 1991: 20) Ross's directing of his gaze was more than a mere mode of representation: it was "an effect of a heterogeneous network of discursive, social, technological, and institutional relations" (Crary, 1991: 48).

More specifically, implicated in Ross's reports about what he saw were, among other things, a history of American industrial growth and the migratory effects it encouraged—various industries drawing immigrants from different parts of the globe and, at different times, displaying different vulnerabilities to exploitation, and confronting differing levels of exclusion—and a prevailing discourse on race and nationality. Ross's complaints about unassimilable races functioned within a domain of "knowledge" and a spatially predicated story. What he saw reflected a convergence in the twentieth century of racial science and racial nationalism (Higham, 1955: 134); he wholly accepted and recycled an already scientifically questioned typology of racial types, and his model of global space privileged a nation-state, geopolitical cartography.

By contrast, today's immigration alarmists argue on cultural rather than race or biological grounds. They invoke an amalgam of undigested sociologisms, anthropologisms, and political theories (from Alexis de Tocqueville onward) to question the ability of American society to assimilate culturally the current influx of people to (what they construct as) an American cultural core. And they posit this cultural core as a foundation that makes possible the American democratic ethos and the functioning of the American economy. Moreover, in keeping with their shift from the science of race to the social science of cultural assimilation, they evince none of Ross's confidence in subjective perception. They still construct peoples within a state-oriented cartography, but what was for Ross a very specific bodily threat has become for them a demographic one. The strange bodies have become abstracted and molarized; the threat is to America's demographic entity, a "population," not to an exemplary and sightly citizen body.

In short, by the time the contemporary Rosses arrived on the scene, the once visible ethnoscape had dissolved into conceptual and statistical abstractions. Certainly, aspects of the discourse of racial science remain; Peter Brimelow, for example, refers often to "stock," but rather than emphasizing an influx of different racial types, he employs locational and anthropological figures of speech, referring for example to "four 'cultural hearths' . . . delineated by linguistic geographers" (1995: 179) from which American cultural diversity had been constructed by the mid-twentieth century. This manageable level of diversity is a comfortable "balance" for Brimelow. It is what he sees the current influx threatening to destabilize.

Unlike Ross, Brimelow sees no grotesque bodies. Inflammatory racial figures occasionally break through his discursive sangfroid (he refers, for example, to an INS waiting room that is "teeming" with people who are "almost entirely colored"—1995: 28), but operating within the modern episteme, inflected by the displacement of subjective perception by technologies of data collection, Brimelow relies on the self-evidence of his data displays rather than his senses. What are threatened are not America's "good looks" (Ross, 1914: 287) but the numerical domination of the white Americans. Brimelow constructs a graph, showing the projected increase of the population (if current rates of immigration continue). The threat to America's whiteness comes into his discourse figuratively here rather than semantically, for the graph is in the form of a black wedge on top of a gray area, representing normal growth (47). He also constructs a graph with a "pincer shape," (again with black color growing larger) representing the extent to which Asian, Hispanic, and non-Spanish blacks are squeezing out the white majority (63). Reflective of his quest to achieve epistemic authority for his version of nativism, the graphs are included in a section entitled "Truth."

Although separated by a half-century and operating within different epistemes, the two Jeremiahs, Ross and Brimelow, are strikingly similar in their warnings about a national catastrophe. It has been clear for centuries that a combination of political and economic forces is primarily implicated in creating the flows of people from one to another global location, and the twentieth-century flows are no exception; they can be understood in terms of the demands of capitalist producers and the collaboration of governments, which, in varying degrees, comply with those demands. The significant actors—capitalist enterprises and migrating workers—function within a larger structural imperative of modernity, the process of decolonization that, in Etienne Balibar's terms, has created a "new political space." It is, he notes,

> not merely a space in which strategies are formed, and capital technologies and messages circulate, but a space in which entire populations subject to the law of the market come into contact physically and symbolically. (Balibar, 1991b: 43)

Ignoring this larger structural dynamic, both Ross and Brimelow pick up the story at the level of contact. Reaching into the past to imagine its genesis, they tell a story of migration that is more biographical than economic and structural. They construct immigration as a series of perversely motivated, individual decisions. Romanticizing the earlier, northern European immigrants, for example, Ross describes them as "home seekers" in contrast with the later flows of more "common stock," e.g., Italians, who come as "job hunters." It is greed that brings them to America (95).

Brimelow has a similarly romantic view of what he calls "colonial stock Americans" (they get to be "Americans" as soon as they hit the shore), who "had things rolling along pretty well before mass immigration began" (1995: 159), and he specifically argues that current immigration "does not seem to be affected very much by the economic conditions in the United States" (33). His preferred model of the influx is permissive U.S. immigration policy as the enabling condition and economic greed as the immigrant motivation. He implies that destination USA is a result of "alien" decision making: "Whether these foreigners deign to come and make their claim on America—and on the American taxpayer—is pretty much up to them" (5).

Despite all his data displays in the part of his *Alien Nation* entitled "Truth," Brimelow constructs the cultural core of America with his grammar, not with his evidence. He asserts, for example, that "slowly, over generations, America changed the Irish" (215). "America" in this grammatical construction is located as a unified actor/entity. Whereas what constitutes "America" at any moment are the forces contending to shape it (Irishness, among other cultural practices contributed to that shaping), Brimelow fabulates an arbitrary cutoff to the shaping process. Shortly after Anglo colonists arrive, "America" becomes a culture. This fixed unity then acts upon others or is, in turn, threatened by an alien presence impervious to its ability to assimilate it. To appreciate more fully the fabulation involved in Brimelow's arguments we must turn from grammar to narrative.

Narrative Contentions

The process of "constituting Americans" (Wald, 1995), especially struggles over how the national story should be written to connect personhood with national identity, has been particularly contentious during periods in which the boundaries of the self have been altered. Theodore Roosevelt's gloss on "the winning of the West" was written during a period in which the boundaries of the working body were being extended. Specifically, Roosevelt's role in attempting to author American nationhood and personhood is associated with a crisis of masculinity at the turn of this century. As the Industrial Age increasingly lent mechanical extensions to the working body, there were expressions of concern about the depletion of masculinity. Such significant cultural actors as Thompson Seton, a cofounder of the scouting movement, concerned themselves during this period with the craft of making men an "antidote to anxieties about the depletion of agency and virility in consumer and machine culture" (Selzer, 1992: 149). As it is put in the first *Boy Scouts of America Handbook*, it is necessary "to combat the system that has turned such a large proportion of our robust, manly, self-reliant boyhood into a lot of flat-chested cigarette smokers, with shaky nerves and doubtful vitality" (quoted in Selzer, 1992: 149). The anxieties expressed at the time were organized around a confusion of agency, as "men" enacted their work with the increasing aid of mechanical prostheses that, on the one hand, extended bodily capacities but, on the other, ambiguated issues of agency and value. Telling the American story as the story of the "winning of the west" was among Roosevelt's solutions to what he saw as a crisis in nationhood and national personhood.

Not surprisingly, various nationalist, anti-immigration Jeremiahs have invoked Roosevelt's mythic treatment of the Euro-American movement westward. Brimelow does so explicitly; his "commentary" (Foucault, 1984a) invokes Roosevelt's mythologizing as if it were an ethnohistorical investigation that traces a "perfectly continuous history" of Anglo-Saxon settlement (1995: 210). Brimelow's purpose is to argue that as regards important nation-building epochs, "America" has been effectively ethnically homogeneous; the westward settlement of English-speaking people, he avers, quoting Roosevelt without criticism, was "the crowning and greatest achievement," having made America part of the "heritage of the dominant world races" (1995: 210). Thus, for Brimelow, the threat of nonwhites and non-English speakers is to a cultural homogeneity seemingly established by the Rooseveltian fable.

Ross also worried about the "loss of political like-mindedness" engendered by the addition of immigrant aliens, but for him the primary threat was to the American bloodlines, which he imagined had been created by the rigors of the western adventure: "The blood now being injected into the veins of our people is 'sub-common' " (1914: 285). Thus, for example, he thought that Jews make poor Americans because they are not fit to haul canoes through the wilderness:

> On the physical side the Hebrews are the polar opposite of our pioneer breed. . . . it will be long before they produce the stoical type who blithely fares forth into the wilderness, portaging his canoe, poling it against the current, wading in the torrents, living on bacon and beans, and sleeping on the ground, all for "fun" or "to keep hard." (Ross, 1914: 290)

Roosevelt's *The Winning of the West* (1889) certainly supports the inferences of these two differently situated but exemplary immigration alarmists, but there is another element of his legendary history that bears scrutiny. There is a remarkable disjuncture in Roosevelt's text, a telling economy of "Indian" presence and absence in the West. Constructed in part as a spatial history, Roosevelt's fable depopulates the western landscape. Reminiscent of the Zionist reference to Palestine as a "land without people" is Roosevelt's reference to the Native American-occupied West as part of "the world's waste spaces" (1889: 17). Insofar as "Indians" had a significant presence during the "spread of the English-speaking peoples" (17), it was only as occasional visitors:

> The white settler has merely moved into an uninhabited waste; he does not feel that he is committing a wrong, for he knows perfectly well that the land is really owned by no one. It is never even visited, except perhaps for a week or two every year. (Roosevelt, 1889: 119)

However, in the places where Roosevelt's analysis becomes an ethnohistory (albeit a legendary one), the West becomes repopulated with "savage and formidable foes" (30), against whom "the English race" maintains its integrity by driving them off or exterminating them rather than, like the Spanish in other colonial venues, "sitting down in their midst" and becoming a "mixed race" (30). In its pseudo-, ethnohistorical moments, *The Winning of the West* is a romantic soldatesque in which brave pioneers fight their way westward, impeded at every step by the Indians' "fierce and dogged resistance" (40) until they gain what is rightfully theirs. But, when justice becomes the focus in the text—"the settler and pioneer have at bottom had justice on their side" (119)—the "fierce and dogged" foes again disappear, and what has been conquered turns out to have been merely "nothing but a game preserve for squalid savages" (119).

Ethnohistorical Challenges

Roosevelt's drama of the English-speaking people versus the "squalid savages" deserves further scrutiny not only because it has been appropriated in Brimelow's anti-immigration tract but also because it is radically contradicted by both the history of English-speaking peoples and the history of the Euro-Native American encounter in the West. It should be noted, first of all, that the "English" spoken by these people who supposedly won the West was not a cultural property that divided the Anglo-Saxons from other peoples. Indeed, the history of English, like the history of a "people," is a history of acculturation and coinvention. What Roosevelt called a perfectly continuous history of English-speaking people looks discontinuous, interculturally provoked, and often accidental and arbitrary from the point of view of the articulate noises they have made.

What has been historically produced as "English" is "not only the product of dialects brought to England by Jutes, Saxons, and Angles but also the languages of Romans, Scandinavians, and Celts, in an earlier period" (Baugh and Cable, 1951: 72) and French in a later period (93). The history of English in England is a history of the linguistic amalgamations following invasions and other cultural encounters. Without going into an elaborate philological analysis, a focus on the various episodes of the latinization of English is telling. Three historical epochs are primarily involved. First was the Roman conquest, which brought classical Latin into the language mix in Britain, then the spread of Christianity, which infused medieval Latin into English, and then the development of Renaissance science, which added significantly more Latin to English (Baugh and Cable, 1951).

The story of what H. L. Mencken called "the American language" (1943) is similarly telling. What Roosevelt called a perfectly continuous history of English speakers was more aptly described by Mencken as "two streams" of English. American English diverged from the English variety as a result of new circumstances, e.g., the need to describe unfamiliar landscapes and weather (3) and as a result of the contacts among people speaking different languages: French, Dutch, German, Spanish, etc. (108). Not only did the mixing of peoples produce new words but the circumstances of the encounters produced new contexts for old words, changing their meanings (121). American English had diverged significantly by 1812, and as a result, "almost every English traveler of the years between the War of 1812 and the Civil War was puzzled by the strange signs on American shops" (12).

Most significantly for purposes of confronting Roosevelt's story of the winning of the west by the English-speaking peoples, despite attempts to standardize American English in order to build a unique national culture (Noah Webster's primary motivation—Mencken, 1943: 9; Baugh and Cable, 1951: 360ff), what resulted was a hybrid tongue, a product of cultural encounters, with Native American language speakers among others. As Mencken noted, "the earliest Americanisms were probably borrowed bodily from Indian languages" (104), and it remains the case that many place, animal, and food names, as well as action and situation words come from Native American languages.

Rather than having been merely driven off, Native Americans left lasting cultural markers on "America." Apart from contributions to American English, Native American agricultural practices, alliance strategies, military technologies and methods, and other cultural practices helped create what are now both European and American institutions and practices (e.g., Weatherford, 1988). Certainly, many of the Native American cultures became to some extent Europeanized, but it is also the case that English colonial culture became, in part, Indianized, with lasting historical effects (Axtell, 1981: 273).

Native Americans have had a significant cooperative role in constituting the "America" that was shaped as it was extended westward. A genealogical as opposed to legendary account of the constitution of the Native American as other by Euro-Americans reveals an initial period of in some ways respectful "foreign relations" (despite European conceits about cultural superiority). For roughly one hundred fifty years before "American independence," colonists negotiated agreements with Native American tribes as if they were other nations worthy of recognition, and the various Native American nations (nations that were dispersed into autonomous rather than centralized tribal collectives) were important players in the struggles among different European colonials (Rossignol, 1995: 219).

Native Americans were resituated as domestic hindrances during the Jacksonian period, when Congress and the president, supporting Euro-American demands for territory, chose to ignore the earlier treaties and subsequent legal decisions that had granted tribes a degree of nationhood with respect to their territorial practices (Washburn, 1964: 119). And various forms of American "knowing" accompanied the political impetus for the changing construction of the Native American. American anthropology, for example, was deeply implicated in the process through which Native American peoples had their identities reordered as they were changed from "nations" into "races," where in the context of the former, Euro- and Native American relations were "foreign policy" and in the context of the latter, "domestic policy." After a period of ambiguity in which "American governments and ethnographers vacillated ambivalently in their conceptualization of Indian Otherness" (Borneman, 1995: 667), both were ultimately complicit in wholly domesticating "Indians" within sociological and cultural frames that effaced the national frontiers of the North American continent.

Roosevelt's spatial history to the contrary notwithstanding, the winning of the West involved, among other things, the changing of a legal frontier into a domesticated region with an accompanying alteration of the western ethnoscape. Moreover, while Roosevelt represented the movement west of the English-speaking peoples as a series of violent conquests, in which "The Indians have shrunk back before the advance only after fierce and dogged resistance" (1889: 39), ethnohistorical inquiry reveals instead a cultural encounter at a frontier that served as a "school" (Axtell, 1981: 133) in which Native Americans assisted Euro-Americans in their adaptation to an unfamiliar landscape and a domain of spatial encounter in which "Indians and Old World invaders met, traded, and fought, sometimes with each other, sometimes with themselves. As they struggled to control a particular corner of the continent, they created new landscapes, new property systems, new social relationships, and new political institutions" (Cronon et al., 1992: 7).

The Euro-Native American cooperation was more extensive than what was ultimately produced as various ways of living in the West. Despite the popular assumption that the West was "won" by overcoming Indian resistance, in various ways Native Americans assisted in the Euro-American westward advance. The myth of the self-reliant, pioneer/Indian fighter that has been a significant part of the legendary American nation-building story is belied by historical investigations into the effects of "The Covenant Chain," a treaty between Iroquois nations and the Euro-American colonists. The confederation between the Iroquois and the colonists not only helped the English colonists defeat the French (as well as helping to keep the peace between colonists and Native Americans in the eastern zones) but also helped to open the western regions for English settlement (Jennings, 1984: xvii).

The collaborative story by Francis Jennings of the movement westward dispels a series of mythic constructions of American nation-building: the one that arrogates all significant achievements to the "white race," the one that constructs American institutions as culturally homogeneous, and most essentially, the Rooseveltian myth of the "Indians" as barriers to westward expansion.

Conclusion

It remains unclear if the age of nationalism is near an end, but one of its primary legacies remains well entrenched. The story of a unified national culture, designed to legitimate the ethnic and spatial boundary policing of the modern state, retains its force. As a result, contemporary "strangers in the land" are constructed as threats to legendary and anachronistic national imaginaries. The account I have offered—of the highly contingent and often arbitrary commingling of peoples and the resulting coinventions responsible for what have been historically rendered as autonomous cultural achievements—is meant as an intervention. The aim, at the level of writing, has been to disrupt such national imaginaries and, at the same time, to offer an alternative language and thus an alternative vision.

State stories are generally consolidating discourses on national culture. They impose alienating scripts that construct the immigrant-other as a danger. Such scripts are, in the terms employed by performance artist Krzysztof Wodiczko, a package of "dangerous metaphors." His artistic enactments—various media generating prostheses carried or worn by immigrants as they move about in public space—are meant to "disarm and deactivate them [the metaphors]" (Wodiczko, 1995: 208). The analysis here is meant to serve the same purpose. Culture is a dynamic that moves on, despite, not because of, state cultural productions and national master narratives; it emerges from encounters and negotiations. Unified and fixed national cultures are fictions, products of national fantasies. Once one relaxes territorial models of identity and recognizes the amoebalike existence of cultural boundaries, there can be no culturally dangerous others, only dangerous ways of estranging others.

2

Constitutional Tales: Capitalist Origin Stories and U.S. Democracy

Carl Swidorski

- In 1776, Samuel Loudon, editor of the New York *Packet* and a supporter of independence, published a loyalist's reply to Thomas Paine's *Common Sense*. Vigilantes broke into his house, destroyed the printing plates, and burned fifteen hundred copies of the pamphlet. All the new states passed wartime statutes prohibiting publication of materials supporting British authority over the colonies, even forbidding derogatory comments on the continental currency (Linfield, 1990: 16).
- Benjamin Bache, grandson of Benjamin Franklin and editor of the Republican Philadelphia *Aurora*, was tried for common-law seditious libel in 1798 to silence his criticism of the Adams administration. Already the target of economic pressures and mob violence, Bache died during his trial. His successor, William Duane, was then indicted for sedition under the new Alien and Sedition Acts. Prosecutions were initiated against leading Republican, papers throughout the country. Several were driven out of business, including all three in New York (Linfield, 1990: 24).
- The longest prison term, two years, was given to a laborer in 1799 for putting up a sign that said, in part, "No Stamp Act, No Sedition ... Downfall to the Tyrants of America, Peace and Retirement to the President" (Kairys, 1993: 49).
- Oberlin became the first college to admit women in 1833 but it did not allow them to speak in class (Tedford, 1985: 42).
- Abner Kneeland was found guilty of blasphemy in 1834 for circulating a paper in Boston containing ideas contrary to the Christian religion (Tedford, 1985: 52).
- The abolitionist *Illinois Observer* was attacked by mobs on several occasions and finally in 1837 its editor, the Reverend Elijah P. Lovejoy, was murdered. Southern states legally restrained freedom of speech in the antebellum era by providing fines and imprisonment for individuals advocating the abolition of slavery (Tedford, 1985: 48).

- In 1862, Secretary of War Edwin Stanton, displeased by an article in a Washington, D.C. paper, the *Sunday Chronicle*, confiscated its printing presses, destroyed all editions of the paper, and arrested its editors (Linfield, 1990: 24).
- Susan B. Anthony and fourteen other women voted in the November election in Rochester, New York, in 1872. All were arrested for violating the Civil Rights Act of 1870. Anthony was not allowed to speak in her own defense at the trial (Hoff, 1991: 153).
- Between 1880 and 1930 over four thousand labor injunctions were issued by courts. Most prevented peaceful picketing, barred boycotts, and even the use of the word "scab." Some injunctions barred union meetings and strikes, and occasionally included extreme measures such as "barring striking clothing workers in New York City from 'standing in the street within ten blocks . . . of the plaintiff's business' although this area was the center of the New York City men's clothing industry and included the strikers' headquarters" (Goldstein, 1978: 19).
- In 1894, the Reverend William F. Davis was incarcerated for attempting to preach the gospel in Boston Common. The Massachusetts supreme court, in a decision upheld by the U.S. Supreme Court, affirmed his conviction in an opinion written by Oliver Wendell Holmes. To Holmes, the legislature had absolute authority to forbid public speaking on public property (Kairys, 1993: 42–43).
- During World War I Beethoven's music was banned in Pittsburgh. Los Angeles forbade all discussion of peace in the schools. The producers of the film *The Spirit of '76*, which showed scenes unflattering to the British army during the American Revolution, were convicted of attempting to cause insubordination in the armed forces and sentenced to ten years in prison. A man was sentenced to twenty years in prison for distributing a pamphlet urging voters in Iowa not to reelect a congressman who had voted for the draft. Socialists were denied the seats they were elected to in the New York state assembly and the U.S. Congress while the presidential candidate of the Socialist Party, Eugene V. Debs, was sentenced to twenty years in prison for a speech critical of U.S. participation in the war (Murphy, 1979: 128–32).
- In 1936, Jack Barton, local secretary of the Communist Party in Alabama, was sentenced to one hundred eighty days of hard labor for possessing "communist material," including such publications as *The Nation* and *The New Republic* (Goldstein, 1978: 219).
- Six college professors and eight schoolteachers were fired in New York during 1952 for their political beliefs, part of a continuing attack on the education profession during the decade. A member of the education board stated there was no need to prove the teachers were communists because "formal membership does not prove non-dedication" (Belfrage, 1973: 177).
- During the Vietnam War era, local police, the FBI, and the CIA mounted a full-scale effort to disrupt and silence the underground press. The editor of the Miami Daily Planet was arrested twenty-nine times on obscenity charges. The Houston *Space City* offices were bombed and burglarized. The Jackson,

Mississippi, Kudzu had eighteen of its staff attacked and beaten by police (Linfield, 1990: 149).
- In 1985, sixteen people, including three nuns, two priests, and one minister, were indicted on seventy-one counts for giving sanctuary to Central American refugees. Most of the evidence used against the defendants was gathered through government surveillance. Eight of the eleven who stood trial were convicted (Curry, 1988: 304).
- Until 1990, gays, lesbians, and bisexuals were automatically denied visas to enter the United States, whether as tourists, for professional reasons, or as immigrants (Ethelbrick, 1995: 360).

When I teach my civil liberties course each year it comes as no surprise to me that my students do not know about any of the events above. Most of my professional acquaintances, including lawyers, also are completely unfamiliar with the history of political repression in the United States. But I am not surprised because they are "products" of an education system that teaches the story of U.S. history as a "march of liberty" with the Constitution providing "a legal framework in which the orderly expansion of liberty could take place" (Urofsky, 1988: 969).

The Constitutional Tale

The story of the Constitution is usually told as a circumscribed political narrative about freedom from government and the protection of individual rights through law. It is far less common to discuss the Constitution as a product of social struggle let alone as an economic document closely related to the development of U.S. capitalism. The dominant story of the Constitution serves an important educational and thus ideological function in U.S. politics. The Constitution is a way of knowing, of making sense out of the world that we all learn as we progress through the education system. This way of knowing about U.S. politics has been characterized as "a kind of bourgeois fairy tale" in which political and economic struggles are subsumed in a discourse about legality. In this tale, politics and morality become reduced to the maneuvering of lawyers and judges (Ollman, 1990: 6).

Antonio Gramsci argued that the modern capitalist state needs to validate itself ethically to both elites and the society as a whole. To maintain power the dominant class must have its interests "conceived of and presented, as being the motor force of a universal expression, of a development of all 'national energies' " (1971: 182). The U.S. constitutional story also serves of that ethical validation. The tales we learn about it in elementary and secondary school, college, and church, at civic functions, and through the media are part of the process through which the dominant classes try to exercise hegemony. Through these channels, we learn that politics in the United States is conducted legally. We are a nation of laws, not "men." These discursive practices about "having" individual rights legally protected under the Constitution help legitimate existing power relationships. They discourage the kind of political activity that empowers people to act collectively to make sure they "have" such rights rather than as individual litigants "petitioning" for their rights. Belief in the "rule of law" and its accompanying constitutional concepts of individual rights, equality, and justice inhibit people from looking at the law as an arena of political and economic struggle. This ideological attachment to the rule of law has even had significant effects on the political strategies chosen by reformers and dissidents (Swidorski, 1994).

The tale of the U.S. Constitution is a metastory. It is integral to our political institutions and national culture. It is the kind of story that people live by and some die by. It helps reproduce existing patterns of institutionalized daily life by "freeing" people from thinking and acting. It is a story above all about freedom and individualism set within premises of material progress. It is a story that unthinkingly accepts the equation of freedom with capitalism.

The First Amendment component of this constitutional tale is particularly important because it provides a link to the key legitimating concept of democracy. Freedoms of speech, press, association, and religion are seen as the foundation of a democratic state and society. We are "free to choose" our political leaders and hold them accountable. We are free to choose our own personal beliefs and associations, which the state cannot unduly interfere with. Finally, the political dimensions of freedom are connected to the marketplace as we are free to choose our jobs and the products that bring meaning to our lives. This market connection is often implicit but sometimes becomes an explicit component of constitutional reasoning as in the First Amendment "marketplace of ideas" analogy. Furthermore, there often is an American exceptionalist subtext to this story. First Amendment freedoms are portrayed as the linchpins of "our" democracy. "We" have a tradition of human rights enshrined in the Bill of Rights but "they" do not have, protect, or value individual rights as we do.

As commonly told, First Amendment freedoms are part of our political heritage, present at the creation and progressively expanded over time through enlightened leadership. Our Founding Fathers wrote individual rights into the Constitution and created the Supreme Court as an institutional mechanism for protecting them and checking the power of arbitrary government. U.S. history is a story of the gradual enlargement of these freedoms through the leadership of the Supreme Court and other enlightened public officials and intellectuals. While there have been tragedies in this story, such as the Japanese internment episode, or aberrations, such as the McCarthy era, the fundamental development has been a "march of liberty." Rarely is the story one of political-economic struggle among contesting groups or classes. It is a story of decontextualized politics and abstract rights.

There is a continuum of versions of this story ranging from rather crude Fourth of July speeches and editorials, to the often tepid social studies curriculum of our schools, to the sophisticated explanations of social scientists. Yet all versions share the fundamental elements of portraying the Constitution as the foundation of our democratic society, a document that enshrines individual rights and creates institutional mechanisms for protecting them.

Finally, these constitutional stories contain some of the ironic elements identified in the introduction to this volume. For example, the story often contains a fundamental "tension," a term much preferred by mainstream storytellers to contradiction. Here, a nondemocratic institution protects individual rights central to a democracy from, in a further irony, a majority.

Ambivalence about the judiciary is the inevitable product of the paradox of judicial power in America, for it reflects the inherent tensions of a political system that enshrines both democracy and legalism. Americans expect the judiciary to fill a political vacuum by providing cohesion for a pluralistic society and acting as the guardians of the public interest. In serving this role, the judiciary is expected to interpret the Constitution, statutes, and common law of the land in a way that transcends overt politics and the more transient winds of popular opinion (Ross, 1994: 3). This narrative is part of the larger liberal metastory of legitimating the political economy by delegitimating the state. In this case, an institution of the state performs the role of checking the state and empowering the individual citizen/consumer. The political system remains glorious because the Supreme Court defends and upholds the Constitution against the danger of the evil state.

Understanding Why The Tale Is Told

I believe an analysis rooted in Marxism can help us make sense of why these tales about the Constitution are so pervasive in our culture despite a much more complex and contradictory historical legacy, which includes selective repression. Contrary to some contemporary "post-" narratives that neglect or caricaturize Marxism, I find it both theoretically useful and necessary. Marxism is not a "model of fixed and known . . . positions, which in general had only to be applied" while dismissing all other kinds of thinking as "bourgeois." It is a "body of thinking" that is "active, developing, unfinished, and persistently contentious." While it is radically different from other approaches, at the same time it has "complex connections with them, and . . . many unresolved problems" (Williams, 1977: 3–4).

Raymond Williams's contributions to Marxist theory are especially important in dealing with the Constitution as an educative-cultural document and set of narrative practices. Of particular importance is his theory of cultural materialism, which he described as "a theory of the specificities of material culture and literary production within historical materialism" (Williams, 1977: 5). Conventional narratives either idealize the Constitution or treat it primarily as a political document separated from much of its socioeconomic context. Williams critiqued the practice of sharply demarcating social processes into political, social, cultural, economic, and psychological spheres. He "materialized social processes that had been seen as ideal or immaterial and developed a widened conception of productive forces" (Peschek, 1993: 20). To Williams,

> any ruling class devotes a significant part of material production to establishing a political order. The social and political order which maintains a capitalist market, like the social and political struggles which created it, is necessarily a material production. From castles and palaces and churches to prisons and workhouses and schools; from weapons of war to a controlled press: any ruling class, in variable ways though always materially, produces a social and political order. (1977: 93)

And certainly in the United States, the Constitution, at one and the same time a political-economic practice, cultural symbol, and educational process, has been a major means of maintaining and reproducing the political order.

The story of the Constitution is therefore part of the class and group struggle over the particular political order we should have. It is not surprising that the content of that story is contested terrain in which politicians, intellectuals, civic leaders, and ordinary citizens all play a role. One of Williams's most famous formulations was that "culture is ordinary" (1989: 3). In a similar fashion, the Constitution is ordinary. It is constituted by the everyday activities of people who include not just Supreme Court justices but ordinary citizens. This is especially true of First Amendment practices.

Gramsci's concept of hegemony is important to understanding this aspect of the Constitution. Hegemony is "not only the articulate upper level of 'ideology,' nor are its forms of control only those ordinarily seen as 'manipulation' or 'indoctrination.' " Rather it is "a whole body of practices and expectations, over the whole of living. . . ." The reality of the social order "is a lived system of meanings and values—constitutive and constituting—which as they are experienced as practices appear reciprocally confirming. It thus constitutes a sense of reality for most people in the society . . ." (Williams, 1977: 110). This social process in not merely one of domination and subordination. It also is one of resistance and creativity. It is a contradictory process of adjustments by those in power to maintain cultural hegemony and the continual failure to do so in the light of "ordinary" experiences of those who resist in myriad ways. Gramsci and Williams provide theoretical foundations to help us make sense of mainstream stories about the Constitution.

Political scientists, for example, tell particular constitutional stories. These are not objective tales on the one hand, nor are they the product of some capitalist conspiracy or the effects of deterministic social structures on the other hand. Rather, they are part of the ongoing active struggle over creating history and the meaning of history (Carr, 1962). Political scientists, as intellectuals, occupy a particular, privileged position within that struggle. They primarily have defended the existing social order, tried to reform the state by strengthening it, and entered into symbiotic relationships with the state and corporate America (Lowi, 1985, 1992; Seidelman, 1985; Roelofs, 1992).

The public law subfield of political science has been part of that practice. Its tale of the Constitution has been one of the progressive development of doctrines that preserve the Constitution and enhance individual liberties or, alternatively, a decontextualized narrative about discrete elements of the judicial process. It has tended to emphasize the Supreme Court, separate politics from economics and society, and be atheoretical (Hensley and Rhoads, 1989; McCann and Houseman, 1989). Sometimes, the field takes on the veneer of Constitution worshiping:

> Judicial review is undemocratic. But the Court's power stems from its duty to give authoritative meaning to the Constitution. . . . As a guardian of the Constitution, the Court sometimes invites controversy by challenging majoritarian sentiments to respect the rights of minorities and the principles of representative democracy. . . . At its best, the Court appeals to the country to respect the substantive value choices of human dignity and self-governance embedded in our written Constitution. (O'Brien, 1993: 408–09)

The field has shied away from issues of class, economics, and ideology. It has not seriously engaged research grounded in functional sociology, Marxism, and legal history that challenge many of its assumptions (Smith, 1988). Even though there has been an alternative tradition in the profession from the beginning (Smith, 1907; Boudin, 1911; Beard, 1913), one that remains active and visible today, the mainstream of the profession largely has ignored it.

These patterns of emphasizing one set of stories while avoiding others are reinforced through the disciplinary practices of graduate training, socialization into the profession, advancement in academic rank, and professional development and status (Ricci, 1984). They also occur within a broader context of changing relations between the academy and the capitalist economy. Universities increasingly have become responsible for "educating" a significant proportion of the population. Science, math, administration and management, business, informational technologies, and other vocational subjects have replaced the arts and humanities as the core of higher education. Universities have assumed more of the research and development tasks of private industry. The academy itself has been reorganized along the lines of corporations with more formal rationalization, increased hierarchy, more professional managers, and closer ties with the corporate business community (Ollman, 1993). Thus the "responsibility of intellectuals" is rooted in their particular place in the continuing struggle over the social order (Chomsky, 1967). The conventional story about the Constitution and First Amendment is not that surprising, therefore, if one approaches the issue from the perspective of cultural materialism. The political science profession's particular tales are part of the ongoing struggle over the political order.

An Alternative Narrative

Relying on the theoretical heritage of Gramsci and Williams, I will briefly sketch a counternarrative to the mainstream story about the First Amendment, one rooted in historical materialism. In the study of the civil liberties, "history and theory are mutually illuminating" (Orren, 1995: 386). The mainstream approach to civil liberties usually says a few obligatory words about the Founding Fathers' commitment to political freedom and then begins its story in earnest with the "origins" of civil liberties in the Supreme Court's belated recognition of a constitutional status for freedom of speech in the cases immediately following World War I. But the struggle over civil liberties should be situated in the larger context of the material and ideological struggles associated with the development of liberalism and capitalism beginning in the sixteenth and seventeenth centuries and continuing until today.

I will put forward, and briefly argue, four propositions. First, the issue of civil liberties faced by the revolutionary and constitutional generations must be historically situated in the larger context of class and group struggles both of that era and the previous two hundred years. Second, civil liberties were salient and related to important public issues between 1787 and 1919, not a narrow policy issue developed by liberal Supreme Court justices, influential academics, and interest group leaders after World War I. Third, labor was at the heart of First Amendment developments in the United States, especially between the Civil War and the New Deal. Fourth, civil liberties have been the product of popular struggle more than enlightened elite leadership.

First, civil liberties "have been the locus of intense historical struggles, the swaying to-and-fro motions of the contest between social classes. Each precedent signifies a contest between privilege and liberty, lost, gained, or held in the balance; and certain precedents have been signed in blood" (Thompson, 1980: 230). This struggle in the two centuries before the American Revolution included the efforts of the "bourgeoisie to gain political power, a struggle in which freedoms such as speech and worship were critical to the task of overcoming the power of Crown and Church" (Swidorski, 1995: 165). In the United States, an element of the ongoing struggle in the latter 1780s was that over the Bill of Rights and the new Constitution.

These were not benevolent gifts from enlightened Founding Fathers committed to broad notions of human freedom and democratic equality. Rather, they were the product of a fierce popular struggle over the ratification of the Constitution, a struggle that reflected the pronounced sectional, class, and interest-group rivalries that emerged during the Revolution. Also, the Bill of Rights embodied only a limited commitment to civil liberties reflecting the historical context of the times. For example, the First Amendment was seen as primarily codifying preexisting law and prohibiting only prior censorship, not as offering a twentieth-century version of broad individual freedom to speak, write, and act as one chose.

Second, even though "no right of free speech, either in law or practice, existed until a basic transformation of the law governing speech in the period from about 1919 to 1940" (Kairys, 1982: 141), civil liberties issues were salient as part of broader struggles during the nineteenth century. Civil liberties were important to abolitionists, supporters of the first women's movement, African Americans, populists, and workers. In most of these struggles, the individuals involved did not see themselves as fighting for a narrow category of political rights that we now identify as civil liberties. They were fighting for political, social, and economic interests that they often characterized as their rights or liberties. They may have traced the origins of these rights to eighteenth- and nineteenth-century republican traditions, to a nineteenth-century immigrant socialist or anarchist political culture, or to long-suppressed African traditions that newly emancipated African Americans now articulated in the language of Radical Republicanism. They saw these popular notions of rights as important to their everyday lives and connected them to broader concepts of democracy, equality, and human liberty. Rights were not only functional to representative democracy, in the more narrow sense of twentieth-century civil libertarians; they were embodied in the notion of human freedom and struggle against the privileged.

Furthermore, just because the nineteenth century was not characterized by legal battles over civil liberties in the courts does not mean that struggles over these rights did not occur. A variety of nonstate sanctions, including economic coercion (such as blacklisting, yellow dog contracts, and the sharecropping system), socialization pressures (through the church, schools, press, and family), and political terrorism restricted the liberties of African Americans, trade unionists, abolitionists, populists, and women activists. Thus even in the absence of official state repression, civil society used a variety of methods to suppress dissent. When such sanctions were not sufficient, local criminal laws and police forces were used. Sometimes regional police forces had to be called in if local police were sympathetic to these movements. Less frequently, but often decisively, the coercive force of the national state, in the form of the U.S. military, National Guard, and court injunctions, suppressed the liberties of dissenters. Thus, civil liberties were contested throughout the nineteenth century even if the law refused to officially recognize them as constitutional rights.

Third, "American constitutional development has been inextricably connected to questions of labor . . ." (Orren, 1995: 377). This is especially evident in the area of speech, press, and association. Even before labor-capital conflicts became a major national issue after the Civil War, basic rights of association were denied workers in the antebellum era. Unions were treated as criminal conspiracies by the courts until the 1840s and 1850s. Even after the decline of criminal conspiracy doctrine, courts remained hostile to the activities of workers. The most infamous manifestation of judicial hostility was the labor injunction that was used so extensively that the period from 1880 to 1930 came to be known as the era of "government by injunction." Over four thousand injunctions were issued during this time (Forbath, 1991: 61). The injunction became "an enveloping code of prohibited conduct" (Frankfurter and Greene, 1930: 200). Many injunctions "were directed against speech and prohibited 'opprobrious epithets,' language that was 'bad,' 'abusive,' 'annoying,' or 'indecent,' and words such as 'scab,' 'traitor,' and 'unfair.' Some judges even held that picketing per se [was] unlawful." Furthermore, speech issues were raised in "scores of decisions . . . from all levels of the judicial system in the generation before World War One . . ." (Rabban, 1981: 553, 522). Many of these cases involved the attempts of workers to assert their rights, ranging from resistance to injunctions restricting the ability to communicate to the free speech fights of the Industrial Workers of the World (IWW). The general Supreme Court response to such claims was to neglect the First Amendment issue or limit the meaning of speech and thus, as in the nineteenth century, not officially recognize their First Amendment status.

During the crucial period of 1919 to 1940, when the struggle for Supreme Court recognition of First Amendment rights was being contested, labor was central to the struggle. The American Civil Liberties Union reported that in the 1920s, "Of the infringements of civil liberties against which organizations in this field protest, nine out of ten involve rights which labor asserts in its contest with employers or civil authorities" (Baldwin, 1930: 85). When the Supreme Court finally established a clear constitutional right to freedom of expression in public places as a right of citizenship, it was in the labor case of *Hague v. CIO* (1939), which involved

Fig. 2.1. The law confronts the First Amendment, 1912. *Courtesy of Archives of Labor and Urban Affairs, Wayne State University.*

the right to distribute union literature on the streets of Jersey City. A major reason for the key role of labor in this historical struggle was that freedom of communication and association was central to the ability of workers to organize unions, a point asserted by workers throughout U.S. history and finally recognized by Congress and the Supreme Court in the 1930s. Thus a contextual history of First Amendment rights in the United States must include the centrality of labor in its development.

Finally, civil liberties have been gained more through popular struggle than through elite enlightenment. The major advances in civil liberties as constitutional rights occurred during the 1930s and 1960s, both periods characterized by widespread popular struggle utilizing civil liberties as a means to influence the policies adopted by elites. Moreover, historically those in power, whether in the state or the corporate world, have vigorously resisted the spread of civil liberties for selected groups perceived to be threats to their established power. The surveillance state of the twentieth century was foreshadowed in the practices of labor spies, blacklisting, and private "police" terror used by companies against the nascent labor movement in the nineteenth century. The establishment of a surveillance state in the twentieth century and the selective repression of groups, normally on the left, who are perceived as posing significant threats to the status quo, is dramatic evidence of the limits of the elite's commitment to civil liberties. Unionists, struggling to improve the basic conditions of their lives in the early decades of the twentieth century, Martin Luther King Jr., leading a nonviolent campaign for human dignity in the 1960s, and religious activists, opposing U.S. policy in Central America during the 1980s, have all been subject to illegal surveillance and "counterintelligence" operations. They all learned that there is a price to pay for exercising civil liberties. They all found out that civil liberties are not something we "have" but something we struggle for.

Conclusion

The metastory of the Constitution, especially of First Amendment freedoms, as foundational to U.S. democracy is deeply ingrained in our culture. The major problem with the narrative is not that constitutional freedoms are a hoax or that they are unimportant but rather that they are treated as if they are simply "there"—bestowed on us by enlightened leadership and ahistorically ever-present. Such a metastory is disempowering. It ignores the historical struggles among and between groups and classes that are foundational to the development of civil liberties. It is silent about repression and resistance. It may lead to the diminution of the very liberties that are needed if we ever are to have a meaningful democracy.

3

Pluralizing The American Dream

Miriam B. Rosenthal and Sanford F. Schram

Hope is the only universal liar who never loses his reputation for veracity.
—Robert Ingersoll, quoted in *Truth Seekers* (1892)

Once again, we are reminded that some of the most politically influential stories in national politics are told about the American Dream (Hochschild, 1995). For example, the Republicans' choice for their 1996 National Convention was the focus group-tested theme of "Restoring the American Dream" (Kolbert, 1995). Although for many the American Dream is just that—only a dream—its pervasiveness alone makes it a real force in policy discourse. And even if we are suspicious of its value as a way of articulating policy concerns in the contemporary state, its potency encourages us to see what can be done with it to promote political possibility in an age of diminished expectations (Newman, 1993). Often a dream about personal accomplishment and success, sometimes a dream about inclusion and collective well-being, the American Dream is still a powerful idiom for a variety of worthwhile political agendas.

While the power of the trope is unquestionable, the content of the Dream is contentious—sometimes a celebration of equality and democracy, sometimes a paean to individualism. When Martin Luther King, Jr. said he had a dream, he articulated a vision of the American Dream different from that of the people who resisted his attempts to create a more inclusive society. Yet there is some question whether King was conceding too much to the established order of race relations by articulating his call for inclusion in the historically assimilationist idiom of the American Dream. Indeed, because of its fertile character, the American Dream has often been a site for constructing personal identity and articulating individual goals in profoundly conventional ways that reinforce commitment to the established "civilization of productivity" (Connolly, 1982). King may have had a dream for a just American society, but Colin Powell's "American Journey," narrating his rise from the

Bronx to the upper echelons of state power, is arguably more consistent with the more popular versions of the American Dream that stress that individuals can be personally successful within the established order as it is already constituted (1995). Both these versions, and others as well, continue to be invoked in policy discourse, and while they strike a chord with many Americans, growing numbers of people question whether the American Dream will be realized for them (Hochschild, 1995; Newman, 1993).

Yet, even as we hear and read so much today about the American Dream, achieving it, losing it, restoring it, it is not just its content that is contestable. So is its form. In what follows, we ask whether it makes a difference if the American Dream is treated as ideology or as discourse. Wendy Brown has succinctly captured the distinction between ideology and discourse when she writes of gender biases of American political culture:

> Liberalism will appear here as both a set of stories and a set of practices, as ideology *and* as discourse, as an obfuscating narrative *about* a particular social order as well as a narrative *constitutive* of this social order and its subjects. These two apparently antagonistic formulations—the former associated with a Marxist theory of ideology and the latter with Foucault's critical replacement of that theory with the notion of discourse—are both important to apprehending the operation of gender in liberalism. (1995: 142)

Brown is raising the important point that ideology obscures the reality it depicts while discourse is constitutive of that reality. As the former, the American Dream leads us to think that we can have what we may not; as the latter, the Dream helps constitute us as desiring animals who just happen to have the desires implied by the Dream, and then leads us to act on them. In what follows, we contrast the value of treating the American Dream as either obfuscating ideology or constituting discourse.

We look at the Dream as ideology and discourse in two major versions of the American Dream in mass market texts specifically designed to influence policy discourse today—one offered by the Republicans of the 104th Congress in their follow-up to the Contract with America entitled *Restoring the Dream* (House Republicans, 1995) and the other offered in response by the Democratic former governor of New York State, Mario Cuomo (1995).

These two different tales about the American Dream have significant similarities. Both underscore the continuing popularity of the Dream as a way of framing national policy discourse ideologically and discursively. Both exemplify how the Dream operates as ideology to mystify current conditions and their relationship to past practice. Both offer stories of the Dream as in jeopardy and needing "renewal." Both offer classic policy stories of rise-and-decline for purposes of motivating public concern and implying that we get back to what we have lost (see Stone, 1997). Therefore, both are stories of movement and change that are more than tales of growth and decay; they also are tales of "journey" that suggest, as in many of Western civilization's most cherished epic tales, how we have lost our way and need to find our way back home. Both therefore use the American Dream as a way of rewriting policy history in order to legitimate their policy proposals in terms of origins, original intentions, historical legacy, and the other valued goods that come with being seen as the logical heirs of history and continuity. Both perform important ideological functions mystifying how the existing political economy got to be the way it is and what its current condition is actually like.

Both also represent how the Dream works discursively as a set of terms for narrating people's personal biographies in a collective history in a way that suggests how the American Dream is a story that some people specify and others are expected to live out. In both cases, the Dream is used to imply a particular type of self as the person who qualifies as the American who gets to dream the Dream. In both cases, therefore, the Dream performs an important discursive function, constituting the self who is legitimated as deserving of the benefits of being a participant in the American political economy.

These two versions of the Dream also differ. The Republican version promotes a restoration of competitive individualism as appropriate for the "end of history" with its brave new world order of a global postindustrial capitalism and the opportunities that come with an "emerging information society." The Cuomo alternative harkens back nostalgically to a lost sense of community that should serve as a basis for a more inclusive society, ensuring all citizens equal opportunities for advancement in that new world order. These texts then offer variations on the old theme of who gets to dream the Dream. Each therefore has its own ideological and discursive effects. Each obscures the historical development of the structural conditions of the political economy, while each constitutes a particular self who is expected to act out the Dream that is suggested to still be possible within that structured political economy.

We conclude with considerations on how to get beyond this limited set of the American Dream by trying to pluralize it. For us, pluralizing the Dream means suggesting how it can take other forms that are more attentive to how other selves may get to enact their own versions more geared to current realities of what it would mean to have "made it" in America.

Whose Dream Is It?

As with homilies from the Bible, the American Dream is not only descriptive and performative, but also prescriptive and inspirational. It has been used to teach newcomers how to act and what to expect by means of the telling of the stories of individuals and of America. We are told that there is a moral to these stories, along with an implicit covenant that rewards the faithful or the fortunate.

Its tutelar function, predating the popular stories by Horatio Alger in the latter part of the nineteenth century down to today, should not be trivialized. The American Dream has often been something that some people get to define and other people only then get to pursue. For instance, the "greenhorn" of mass European immigration in the late nineteenth and early twentieth centuries could become a "real American" by pursuing the American Dream as expressed by others. Some get to direct the play while others become cast members who can gain credibility only through participation in the "Dream" as it has been articulated in a wide variety of media ranging from corporate advertising to textbooks (Ewen, 1976).

Today, the American Dream is still being invoked in contemporary policy discourse by House Republicans and critics such as Mario Cuomo, each using the Dream to obscure ideologically the relationship of current problems to past practices and to constitute discursively the American populace in politically convenient ways to mobilize action on behalf of their policy prescriptions. They are the spinners of the Dream and the American people become those who are simultaneously deceived and constituted by the versions of the Dream that are spun.

Ideological Dreams

An ideological analysis is one way of achieving critical distance from the American Dream. The ideological legitimates its object of concern by masking its origins, obscuring its past, and mystifying its history. In this, the ideological is complicit with myth. In "The Eighteenth Brumaire of Louis Bonaparte," Marx wrote:

> Men make their own history, but they do not make it just as they please; they do not make it under circumstances chosen by themselves, but under circumstances directly found, given and transmitted from the past. The tradition of all the dead generations weighs like a nightmare on the living. And just when they seem engaged in revolutionizing themselves and things, in creating something new, precisely in such epochs of revolutionary crisis they anxiously conjure up the spirits of the past to their service and borrow from them names, battle slogans and costumes in order to present the new scene of world history in this time-honored disguise and this borrowed language. (1972: 437)

While the material conditions for revolution are transmitted from the past, so are the ideas that structure consciousness. Antonio Gramsci's ideological critique of the "common sense" stresses its roots in the traditional culture, thereby also making ideology out to be akin to mythology. Both ideology and mythology operate through illusion. Yet Marxist ideological critique has traditionally emphasized how ideology is different from mythology, particularly in its political role of structuring *consciousness* in explicit, more textual forms of representation that inform everyday practice in more prosaic ways than heroic myths of an alleged glorious past that often are directed at infiltrating our collective *unconscious* (Jameson, 1981).

In today's mediated society, ideology is disseminated in good part through the electronic mass media that colonize our consciousness to the point that it is only in our dreams that we come face to face with desires we might otherwise have (Ewen, 1976). In our waking dream world (of consciousness), the American Dream helps give shape to this mediated understanding of ourselves and our relationships to others. In particular, as ideology, the Dream has historically played a key role in the creation and stability of the "American Way" by legitimizing those desires delivered from the media and channeling them into publicly acceptable paths, most often geared toward material success. The Dream as mass-mediated ideology is then a false, but conscious, consciousness (rather than an unquestioned unconsciousness) that imputes to people the desires of the media and mobilizes individuals to participate in the commercial society of exclusive consumption founded on a competitive individualism.

Thorstein Veblen (1953) also wrote about false consciousness and the emulative habit of life that characterized American workers in a way that sheds light on the American Dream. Veblen wrote that the working class is more interested in emulating the leisure class than supplanting it or revolting against it. He pointed out that the key event in the modern history of the leisure class was its involvement with private ownership. It is then no accident that one of the most popular interpretations of achieving the Dream is the emulation of the rich through homeownership. "Everyone should be able to own their own home—it's the American Dream," or so say many public actors when pronouncing on public policy. The home has become a fetishized incarnation of the Dream.

For Slavoj Zizek (1989), ideology, to be sure, engenders something more than a false consciousness, an illusory representation of reality. Zizek also emphasizes that the fetish is not what it seems—it is, we could say, both more and less than a mask. "The mask is not simply hiding the real state of things; the ideological distortion is written into its very essence. When we see something the way it really is, then it dissolves itself into nothingness, or more precisely it changes into another kind of reality" (1989: 28). From this more Lacanian psychoanalytic point of view, the American Dream embodies the sublime object of desire (the Thing), it becomes the unachievable, the impossible-real fetishized object (the big Other). Its vast allure hides the fact that there is nothing behind it. It is an illusion that fills an empty space—it is therefore a "real illusion." Zizek adds that people might cynically still pursue the illusion even as they know it is only illusion.

The Dream becomes a real illusion that people are committed to pursuing even as they know it cannot bring them the fulfillment and inclusion the Dream once implied. Now they pursue it for the status it represents. It symbolizes itself—achieving the Dream means just that—success becomes an end in itself. We might then ask: when is a house not a home? When it is nothing more than a house to be bought and sold on the open market and when it is valued for its ability to signify the status associated with conspicuous consumption more than its ability to be a home. The propertied learn to live with their homelessness and the Dream is still pursued, but now not as the embodiment of some real accomplishment of inclusion and fulfillment but as a symbol that signifies the status associated with success in an acquisitive society.

The power of the American Dream, therefore, can persist even in these cynical (almost postideological?) times. Newt Gingrich and the House Republicans have successfully used the Dream as their own "sublime object of ideology"—perhaps not as a home but as the equally illusory "free" market. They purport to use what they call common sense to rightly restore the Dream (read "free" market), which they argue had been endangered by such things as budget deficits and unwed mothers. The "free" market is freed from responsibility for the country's economic malaise. In part, the ideology suggests, this is because the market has not been free in recent years, but was held hostage by a tax-and-spend welfare state instituted by liberals. This text, therefore, creates its own imagined and hoped-for "freed" market that is a yet to be realized "free" market. It then specifies how it is not free from government and finally tries to imagine how this "banal" object of desire can be materialized through policy change. The House Republicans' ideological text is dedicated to shoring up the common sense of things and buttressing its ability to mask the illusions of a new age of free market capitalism, creating along the way blind spots about the consequences of its "freed" market—deindustrialization, capital flight, and the deterioration of local economies.

While Cuomo's version of the Dream is less interested in freeing the economy, there is still the question of whether it is also too willing to accept and thereby obscure the structural insistences of the changing postindustrial economy. Cuomo tells us he still has reason to believe that the existing political economy can provide economic success, social security, and personal fulfillment for all who play by the traditional rules of work and family. Like the House Republicans, Cuomo very much seeks to demonstrate that today's circumstances can be understood in terms of certain stories about the history of the nation, its origins, its promises, and its traditional cultural values and enduring social practices.

Cuomo plays Horace Kallen to the House Republicans' Horatio Alger. While Alger's late-nineteenth-century stories glorified assimilation based on the adoption of the values of American individualism, Kallen's early-twentieth-century writings criticized the idea of assimilation through a "melting pot" that implied a shared sense of community. Kallen offered the idea of a symphony as an alternative metaphor and stressed that what made America strong was its commitment to cultural pluralism instead of assimilation. Cuomo shares Kallen's belief that the United States is accommodating to diverse peoples and cultures. He speaks in terms of how the United States as a nation of immigrants is a land of opportunity where a sense of helping each other succeed provides the country with its own particular version of community and public sense of family. In this sense, even as he invokes his mother's words about caring for others, Cuomo sees immigrants as people who want to succeed according to rules set by those who came before them. The American Dream is a Dream "Americans" (read people in power) dream for those who wish to become Americans.

Cuomo therefore remains not just an optimistic proponent of the cultural pluralism; he also is trapped within the prevailing ideology of our "civilization of productivity." Like the House Republicans, he still sees economic growth that provides workers the ability to support themselves as the one and only legitimate avenue for realizing the historically legitimated idea of the American Dream. Cuomo no less than the House Republicans is unwilling to consider that the "work dogma" can no longer be insisted on in a changing economy that does not need as many workers as its predecessor (Aronowitz and DiFazio, 1994). He, too, ends up using the Dream as ideological obfuscation to suggest that past practices can still legitimate contemporary circumstances.

Discursive Dreams

What if we pursue the idea that the American Dream is more an artifact of discourse than ideology? In other words, the American Dream may not just obscure the real relations of power operating in civil society but also may be a potent force for helping to constitute those relations, particularly as a form of disciplinary power that helps constitute practitioners of the Dream as particular types of dreamers who by virtue of invoking the Dream construct their self-identity in terms of the Dream and organize their sense of self and their self-pursuits in order to realize the dictates of the Dream.

Roland Barthes (1972) was for a time able to use myth for purposes of critique especially as a way of highlighting how representational practices turned culture into nature and made the changeable seem unchangeable. Yet he eventually came to question the mythological/ideological approach on the grounds that it overlooked how the politics of representation lie not so much in how mythology and ideology naturalized culture as in how discourse constructed those very objects of cultural concern. Also, where ideology and mythology admit to a certain element of the (un)conscious, the discursive approach puts less stress on the states of mind and motives (conscious or unconscious) of the authors of any particular textual representation. From the discourse point of view, the author is not in full control of the text and is unable to police all of its possible interpretations as the discourse is inevitably open to multiple readings. More critically, there is emphasis on how the author operates as a function or effect of the text rather than its producer (see Foucault, 1984b). Authors did not consciously obscure reality as much as discourse helped make plausible the idea that the author might be doing so and in the process helped constitute both the identity of the author and the object of their concern. Both dream and dreamer take the form as artifacts of discourse, as effects of a nonagentistic form of power.

In this sense, the politics of the American Dream are embedded in that discursive practice and how it is deployed more so than in terms of who gets to deploy the Dream and why. Neither does the Dream any longer point to some imagined past, nor does it mystify or act as a necessary supplement for rationalizing fetishized objects. Rather than focusing on the Dream as some fixed, if ambiguous, representation that is articulated in texts, "American Dream" becomes a discursive practice subject to iteration and transformation, something that is transformed while we use it and in turn something that then transforms how we are identified. (A highly visible case is the author Horatio Alger whose name has come to stand in for the success-oriented youths he wrote about. Today, to be "Horatio Alger" is to be someone who succeeded through hard work. Alger gets constituted by his own Dream discourse as the dreamer he was, this time dreaming for himself rather than his characters and perhaps suggesting that the American Dream is really about self-promotion after all.) And while it has mythological and ideological implications, these are results of discourse rather than conditions of its possibility.

It is therefore not so much Republicans and Cuomo anymore as dreamers—i.e., those who use the discourse of the American Dream to make their policy prescriptions. Dreamers all, though they dream in different directions, just as they sleep in different beds, they now become strange bedfellows dreaming the dream of the American Dream and articulating Dream discourse in ways that do not so much represent reality in some ideologically tendentious way or some mythologically idealizing way as in some Dream-constituting way. We become artifacts of the Dream as much as the Dream is an artifact of us. (We all become "Horatio Alger," constituted by the discourses with which we are associated.)

In *Restoring the Dream* the House Republicans therefore define themselves along with the American Dream as possessing "the basic optimism that the future will be better than the past, that anyone in America, no matter what their income level, or where they were born, or what their skin color is, can succeed through perseverance, education, hard work, thrift, and taking risks" (37). This is another way of saying that America is still a land of opportunity and Republicans are still the party of dynamic capitalism. By invoking the Dream, Republicans define themselves as dreamers of that particular Dream as much as they define their particular version of that Dream.

A quintessential Republican self is implied by the Dream in this narrative. Dream discourse constitutes its citizenry as biography in history. We are self-actualizing selves who are living long after the "Golden Age" of free markets confronting stagnation and the need for policy change to scale back government and jump-start an "opportunity society." The Dream does this by inscribing its promises on our bodies, ensuring us each as individuated disembodied individuals the opportunity do better for ourselves, if only we would try on our own according to the strictures of self-sufficiency implied by the Dream. This Dream constitutes us as colorless, genderless, classless dreamers of personal advancement, overlooking how we might be a very diverse group of highly individualized persons differentially situated, not all well positioned to take advantage of the opportunities for exclusive consumption offered by the House Republicans' market society. Less important is the particular version of the Dream as a misreading of the American Way of Life than the fact that Republicans reinscribe the legitimacy of the Dream and its importance in defining who affirms that way of life and who challenges it. To dream the Dream is to invoke the discourse, which is to reaffirm the extant self-understandings such a discourse helps constitute. It is to be enlisted as a Dreamer who embraces that identity.

At the same time, this discourse of anonymous disembodied agents of self-actualization paints the nation as another corporealized entity with its own trajectory of decline. It momentarily stabilizes the state as the welfare state, while imputing obesity to the bloated federal government. This same candidate for Weight Watchers is then cast as our collective enemy: "Nothing has eroded the American Dream for so many of our citizens more insidiously than the $5 trillion modern welfare state. The welfare state seems almost designed to destroy the institution of fatherhood in America today. It seems designed to trap Americans in a cycle of dependency, rather than to encourage individual responsibility" (House Republicans, 1995: 52). For them, to dream the Dream is to reinscribe the implied version of autonomy that the "self-made" man of the American Dream is to be—beyond state control, free to make oneself as successful as one can be.

The Republican Dream constructs real identities, marginalizes others, anthropomorphizes the state, depicts policy problems, and selects solutions, all so as to reinforce a neo-laissez-faire government. This variation of Dream discourse offers its own version of the classic policy story of growth and decay, this time in the idiom of anxious economic actors who are part of a collective history of economic decline wrought by government meddling. We are strongly (and hyperbolically) warned: "Make no mistake about it, if this trend is not broken and reversed, the American Dream will simply cease to exist" (House Republicans, 1995: 52).

Exercising his "negative capability" from outside public office, Cuomo (1995) articulates other aspects of Dream discourse—fairness, equity, equal opportunity (Remnick, 1995). His picture of the American Dream is one that has a larger, more inclusive middle class with a communal sense of obligation. His Dream imagines us as a collective body—the body politic (Warner, 1992). Cuomo points out that we have exhibited "our" greatest strengths when "we" have pulled together during times such as the Great Depression and World War II. He argues that individualism, alone, does more to harm us than to help. His solution is for a return to a new sense of national community. And just before the end, the text says what the Cuomo variation seems to have always been saying even before it was ever spoken: "We need to think of ourselves as a family" (155).

Cuomo continues his use of the collective corporeal construction when he turns to criticizing the Republican vision. He accuses the Republicans of using the welfare issue to drive a blunt political wedge between the middle class and the poor. He offers an economic metaphor for reuniting the country. He suggests that instead of castigating and punishing the poor, we ought to offer them incentives to work and keep working by continuing the Earned Income Tax Credits, allowing health care benefits for the working poor and encouraging the continued development of innovative reform plans on the part of the states, recognizing that reforms will not bring immediate cost savings, but they will be valuable investments in people.

Yet, like all discourses, these versions of the Dream contrive their coherences that, among other things, make our biographies fit its history of decline and its narrative plea for a return to home. In either case, whether it is a discourse of disembodied self-actualizers or a discourse of a collective entity, there are silences in the text that amount to cultural exclusions that may continue to marginalize those who do not pursue the Dream of individual achievement or personal advancement as conventionally defined by the civilization of productivity. Dream discourse puts us all, even a thoughtful Cuomo, at risk of becoming committed to constituting policy in the narrow terms of equal opportunity for those who are willing to prove themselves to be self-reliant according to ascendant standards. The American Dream in these variations therefore offers a limited choice: either individuated, replicable self-reliant selves of exclusive consumption or an assimilated whole dedicated to assimilating the assimilable. More troubling, it is a "Hobson's choice"—one that is made for us. From Horatio Alger to contemporary tracts, the Dream is a dream that we dream according to terms that have been pre-set, thereby constituting us in the image of someone else's Dream.

Conclusion

The stories we tell about the American Dream are representations of what America was, what it is to be. Given the pervasiveness and power of these stories, America is then itself a dream. It is as Benedict Anderson (1983) has called all nations—an "Imagined Community." America the beautiful . . . dreamer. America as constituted in Dream . . . Discourse. It is a dream that has many variations: the Shining City on the Hill of Ronald Reagan, a Tale of Two Cities of Mario Cuomo, Gingrich's restored free market, the House Republicans' free-fall American Dream geared toward individualistic personal responsibility and opportunity in the face of encroaching decline. Perhaps the Dream is the many different individual stories of hope by people who are living their lives and doing the best they can.

The American Dream can be understood as both ideology and discourse. In both cases, we need to consider how to pluralize its possibilities and thereby allow it to constitute us in more inclusive ways. We need therefore to learn to dream other dreams and, perhaps, not just as Americans living in the United States but as people living on this planet. Yet if current dreamscapes of Republicans and Cuomos are any sign of the discursive diversity of the American Dream, then it is a recurring dream that verges on nightmare. Of late, the Dream, as a discursive practice, has become a self-canceling signifier—i.e., a Dream that points toward its own illusory status as an increasingly unattainable state of being (see Baudrillard, 1994b). The Dream becomes a specter haunting our "civilization of productivity" reminding us to mourn what has been left out or what has gone unfulfilled (see Derrida, 1994). It is time to imagine other ways of writing the narrative for "Americans"—ways less tied to the economistic and assimilationist strictures that plague so many versions of the Dream.

Part II
Institutions, Actors, and Narratives

4

The Storyteller in Chief: Why Presidents Like to Tell Tales

John Kenneth White

Over the years, I have become increasingly convinced that the American presidency has less to do with the structures of office than with how its occupant performs as an embodiment of the American populace, representing hopes and fears through the arts of communication, particularly the craft of storytelling. Initially, most academics took a highly formalistic approach to the office, reflecting a preoccupation with how certain powers came to be and how the various custodians of the presidency utilized these powers. Edward S. Corwin (1957), a leading scholar in the 1950s, set a high standard with his comprehensive examination of the institutional origins and development of the presidency. By the 1960s, however, presidential scholars understood that power was a much less solid and more malleable quality than previously thought. Richard E. Neustadt (1960) in a path-breaking book described how chief executives derived their authority from their effectiveness in negotiating with elites and convincing the mass public about what they saw as the direction the government should take.

In recent years, scholars have focused more on leadership qualities, especially those linked to the immersion of presidents into the mythologies and symbols of the nation. James David Barber (1972) provided a masterful book that recognized the presidency as a reflection of its occupants. Stephen Skowronek (1993) focused on the leadership qualities of each of the forty-one men who have occupied the White House, and how they have put their brand on the politics of their time.

Still there is more to be done to enhance our understanding of the presidency and, in some cases, correct misunderstandings that have arisen over the years. Eric Goldman (1969) undertook to address the latter when he argued that general misperception of the president's role as legislator-in-chief formed the "tragedy" of Lyndon Johnson's tenure. In Goldman's view, Johnson saw the presidency as a means to an end—i.e., keeping score of the number of bills that successfully cleared the many congressional hurdles. But "getting things done" is just one part of a president's legacy. Another important function of the office is the incumbent's ability to "tell the tales of the state." The presidency affords its occupants the opportunity to play a unique role as the nation's storyteller in chief. Often that means reaffirming the essential character of the American ideology, or more cynically, telling folks what they want to hear. By singling out individuals that exemplify the American character, presidents use a political shorthand to communicate with the public. Jeffrey Tulis understood this aspect of the office in *The Rhetorical Presidency* (1987). I have expounded upon a similar theme in *The New Politics of Old Values* (1990). What both books make clear is that of our recent presidents, no one was better at doing this than "the Great Communicator," Ronald Reagan, and there is much that the academic community can learn from his presidency—not only about the American polity, but also about ourselves.

For years, I have recounted an incident during the Reagan presidency that I consider emblematic of those years. In April 1987 during the height of the Iran-Contra affair, Reagan sought refuge from his trials in Washington by traveling to the heartland. Reagan told an airport crowd in West Lafayette, Indiana, about a boy named "Billy." It seemed that while Billy's father was an avid reader of the Sunday newspapers, son Billy preferred an afternoon game of baseball. To stall his son for a while, Billy's father told him to reassemble a newspaper map of the world that he had cut into tiny pieces. Reagan (1987) reported that after just seven minutes Billy completed the task. Asked how he did it so quickly, Billy responded, "On the other side of the map there was a picture of a family, and I found that if you put the family together the world took care of itself." After that, father and son went outside to play ball. When Reagan finished, the crowd applauded. But every time I tell the story, students snicker at Reagan's tall-tale.

Reagan's story about Billy is not simply a moral lesson about family life. True, Reagan was a gifted storyteller, but the story about Billy and the Reagan years say much about the presidency and the public. It is often said that in a media age, the president acts as the "national host." Certainly, Bill Clinton has been on many a cable television program, with appearances on *Larry King Live, Donahue,* C-SPAN, and even MTV. But even before the television era, every president was an entertainer to some extent. As John Adams once observed of his predecessor George Washington: "If he was not the greatest President, he was the best Actor of the Presidency we ever had. His Address to the States when he left the Army: his solemn Leaven taken of Congress . . . his Farewell Address to the people when he resigned his Presidency. There were all in a strain of Shakespearean and Garrickal excellence in Dramatic Exhibitions" (quoted in Hughes, 1973: 89).

Certainly, Reagan's training as a Hollywood actor served him well in the presidency. A Des Moines businessman praised his acting skills: "The reason this country is getting better is because we've been led to believe it's getting better. I believe we can be led into doing that. I believe Reagan projects that" (quoted in Galston, 1987: 20). Punctuating Reagan's tales were heroes who said things everyone wanted to hear. As a presidential candidate in 1980, Reagan told audiences about the B-17 pilot whose plane was attacked by the enemy during a World War II bombing run. One crew member was badly wounded and could not be extricated from the damaged bull-turret. As the aircraft lost altitude, the commander ordered the crew to bail out and then laid down beside the injured man, saying, "Never mind, son, we'll ride it down together." Reagan ended with a flourish: "Congressional Medal of Honor posthumously awarded" (quoted in Rogin, 1987: 5–6).

Unfortunately, there is no record of any such B-17 incident or any Congressional Medal of Honor. And because both men died, many wondered who had lived to spread the word. It was later discovered that Reagan's account bore a striking resemblance to the plot of the 1944 movie *A Wing and a Prayer*, whose star, Dana Andrews, says, "We'll take this ride together" (see Wills, 1981: 412). Despite the story's having been proved false, Reagan did not drop it. On a visit to West Germany in 1982, he told it again to U.S. soldiers stationed there—this time contrasting the heroism of the airmen with the dastardly deeds of the Soviets.

Why did Reagan's stories resonate with so many Americans? In part, because he told us how good we were. In so doing, he enunciated his faith in "American Exceptionalism"—namely, that the United States is a special place set apart from the rest of the world. In the nineteenth century, Herman Melville compared Americans to the biblical tribes of Israel, calling them "the peculiar chosen people . . . the Israel of our time" (quoted in Cronin, 1980: 161). A century later Reagan used nearly identical words: "Think for a moment how special it is to be an American. Can we doubt that only a Divine Providence placed this land, this island of freedom, here as a refuge for all those people in the world who yearn to breathe free" (remarks by the president and first lady in a national television address on drug abuse and prevention, Washington, D.C., September 14, 1986)? These statements symbolize something more than mere platitudes. After visiting the United States in the 1920s, G. K. Chesterton concluded: "America is the only nation in the world that is founded on a creed" (1922: 8). At the core of the "American Creed" is a belief in the malleability of the future by the individual. A shorthand phrase evokes this sentiment: the American Dream.

The American Dream is as old, and as young, as the United States itself. Historian James Truslow Adams wrote that John Quincy Adams believed his country stood for opportunity, "the chance to grow into something bigger and finer, as bigger and finer appealed to him" (1935: 174). Little has changed since. Like the sixth president, people still hope that their lives (and those of their children) will improve. Often the American Dream has become enmeshed in a glorification of materialism. James Q. Wilson described how Southern Californians were wont to display the fruits of their labors: "Each family had a house; there it was for all to see and inspect. With a practiced glance, one could tell how much it cost, how well it was cared for, how good a lawn had been coaxed into uncertain life, and how tastefully plants and shrubs had been set out" (1967: 40). When asked in a 1986 poll what the American Dream meant, most people spoke of education and property: 84 percent said it meant getting a high school education; 80 percent said it was freedom of choice; 70 percent said it was owning a home; 77 percent thought it was their children's receiving a college diploma; 68 percent said it was getting a college education for themselves; 61 percent said it was "doing better than my parents"; 58 percent said it was owning a business; 52 percent said it was symbolized by going from ordinary worker to company president (Roper, 1987: 1).

Today, Americans of every political stripe extol the American Dream. Accepting the Republican nomination in 1960, Richard Nixon declared: "I believe in the American Dream because I have seen it come true in my own life." A generation later Bill Clinton echoed similar sentiments. Standing before the Democratic Convention in 1992, Clinton recalled how his father died before he was born, how his mother became a nurse, how with manic determination he won entry into prestigious universities, and how as governor of Arkansas he used the values of opportunity, community, and responsibility to make a better life there. Born in Hope, Arkansas, Clinton ended his peroration with these words: "I still believe in a place called Hope."

Clinton Rossiter once wrote, "The final greatness of the presidency lies in the truth that it is not just an office of incredible power, but a breeding ground of indestructible myth" (1960: 103). From Washington's mythical cherry tree, to Lincoln's log cabin, to Clinton's humble origins in Hope, every president is the living symbol of the American Dream.

The freedom to excel is an important component of the American Dream. But another value also adheres to the American Dream: equality of opportunity. No wonder Martin Luther King, Jr. seized on this American version of egalitarianism to woo supporters to the civil rights movement. Addressing a throng at the Lincoln Memorial in August 1963, King immersed his dream in the American one: "I have a dream that my four little children will one day live in a nation where they will not be judged by the color or their skin but by the content of their character." Americans, however, have been strong in their devotion to equality as something that can be achieved through simple hard work. Glorification of the work ethic has endured throughout the nation's history. A 1991 poll found 67 percent believing "hard work" was the most important factor in getting ahead; only 13 percent thought "luck" was crucial (National Opinion Research Center, 1991).

The values of freedom, liberty, and equality of opportunity are dominant themes in American civic life. Americans are painfully aware of the poverty that grips some parts of the land—often stubbornly so. But they have steadfastly refused to confront the question Bruce Springsteen posed in a song titled "The River": Is the American Dream a lie, or does it represent something worse? If the American Dream fails to come true, most believe they have only themselves to blame. Political scientist Robert Lane's interview with a poor mechanic in New Haven, Connecticut, is illustrative of the prevailing view:

> I could have been a lot better off but through my own foolishness. I'm not. What causes poverty? Foolishness. . . . Believe me, had I used my head right, I could have had a house. I don't feel sorry for myself—what happened, happened you know. Of course you pay for it. (1962: 69)

During the 1980s an Iowa farmer facing foreclosure expressed similar sentiments: "My boys all made good. It's their old man who failed" (quoted in Malcolm, 1987: A1). Indeed, any attempt to deny or limit the American Dream has met with considerable resistance. For example, a 1938 Great Depression-era Roper poll found 67 percent rejecting the idea that there "should be a top limit of income and that anyone getting over that limit should be compelled to turn the excess back to government as taxes" (Roper, 1938). In 1981, the consensus still held: 79 percent did not think that "there should be a top limit on incomes so that no one can earn more than $100,000 a year" (U.S. Civil Service, 1981). A 1984 Roper survey found that 71 percent believed that differences in social standing were acceptable because they resulted from "what people made out of the opportunities they had."

This unquestioning faith in freedom, liberty, and equality of opportunity has produced a fanaticism of sorts. Garry Wills has written that one must adopt the American Dream "wholeheartedly, proclaim it, prove one's devotion to it" (1978: xxii). Wills might have had the House Committee on Un-American Activities in mind. The committee was created during the hysteria about communism in 1945. For three decades, it inquired into the public and private lives of suspected communists—notably, Whittaker Chambers and Alger Hiss. After Richard Nixon's spectacular political debut as an Un-American Activities communist-hunter in 1948, committee membership became highly sought after. But after its injudicious blacklisting of so many Americans, Congress abolished the committee in 1975 on the grounds that it, too, had become un-American.

The Committee on Un-American Activities illustrates the country's rigid political orthodoxy. Daniel Boorstin (1953: 14) rhetorically asks, "Who would think of using the word 'unItalian' or 'unFrench' as we use the word un-American?" As Louis Hartz observed, "When one's ultimate values are accepted wherever one turns, the absolute language of self-evidence comes easily enough" (1955: 58). To illustrate: a 1920 conference on immigrant education declared, "We believe in an Americanization which has for its end the making of good American citizens by developing in the mind of everyone who inhabits American soil an appreciation of the principles and practices of good American citizenship" (*Bulletin of the Department of Education*, 1920). In 1987 the American Federation of Teachers reaffirmed this view, urging educators to abandon a "morally neutral" approach in favor of teaching that "democracy is the worthiest form of human government ever conceived" (Fiske, 1987: 1).

"A Hell of a King"

It is in wearing this ideological straitjacket that the president performs. Several years after leaving the White House, Harry Truman described the presidency as "the most peculiar office in the world" (quoted in Hughes, 1973: 32). British scholar Harold Laski noted that the American presidency "functions in an American environment, that it has been shaped by the forces of American history, that it must be judged by American criteria of its responses to American needs" (quoted in Hughes, 1973: 23). One of the greatest needs of the public is the constant reaffirmation it seeks from the president of the ideological imperatives of freedom and equality of opportunity. Reagan poll-taker Richard B. Wirthlin once advised his client: "By symbolizing the past and future greatness of America and radiating inspirational confidence, a President can pull a nation together while directing its people toward fulfillment of the American Dream" (1981: 1).

The Founding Fathers may have understood this inherent desire when they created the presidency in the first place. Walter Dean Burnham (1989) contends that by fusing the powers of chief of state and chief of government in one person, the president has become "a *pontifex maximus*, a chief priest of the American civil religion." Rossiter (1960) thought being a chief of state meant a series of endless activities that kept a president "running from sunrise to bedtime." These included welcoming foreign dignitaries, laying wreaths at the Tomb of the Unknowns, lighting the national Christmas tree, throwing out the first baseball of the season, presiding at the White House Easter egg roll, greeting the truck driver of the year, and extending good wishes to the poster child of one charity or another. Like so many other political scientists, Rossiter did not disparage the role, but he did not glorify it either. Instead, he considered it a "genuine release from the routine tasks and hard decisions that fill the rest of the day" (1960: 16).

But chief of state is not doing, it is *being*. An effective performance can alter the national mood. Reagan's jaunty optimism translated into an enlarged national self-confidence. Such confidence-building was salutary after the disasters of Vietnam, Watergate, and the malaise of the 1970s. That had consequences that reached into every home according to Reagan pollster Wirthlin: "In being the person who establishes a tone, a president has influence on every American—be it a young person entering the job market, an individual on the margin of deciding whether to study or whether to work, an entrepreneur trying to determine whether to invest in his own business or go to work for someone else" (1988).

Reagan's effective performance as chief of state contrasted with his predecessor, who likened the presidency to a prime minister—often concentrating on being an effective legislator. Lyndon Johnson is a prime example. While Johnson produced many notable legislative accomplishments, British journalist Michael Davie labeled Johnson "uncouth," adding:

> He picked his nose. He was liable, when slumped in a chair, to reach casually and unashamedly into his groin to ease his pants. His phrasing was of a kind not usually associated with the Presidency of the United States. To a reporter who began an interview with a trivial question, he asked, "Why do you come and ask me, the leader of the Western World, a chicken shit question like that?" (1967: 14–15)

On other occasions, Johnson overplayed his role. When LBJ was leaving the White House by helicopter in 1968, a young staff sergeant steered him away from the helicopter he thought he would be riding saying, "Mr. President, *that* is your helicopter over there." Johnson grabbed the sergeant and explained, "Son, they're all my helicopters" (see Koenig, 1986: 13). When the Vietnam War stalled into a stalemate, his support began to wane. But Johnson had already been weakened by his inability to grasp the job of being chief of state.

The importance of popularity is not ephemeral. From its inception of the presidency, presidents have been searching to extend the limited authority given the office by the Framers. Reagan tapped a wellspring of power in the largely ignored chief of state role, particularly by emphasizing the storyteller in chief dimension. So successful was he that the first known instance of President George Bush soliciting his advice concerns it. When forty-seven sailors on the USS *Iowa* died after being hit by an Iraqi missile, Bush was scheduled to address the survivors. Bush readily admitted his discomfiture with the impending ceremony and asked Reagan how he should conduct himself. As president, Reagan won considerable praise for his handling of the *Challenger* disaster, his commiseration with those who lost loved ones on the USS *Stark*, and his remembrance of the World War II heroes at Normandy. Former House Speaker Thomas P. "Tip" O'Neill once said of Reagan, "He wouldn't have made much of a prime minister, but he would have made a hell of a king" (quoted in "Ronald Reagan and David Brinkley," 1988).

If Reagan invested considerable energy perfecting the chief of state role, his fellow countrymen invested a huge amount of time watching him perform. Americans are devoted to the presidency, and they follow the exploits of its incumbents closely because they have so much at stake in the institution's well-being. To the public, the president is the nation made manifest to itself and the rest of the world. Rossiter observed, "Only the Constitution overshadows the Presidency as an object of popular reverence, and the Constitution does not walk about smiling and waving" (1960: 250).

Clinton Agonistes

In a masterful book, Charles C. Thach Jr. (1923) maintained that the Founding Fathers were enamored with "a new theory of executive responsibility based on unity, integration, choice by, and complete responsibility to, the people." He quoted James Wilson who argued that representation was the vital ingredient of the new Constitution:

> The American States enjoy the glory and the happiness of diffusing this vital principle throughout all the different divisions and departments of government. Representation is the chain of communication between the people and those to whom they have committed the important charge of exercising the delegated powers necessary for the administration of public affairs. This chain may consist of one link, or more links than one, but it should always be sufficiently strong and discernable. (1923: 175, 167)

One of the most important linkages a president has with the public is his ability to preach to the choir. Bill Clinton has, no doubt, asked himself: "How can I be more like Reagan?" Certainly, Clinton does not intend to emulate Reagan's conservative philosophy, but he would love to enjoy Reagan's political successes. In two successive presidential elections, Reagan won 93 of the 100 state contests, and he left office with the highest approval rating since Franklin D. Roosevelt (*Gallup Report*, 1989). Clinton has discovered that he can emulate Reagan if, in the words of his speechwriter David Kusnet (1992), he can "speak American." This has proved to be a troublesome task for other Democrats. In 1988, Gary Hart lamented: "I don't want to be president of a country that thinks like Ronald Reagan" (Providence *Journal*, 1989). But four short years later Bill Clinton easily made Reagan's values rhetoric his own. Accepting the nomination, Clinton outlined a "New Covenant" whose purpose was to demonstrate that he shared the voters' collective values and aspirations: "In the end, the New Covenant simply asks us all to be Americans again. Old-fashioned Americans for a new time. Opportunity. Responsibility. Community. When we pull together, America will pull ahead" (1992).

As president, Clinton has made the words opportunity, community, and responsibility his emblem. Like Reagan, he has used ceremonial occasions for storytelling that gives these values resonance. In his 1995 State of the Union Address, Clinton told not one story, but *six*. There was Lynn Woolsey, a single mother from California who found her way off welfare to become a member of Congress. Then came Cindy Perry, a mother of four who passed her high school equivalency exam and teaches second-graders to read in rural Kentucky. Next Clinton recognized Steven Bishop, the police chief of Kansas City, Missouri. Bishop was an Americorps volunteer and innovator in community policing. Then Corporal Gregory Depestre was asked by his commander in chief to stand. Depestre, a Haitian-American, was part of the force that landed in Haiti. Clinton noted: "We must be the only country in the world that could have gone to Haiti and taken Haitian-Americans there who could speak the language and talk to the people, and he was one of them, and we're proud of him."

Clinton was hardly finished. He talked about the Reverends John and Diana Cherry, noting that the church they formed in the 1980s had grown to 17,000 members and had expanded into the high-crime and drug-infested neighborhoods of Washington, D.C. Finally, Clinton recognized Jack Lucas from Hattiesburg, Mississippi. Lucas was badly wounded at Iwo Jima after he threw himself on two grenades and saved the lives of three of his fellow soldiers. At age seventeen, Lucas miraculously survived and became the youngest citizen ever to win the Congressional Medal of Honor. For Clinton, the moral lessons contained in each of these stories was clear: "We all gain when we give and we reap what we sow." He then drew a connection with the New Covenant:

> That's at the heart of this New Covenant, responsibility, opportunity, and citizenship. More than stale chapters in some remote civics book, they are still the virtues by which we can fulfill ourselves and reach our God-given potential and be like them, and also fulfill the eternal promise of this country, the enduring dream from that first and most sacred covenant. I believe every person in this country still believes that we are created equal, and given by our Creator the right to life, liberty, and the pursuit of happiness. This is a very great country and our best days are still to come. (1995)

Conclusion

Clearly, Clinton had learned Reagan's lessons. By 1996, this skilled politician had become one of America's premier storytellers. In becoming the first Democratic president to win re-election since Franklin D. Roosevelt did so in 1936, Clinton had altered the traditional presidential role of party leader established by Roosevelt as he brilliantly used his New Deal coalition to change the face of American politics. At the 1996 Democratic National Convention, Clinton turned the podium over to paralyzed actor Christopher Reeve and gunshot victim James Brady so they could tell the nation about their stories of hope and courage. By inference, Clinton added the biographies of these American heroes (heretofore not associated with the Democratic party) to his now-famous "bridge to the twenty-first century" metaphor that he hopes will encapsulate his second term in office. Whatever judgments historians eventually make about Clinton, it is clear that the transformation of the president as the storyteller in chief was completed during his two terms in office.

5

The Cycle of Representation: The House Republicans and the Contract with America

Sanford F. Schram

As reproduced in the *New York Times* shortly after the November 1994 congressional elections, the "Contract with America" was a set of ten promises Republican candidates for the U.S. House of Representatives made for legislative action they would undertake during the first one hundred days of the 104th Congress:

1. *The Fiscal Responsibility Act:* A balanced budget/tax limitation amendment and a legislative line-item veto to restore fiscal responsibility to an out-of-control Congress, requiring it to live under the same budget constraints as families and businesses.
2. *The Taking Back Our Streets Act:* An anti-crime package including stronger truth-in-sentencing, "good faith" exclusionary rule exemptions, effective death penalty provisions, and cuts in social spending from this summer's "crime" bill to fund prison construction and additional law enforcement to keep people secure in their neighborhoods and kids safe in their schools.
3. *The Personal Responsibility Act:* Discourage illegitimacy and teen pregnancy by prohibiting welfare to minor mothers and denying increased AFDC for additional children while on welfare, cut spending for welfare programs, and enact a tough two-years-and-out provision with work requirements to promote individual responsibility.
4. *The Family Reinforcement Act:* Child support enforcement, tax incentives for adoption, strengthening rights of parents in their children's education, stronger child pornography laws, and an elderly depen-

dent care tax credit to reinforce the central role of families in American society.

5. *The American Dream Restoration Act:* A $500 per child tax credit, begin repeal of the marriage tax penalty, and creation of American Dream Savings Accounts to provide middle class tax relief.
6. *The National Security Restoration Act:* No U.S. troops under U.N. command and restoration of the essential parts of our national security funding to strengthen our national defense and maintain our credibility around the world.
7. *The Senior Citizens Fairness Act:* Raise the Social Security earnings limit which currently forces seniors out of the work force, repeal the 1993 tax hikes on Social Security benefits and provide tax incentives for private long-term care insurance to let older Americans keep more of what they have earned over the years.
8. *The Job Creation and Wage Enhancement Act:* Small business incentives, capital gains cut and indexation, neutral cost recovery, risk assessment/cost-benefit analysis, strengthening the Regulatory Flexibility Act and unfunded mandate reform to create jobs and raise worker wages.
9. *The Common Sense Legal Reform Act:* "Loser pays" laws, reasonable limits on punitive damages and reform of product liability laws to stem the endless tide of litigation.
10. *The Citizen Legislature Act:* A first ever vote on term limits to replace career politicians with citizen legislators. (New York Times, 1994)

"In their own words," as the *New York Times* aptly headlined its summary, the Republicans stressed how "common sense," "business," "family," and "personal responsibility" were to be imposed through the Contract on some other "out-of-control Congress" in order to provide "reinforcement" and "restoration" of the "American Dream." In the end, only number 3 was to be enacted with full force; however, the ultimate power of the Contract may be determined by more than this one policy success.

The success of the Contract may instead be contingent upon what it has represented—e.g., as electoral politics or policy agenda, as a symbolic or material practice. While there may have been a time when such distinctions were meaningful, the Contract's ambiguous status as what we can call a "hybrid imagined agreement" highlights how politics/policy, symbolic/material, text/image, and a variety of related binaries do injustice to representing what is described by them. In fact, the Contract, whether seen as elite political posturing or as popular policy agenda, highlights the problem of representation in politics. In the case of the Contract, its politics lie in the terms it uses to represent its policy agenda. Its power may be assessed by how well it intensifies a self-legitimating discourse that promotes what we can call "orders of disentitlement," that freeing state actors to decide what it is that the "American People" want and who among them is entitled to it.

The political power of the Contract with America lies most especially in its relationship to the term "contract" as it is used in liberal policy, legal, and business discourses. "Contract" is particularly important because it facilitates the presencing of a distinctive self as the kind of person that is assumed to be needed in so many settings by a liberal society, i.e., an individuated self who creates and destroys value through the fulfillment of contractual exchanges (Norton, 1993). The Contract with America's conservative policy agenda, therefore, was ineliminably tied to the implied liberal narratives of consenting citizenry and personal responsibility associated with the political vocabulary of contract (Reddy, 1992).

The Contract with America, irrespective of its inability to achieve all of its agenda, is an important contemporary instance of how liberal theory has become, even more so than in the past, the "common sense" of the United States and how this common sense operates as a ready reserve—i.e., a lexicon of signs, symbols, and images used to reinforce prevailing relationships of power (Norton, 1993). The liberal "common sense" of the conservative Contract, therefore, becomes a political subtext that needs interrogation, but not as an apolitical literary exercise. Anne Norton has emphasized the political value of such analysis when writing about how liberalism has achieved unquestioned authority as the common sense of the contemporary United States:

> Silence concerning the authority of language over the constitution of the self, the realization and expression of the will, permits liberal regimes to maintain the myth of the word, particularly the spoken word, as a neutral instrument for the utterance and realization of the individual will. It enables liberal regimes to maintain established hierarchies by predicating the achievement of equality and the establishment and maintenance of cultural difference on involvement in practices that obstruct or preclude these ends. (1993: 160–61)

The following analysis seeks to break that silence about the self-legitimating liberal politics of contractual language by highlighting it in the conservative Contract with America. In the process, we can begin to examine how even the conservative Contract with America reinforced the hegemony of liberal contractual discourse and how that hegemony perpetuates questionable notions of citizen consent and personal responsibility.

Contracts and Diaries: Dispatches to the Self

Dear Diary: I promised myself that I would log in my reactions to the "Contract with America." Yet, before I do, I offer some prefatory comments on the protean politics of the phrase itself. "Contracting America," as the activity engendered by the Contract, is unavoidably a multidimensional practice referring to the various forms of contracting that are possible in America today. Once we start contracting America, there immediately arises the question of whether we will go all the way—e.g., privatize it to subcontractors, retrench it to a "two-thirds society" (Brown, 1988), or become totally infected by it.

"Contracting America" is at least trebled in meaning—legally binding exchange, welfare state rollback, disease. The idea of contract serves the politics of today in various convenient ways: (1) the reassurances that come with business transactions between ostensibly free and equal parties; (2) the insistencies derived from persistent political pressures to reduce the welfare state; and (3) anxieties attached to contagious diseases given the decline of immunology in a postantibiotic age. In an age in which the modernist impulse to insist on airtight distinctions between nature and culture break down, contract becomes a hybrid implying simultaneously the symbolic and the material, if not the cultural and the natural (Latour, 1993). It is a multipurpose term that has multiple resonances suggesting a variety of possible responses, each of which can be said to "process" the idea of contract in a distinctive way.

"Contract" in America, therefore, as a "hybrid, imagined agreement," is a potent, if unstable, metaphor. America is the contractual society where contract is the metaphor of choice for legitimating so much of what we do publicly and privately, in marriage, business, law, and social policy. Contract is a live metaphor (i.e., used so often) because it is a dead metaphor (i.e., has lost its figurative character and is seen as literal). Yet, in America, contract is catachresis (i.e., a misrepresenting nonequivalence) not metaphor (i.e., a representing equivalence), for contract is contracted by so many in so many dissimilar ways (on catachresis see White, 1979). The power of contract lies in its articulation—i.e., the extent to which it as an expressed representation can be connected with so many different things (on articulation see Hall, 1986; Fiske, 1989). In the contract society, so much is about contract, even if diversely so, and the Contract with America is a quintessentially American discursive practice.

From campaign slogan to policy agenda, this act of contracting America becomes a paradigmatic example of the dangers associated with the borrowing of metaphor across the overlapping, discontinuous discourses of business, law, and politics (R. Schram, 1995). Contracting America underscored how one discourse must of necessity invoke another given the pervasive impossibility of getting beyond intertextuality (Baudrillard, 1994a). In the quest to use discourse as an attempt to make coherent the incoherences of public life, or life generally, one discourse trades on the other, borrowing metaphors for justification, creating an inevitable layering of meaning (Derrida, 1982). Contractarians would probably prefer the formulation that one discourse must inevitably contract with other discourses in order to create meaning. The "metaphors of contract" highlight the "contracts of metaphor." Meaning becomes contingent upon the deferred promise of representation. And the Contract with America inevitably invokes references to the contracts Americans regularly make in the liberal society of commercialized, propertied relations.

To stress contract already suggests how all political discourse is contracted from intertextual articulations with other discursive realms necessitating the indefinite deferral of the contracted terms. Contract itself then is contracted through an intertextuality that defers specifying the definitional terms of contract. The Contract with America traded on the fictions of consent in the social contract theories of liberal political discourse that themselves echo the questionable notions of fiduciary responsibility and reciprocal rights and obligations associated with contracts of business and marriage, labor and slave. Such is one way of characterizing the contagion that is liberal policy discourse today as practiced by conservatives and others. Borrowing the contractual metaphors of catachresis (i.e., metaphors about contract that make the dissimilar similar) from business practice to legal document to policy prescription results in its own linguistic contamination and subversion.

To "Contract with America" is therefore also unavoidably vexed as a linguistic act—is it illocutionary or locutionary? "Contract with America" as a statement in language used by the Republicans is not just what J. L. Austin (1962) called a "constative" (i.e., a descriptive statement). Instead, in name and deed "Contract with America" would be for Austin a "performative" (i.e., a statement that is itself an act). As an enactment, "Contract with America" has more than what Austin calls the "locutionary" force of referencing the world beyond itself. It has either the greater "illocutionary" force of implicating the sender of its message in that act (as in a promise or a contractual commitment) or the even still greater "perlocutionary" force of imposing consequences on the receiver (as in a command or order that by the sheer force of its being spoken in public implicates others who hear it in undertaking a certain act) (Austin, 1962). "Contract with America"—is it illocutionary or perlocutionary? As a performative, does it offer a contract or announce it as a fait accompli?

"Contract with America" in the least therefore highlights how speech acts can have both a performative dimension and a constative dimension (Derrida, 1988). The performative operates in declarative statements that announce a promissory as to what will happen, but these performatives are only made credible if the message is from an authorized sender to a relevant receiver. The constative operates in the authorless descriptions of ongoing events. In the case of the Contract with America, its unstable perlocutionary positioning gives rise to the question: Who is contracting what?

Only what Jacques Derrida (1977) calls a "metaphysics of presence," where volitional speaking subjects are assumed to be the originating source for what they take to be their own ideas, creates the ground to deny how the representations of discourse indefinitely defer meaning by delegating that responsibility to intertextual exchanges. Contract, like the signatories to it, is never but a presence referring to a deferred absence. Signature connotes the authorization of the authorizing agent who is not present but absent and whose signature is thereby required. The idea of signature has proven to be a historic problem for the liberal social contract that whether deployed in founding the American or other liberal political systems had to construct ahead of time the "People" of that nation-state who were then post-hoc taken to comprise the consenting parties to the agreement (Derrida, 1986; Honig, 1991). The state constructs the nation rather than the people construct the state as when the leaders of the American Revolution claimed to be acting in the name of the "American People" who had yet to consent to formation of a new government. Contract symbolizes agreement achieved at some other, often imagined point in time, as likely in the future as in the past. The Contract with America therefore undermined the critical subject position of its central objects of inquiry—i.e., "citizen consent" and "personal responsibility." The Contract with America therefore sought to legislate with welfare reform who qualifies as personally responsible, while denying the extent to which the people represented by the symbol of "America" actually got to be real signatories for a contract made in their name.

In the parlance of liberal political discourse, contracting "America" inevitably also means converting America into a form of property to be bought and sold on the open market (Williams, 1991). The commodity sold here is the reified, repackaged, already processed entity entitled the "American People." Buying into this transaction would actually imply condoning a form of property theft—i.e., aiding and abetting the stealing of the name of the "American People" for purposes of "forging" national public policy in the name of the people who are alleged to have made those policies. Resisting the theft associated with the Contract with America of necessity involves interpretive agonistics that challenge in particular how the Contract with America is a discursive politics that appropriates the "American People" for its own political purposes. To leave the Contract with America uncontested would be to accept how it operates as an economy of intelligibility (a lingua franca of discursive exchange) that maps political space and positions the citizens of the United States as assenters to an imagined request for specific policy actions (Shapiro, 1993).

Contesting the Contract with America therefore starts with challenging it as a conservative discursive practice whose liberal silences are tied to the prevailing common sense about that exchangeable commodity called the "American People." Political struggle over the continuing linguistic legacy of the Contract with America then involves contesting both the commodification associated with contracting "America" and the possessiveness implied by the (body)snatching of that (body) politic that is called the "American People." The right to take possession of that *proper* name and to treat it like one's own personal *property* is like other property rights and is therefore constructed out of law. Possession of the body becomes contingent upon the deeding of the title. Who has title to the "American People" and to what extent and under what conditions are the people who comprise that populace entitled to benefits from the state? To what extent does the power to entitle the "American People" in the linguistic sense promote the power to disentitle some of those people in the political sense?

Just what then are the "orders of disentitlement" in the Contract with America? This is very much a problem of language that is also a problem for politics. For instance: when they say it is time to "disentitle the unentitled," do they mean "to take away *welfare benefits* from the *unworthy poor*" or do they mean it is time "to take away *titles* from *the unnamed*"? While the contemporary political scene suggests the former, the linguistic formulation in question allows for the latter. I want to ask what is to be gained by highlighting that both interpretations are possible from this phrase. What do we learn about the contemporary uses of that phrase when we recognize its duality or how it is doubled-over in meaning? Does the denying of names (i.e., disentitlement of the first order) help promote the denying of benefits (i.e., disentitlement of the second order)? How do these "orders of disentitlement" interact and to what effect? How did the conservative Contract with America reinforce liberal political discourse in ways that intensified notions of citizen consent and personal responsibility that in turn activate these orders of disentitlement?

The corporealization of "America" (see Warner, 1992) implied by the Contract, therefore, inaugurated an imperialistic, if contemporary, form of top-down ventriloquism (on top-down see Fiske, 1993). After one hundred days of legislating in order to fulfill the promise of the Contract, Newt Gingrich, as speaker of the House, got to speak on how the House had upheld its end of this bargain, all the while denying how he had positioned members of the American polity as contractors in his discourse. In his House, "the Contract with America" becomes "the Discourse on America"—the one and only promise that needed to be kept. Never mind that his House was but one House and that policy promises cannot be fulfilled in America unless they are affirmed in two houses and gain the signature of the resident in the White House. Nonetheless, "the Speaker of the House" at least got to keep his promise to himself, even as his pronouncements denied the ways in which his Discourse on America contracts it and makes it a more exclusive group.

The Contract with America was then like a diary entry; it was a memo that Gingrich and other House Republicans wrote to themselves. More than that however, it was a diary entry meant to be read as if it were a letter posted to someone else. It anticipated reading by supplying a subtext that assumes its audience and it did so by implicating that audience in the text. In so doing, this perlocutionary practice denied readers their readership. It was more O. J. Simpson's *I Want to Tell You* than the *Bob Packwood Diaries.* To read the Contract with America was to be denied the opportunity to supply what was missing from the text—i.e., the very act of supplementation that Paul de Man (1986) suggests defines readership. Specifically, de Man defines reading as enacting what is missing from a text but doing so in a way that must of necessity create a new text that is also in need of supplementation, thereby suggesting that all readings should be open-ended and not foreclose the possibility of additional readings. Yet reading the Contract was reading a closed-ended pact Newt Gingrich made with himself only to claim that it was a pact he had made with the "American People." Reading the Contract, the American people found out rather than decided each on their own what that text was supposed to mean for them.

The Contract with America was therefore not just the public equivalent of a bedside diary, it was also the political equivalent of a draft notice—and if not conscription, then a coercive form of enlistment. Enlistment (Clegg, 1989) allegedly signs up those who join voluntarily while conscription enrolls individuals without their voluntarily choosing to join. Yet that is what can be so insidious about enlistments like the Contract with America. It enlisted the "American People" into being signatories to this imagined contract without the people actually signing on to it.

The Self-Referential Text/Image

The Contract's ambiguous status as a constructed agreement with the "American People" is compounded by its hybridity as a "text/image" (Mitchell, 1994). The mostly unread but often visualized Contract with America was an act of both narrative and pictorial representation—i.e., a representation that stages a scene in text and image. Yet its ambiguity as a text/image is something that it as a representation works to erase. It is part of all the denials the Contract tries to enforce about its problematic status. Most importantly, for the House Republicans, the Contract was to be denied as a symbolic election campaign spectacle (i.e., a pictorial representation) so that it could serve a material public policy-making purpose (i.e., a textual practice).

In fact, the Contract's ambiguity as a text/image enables us to suggest how it became unavoidably the non-reflective policy equivalent of Velazquez's *Las Meninas* (Fig. 5.1). Michel Foucault (1973) has helped us understand how *Las Meninas* creates a cultural resource for problematizing the aesthetic experience as one grounded in the idea of the artist as the originating genius for her or his creations (Aronowitz, 1994). *Las Meninas* operates as what W. J. T. Mitchell (1994) has called a "metapicture"—i.e., a picture that makes visible

(1) how all representation is ineliminably self-referential, (2) how each representation cannot but highlight its own constitutive practices, and (3) how it must do so in a way that undermines the unquestioned status and sovereignty of the viewing subject. The metapicture illuminates the problematic status of representations based on the fallacious idea that the represented can be faithfully and objectively depicted by the representative and how such representations must of necessity construct a point of view that makes this lie believable.

For Foucault, the self-reflectivity of *Las Meninas* stems from its being a "spiral shell" that "presents us with the entire cycle of representation" (1973: 11). Its political significance lies with its holding open the gap between (interpreting) language and (interpreted) image in a way that allows the process of representation to be seen as a dialectical field influenced by *both* the viewing (subject) and the viewed (object). As a self-reflective text/image, *Las Meninas* was what Foucault called a "calligram" —i.e., a representation that did not try to erase the ineliminable gap between what can be said and what can be seen.

The Contract with America's nonreflectivity lies in a somewhat parallel dimension of representation, with the attempt of the (House Republican) viewing subjects to impose their univocal interpretation of their viewed object (the "American People"). Yet, the Contract still performs the work of *Las Meninas*, or any metapicture, if only un-reflectively, because it cannot but point to the indeterminatedness of the "cycle of representation" even, or especially, as the (House Republican) representatives try to determine the represented ("American People").

The Contract was a nonreflective *Las Meninas* because it unreflectively denied how it represented some other imagined "real" contract with the "American People" that it claimed it itself actually was. Yet, unavoidably, the Contract became a metapicture, if only a naive one (Mitchell, 1994). It unavoidably highlighted the constitutive practices of its own representational process. In particular, its play on the idea of signature offered a way toward recognition of the inverted character of its representation of the "American People" and thereby undermined the meaningfulness of seeking authorization for interpretation of what it represented in some beginning, origin, or author (such as the parties to a contract or the painter of a picture) who could serve as the authentic, genuine, or original source of meaning (of that contract or painting). In context, the Contract, as a hybrid agreement, was represented in such a way that its representations, lacking an originating referent, could only point back to themselves. The Contract became an unreflective *Las Meninas*, i.e., less intentionally, but still nonetheless, problematizing its own representational status as elite political posturing posing as popular policy agenda.

The congressional representative shown in Figure 5.2 could consult his copy, while the larger-than-life model simultaneously suggested the imagi-

Figure 5.1. Velazquez's "Las Meninas." *Courtesy of Museo del Prado, Madrid. Copyright © Museo del Prado. All rights reserved. Reproduction prohibited without permission.*

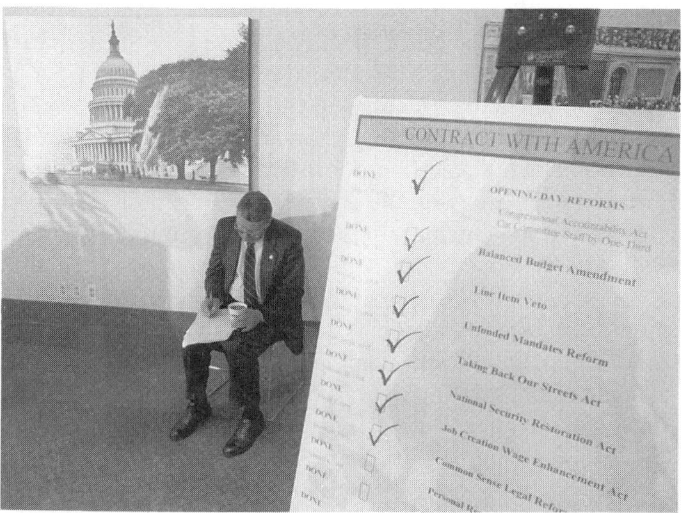

Figure 5.2. The Cycle of Representation. *AP Photo, courtesy of Wide World Photos.*

nary original agreement and served as the standard for the whole of Congress as a representative body against which to measure all lesser copies possessed by individual representatives. The "American People," even as parties to the agreement, were left to participate as passive spectators viewing the image of the written Contract but not possessing their own copies. And even their gaze was scripted for them as they were passive spectators encouraged to see in the ways that the Contract had read them as audience for the Contract.

The Contract was then conceivably a self-referential, undecidable, erased, and arbitrary text/image representation of itself. It was what Derrida (1981) has called a simulacrum—i.e., a model that was its own referent or a representation that referred to itself. Yet it was still not a simulacrum in the sense that Jean Baudrillard (1981) has used the term to refer to acts of signification that rely on the autonomous signal rather than the context-dependent sign. Norton (1993) suggests that Baudrillard uses simulacrum as signal to refer to a sign that is liberated from its referent, divested from history, and unconnected from meaning. Signals, as opposed to signs, send messages that receivers cannot challenge on the grounds that they misrepresent their referent. In this "mode of signification," simulacra operate as decontextualized signifiers that invert the process of referentiality. Simulacra become models that precede that on which they are modeled. The model precedes the referent and the referent is modeled after the model to the point that models are all that there is. Shopping districts come to be modelled after the shopping malls that simulated shopping districts to the point that there are only shopping malls. Public opinion is modelled after the polls to the point that only polls need to be anticipated irrespective of what opinions the public might otherwise formulate (Baudrillard, 1983). Simulacra point to themselves out of any context and do not suggest anything other than themselves.

Yet the Contract with America was arguably not so decontextualized. Contract, as a term of liberal political discourse, of necessity invokes the ready-standing liberal lexicon of established meanings. As such, the Contract like so many signs of liberalism had been integrated into the prevailing common sense. Like the dense, if mute, imagery associated with the liberal order (whether it is the U.S. flag or Constitution), liberal metaphors like contract immediately invoke the mythology of the liberal fabulom that comprises the prevailing sense of place and time (i.e., how things came to be the way they are here and now). In this sense, contract is more mythology than simulation (more mythological simulacrum than real simulacrum). It does point somewhere but its referent is not real referent but instead the mythology with which it is associated. As a semiliberated signifier, contract points to the preexisting understandings of liberal mythology.

It is conservative in its political effects and therefore operates as a conservative-liberal signifier—i.e., operating to conserve the preexisting liberal cosmology on which liberal relations rely for their justification.

Contract then is an inevitably conservative simulacrum destined to invoke the commodifying properties of a contractual society. The Contract with America may point nowhere but to itself, but when it does so it reinscribes the terms for living in that contractual society. It calls for imagining people as embodying the characteristics of "contractual persons" who get to participate in contractual relations to the extent that they can demonstrate that they are self-made persons responsible for their personal property as self-possessions (Reddy, 1992). Right conduct becomes an issue of representation. The Contract with America, as a hybrid text/image agreement, did not so much represent the American people as represent how the American people ought to be represented.

Conclusion: Rewriting Contract

It is time to reconsider the violence done in the name of regimenting people into the contractual society. The contractual origin story needs to stop being told so that political legitimation can be achieved in less exclusionary ways. Carole Pateman has written: "Political argument must leave behind stories of origins and original contracts and move from the terrain of contract and the individual as owner. To look to an 'original' act of contract is systematically to blur the distinction between freedom and subjection" (1988: 232). The Contract with America provides a contemporary instance of such regimentation. It exemplifies how even conservative symbolization can reinforce the prejudices of traditional liberal political discourse. In the process, the Contract intensified the violence done in the name of identifying who qualifies for participation in that contractual society. It exercised the linguistic power to title the "American People" so as to promote the political power to disentitle some of those people. It promotes its own "orders of disentitlement."

Contractual discourse, in this as other instances, affirms the commodification of personhood in terms that favor those who are already positioned to be seen as fulfilling the obligations of contract. This, like other instances of "white mythology," is a surplus absence whose whiteness erases the cultural prejudices that masquerade as liberal, neutral standards that androgynously treat all individuals alike (Derrida, 1982). This masquerade even allows the breaking of contracts to be seen as honoring them. This masquerade creates an allegedly neutral space within which the "orders of disentitlement" work—first erasing citizen consent and then erasing the grounds for legitimating government assistance for those who are made out to be violators of the standards of work and family that serve as the basis for legitimating one's participation in the liberal order. This false neutrality becomes most visible with the one victory of the Contract with America—the 1996 welfare reform that ends the sixty-one-year-old federal entitlement for single mothers with children.

This reform attacks women while the problem of "deadbeat dads" was treated as secondary until President Bill Clinton insisted on some minor enhancements in enforcement. The argument of the authors of the Contract was that aggressive enforcement of child-support orders, even if they are contracts, would prejudice the rights of individuals involved in divorce and child custody proceedings (Berg, 1995). Male problems of contract do not rise to the level of invalidating someone as a contractual person. The needs and rights of some contractual persons are recognized in liberal contractual discourse more so than the needs and rights of others. Liberal contractual discourse needs to be interrogated for how it is contracted from the prevailing mythologies of liberalism. This mythology works to reinforce the sexist, racist, and classist prejudices of liberal political discourse with its implied identity of who is the personally responsible (read breadwinning) and independent (read non-welfare using) citizen. Until then, contractual metaphors will circulate in the public imaginary in ways that do much damage to the entitlement status of single women with children in particular and the idea of a democratically effective citizenry in general.

6

Native Son: Stories of Self-Creation and the Judicial Politics of Clarence Thomas

Leslie J. Vaughan

> Both *Native Son* and *Black Boy* really woke me up. [They] captured a lot of the feelings that I had inside that you learn to suppress.
>
> —Clarence Thomas, 1987

> The real Judge Thomas will come out of the hearings, the *person*, the man who had succeeded against the odds.
>
> —Clarence Thomas, 1991

Within six months of the 1991 confirmation hearings for the appointment of Clarence Thomas to the U.S. Supreme Court as associate justice, those hearings were transformed into his "trial." Anita Hill's accusation at the hearings that Thomas sexually harassed her when they both worked at the Equal Employment Opportunity Commission (EEOC) was the transformative agent. Since then, the hearings have gone on to become a literary and political text subject to extensive interpretation.

The Thomas hearings involved both the spectacle of sexual harassment between black elites and the banality of white racist imagery concerning black sexuality and violence. The combination of the two turned the hearings into a faux trial, employing many of the rules and procedures of a court of law (Kelman, 1991: 798–817), but without a script. Thus, Hill was tried and convicted of professional ambition and "erotomania" (U.S. Senate Judiciary Committee, 1991: 554–60, 565–69), especially in Senator Arlen Specter's prosecutorial interrogation, and Thomas was permitted to try and acquit himself, denying her charges categorically, even while refusing to listen to her testimony. As with many trials involving sexual violence, the victim herself was tried (Bumiller, 1991: 95–112), but in this case the script was written as it was being performed. Through the artful use of American folk narratives,

Thomas wrote a script that discredited Hill, effectively silencing her or, as some would say, rendering her functionally white with his use of the "high-tech lynching" metaphor. Ironically, Thomas managed to constitute his public identity in terms that re-raced his relation to the black experience in America and arrogated for himself a position within its white liberal tradition.

While still retaining a textual reading, this chapter shifts the focus slightly from the hearings as text/event to Clarence Thomas himself as a site of textual interpretation. Thomas himself invited this examination when declaring that "the real Judge Thomas will come out of the hearings, the *person*, the man who had succeeded against the odds." Yet, as with all representation, Thomas's representation acted out a fiction—i.e., made present what was absent (Norton, 1993). Thomas's dramatic performance reinscribed cultural narratives that structure meaning in American political culture. Because we all operate in stories not of our own making, culture, in this sense, according to G. W. F. Hegel, is inscribed in us. But because we put these cultural narratives to different uses or read them strategically, we establish our particularity and our relation to that culture as social and political persons. How Thomas used American cultural narratives and particularized them tells us not only something about that culture but also about his relation to it.

This chapter will suggest that Thomas used several fictions at the hearings. First, there is Thomas's "Pinpoint" story of his overcoming childhood poverty with parallels to the legendary Horatio Alger myth of American success through hard work. Second, there is his use of the story of Bigger Thomas in Richard Wright's *Native Son*. Thomas self-consciously used both to "e-race" his past (Clarke, 1993: 181–98) and his links to African Americans as a people and to reposition himself firmly within the liberal order, at the center of power. The use of literary and folk narratives became legitimating discourses, as tales contributory to power, rather than counternarratives to contest historical racial stereotypes and the liberal myth of "color blindness" in law and policy.

By rereading his own personal success story in terms of the Horatio Alger myth, he offered white senators (Democrats, in particular) the opportunity to renounce their guilt over a shameful American past of racial violence and segregation and, with his confirmation, bring the nation together. In addition, Thomas relied on a misreading of *Native Son* as a justification for his judicial politics of color blindness in law and policy, and downplayed the sexual nature of his offense. Finally by denouncing "the process" itself as "not American" and "Kafka-esque," he appealed to all patriotic citizens to support his nomination and to thus, in some sense, save the political system itself. These strategies of romantic nationalism, heroic paternalism, and political purity became potent allies in the successful effort to introduce his punitive judicial philosophy to the U.S. Supreme Court.

Rewriting the Self

Nine months before the Senate Judiciary Committee hearings in 1991, the question of Clarence Thomas's identity arose. The nominee had had an embarrassingly brief career as U.S. Circuit Court judge of eighteen months, yielding a mere twenty opinions, and had held an undistinguished two terms as the director of the EEOC, noted most significantly for its opposition to affirmation action and its inaction in discrimination cases (particularly age discrimination). From his writings and public speeches before conservative religious and political groups, Thomas's record became more detailed, but also more contradictory (*The Nation Institute*, 1991: 1–35). Appointed as the successor to Associate Justice Thurgood Marshall, Thomas seemed firmly opposed to affirmative action, desegregation of public schools, and federal protection of personal privacy rights, particularly with regard to reproductive choice.

The Bush administration, anticipating challenges due to Thomas's lack of judicial experience and legal competency, decided the best strategy was to emphasize his "character" (Mayer and Abramson, 1994; Danforth, 1994). Yet by the time of the hearings, the question of just who the "real" Clarence Thomas was—a question no longer unthinkable after the tumultuous 1987 confirmation hearings of Robert Bork—became unavoidable as Thomas began backing away from previously held positions on reproductive freedom, a constitutional right to privacy, affirmative action policies as deleterious to blacks, the natural law foundations of the Constitution, and states rights. Senator Howell Heflin, the Alabama Democrat with a reputation for dissociating himself from the Dixiecrats on matters of principle, voiced the concern of many senators and members of the public when he wondered whether another "confirmation conversion" was underway.

Indeed, Thomas's transformation seemed truly startling. In his legal philosophy, he reversed his earlier endorsement of natural law (Thomas, 1989: 63–70), and he stepped away from his position of strict construction in constitutional interpretation that required the Supreme Court to defend constitutional rights aggressively and not invent new ones where the Constitution was silent. He reassured the senators he would not roll back *Brown v. Board. of Education*, despite his adherence to the doctrine of a color-blind Constitution, and would not substitute his own morality or political philosophy for judicial precedent. He spoke frequently of the role judges must adopt. "When one becomes a judge, the role changes . . . you strive—rather than looking for policy positions . . . for impartiality" (U.S. Senate Judiciary Committee, 1991: 267).

Thomas's altered public persona was equally dramatic. At the hearings, according to one scholar, Thomas impersonated, like a trickster or confidence man in alternating guises, the "tom," "buck," and "sambo," images of

African Americans that had long been embedded in American culture to justify white domination (Jackson-Leslie, 1992: 106–9; Jordan, 1992: 120–24; Clarke, 1993). As "pleasing illusions," these invidious stereotypes worked to console anxious whites that he was not a renegade but a black man with whom they could work. In fact, his backers tripped all over themselves in order to avoid racist references and salve white anxiety. President George Bush cynically denied that Thomas was appointed because he was (a) black (conservative), and in his introduction of Thomas to the Senate Judiciary Committee, Senator John Danforth (R-Missouri), Thomas's patron, embarrassingly referred to Thomas' distinctive "booming laugh" and imposing physique (U.S. Senate Judiciary Committee, 1991: 101; Morrison, 1992: xii–xv). The specter of "surplus desire" emerged the more they tried to suppress it (Zizek, 1994).

But Thomas also applied these tropes to others, particularly in reference to those "on the dole" (Handler, 1991: A20), or seeking relief from discrimination as a class, triggering a sustained resistance to his confirmation from many in the black public sphere (*Public Culture*, 1994), who perceived a betrayal of their struggle for civil rights and a move to instantiate himself within the white liberal establishment (Sales, 1992: 176–84; Higginbotham, 1992: 3–39). The opportunity for narrative as opposition became narrative as therapy.

His therapeutic autobiography invoked an Horatio Alger myth, structured as a conversion narrative of his own overcoming of humble beginnings. Recounting his journey from childhood poverty in Pinpoint, Georgia, he told of his education by nuns and of his grandfather's entrepreneurship, from which, he claimed, he learned the value of hard work and discipline, and about racial injustice. It was a life "far removed in space and time from this room, this day and this moment," yet he maintained that his values had remained consistent throughout his life and guided him to the present day. He admitted to no fundamental intellectual or spiritual changes as he "moved on up" from Pinpoint to the federal bench. "I have always carried in my heart the world, the life, the people and the values of my youth . . . fairness, integrity, openmindedness, honesty and hard work." It was a story of hard work and uplift, the building of character from experiences of deprivation and racial exclusion that inexorably brought him closer to the center of American society and made him a firm believer in its fundamental fairness. Consequently, as a true believer in America's fundamental fairness, he remained sensitive to those left on the margins and gave credit to those in the civil rights movement for their labors and for inspiring him. They had given him a "road to travel," and he had "benefited greatly from their efforts" (U.S. Senate Judiciary Committee, 1991: 10).

While all autobiography is an exercise in self-invention, the Pinpoint story substituted fiction for history. By the lie of omission, he credited his grandfather for inculcating him with values of hard work and dignity, while the women in his family, who exemplified it equally, were unmentioned. His mother's labor, picking crabs at 5 cents a pound and cleaning houses to support her children when the father left home, was unmentioned. When their home was destroyed in a fire, he did not recall that the girls stayed with their mother, while Thomas and his brother went to live with their grandfather. He attended Holy Cross, a Catholic boarding school, supported by his grandfather; he next attended John Vianney Minor Seminary, supported by loans, work-study, and scholarship; and then he was admitted to Yale Law School, where he concentrated in tax law, anti-trust, and property law, avoiding all classes having anything to do with civil rights (Williams, 1987: 74). He did not concede to the preferential treatment he received within the family, nor to the effect of affirmative action in his admission to law school. Nor did he trace his political and intellectual journey in the terms he had used previously, i.e., as a personal transformation from self-help (Pinpoint), to self-hate (Holy Cross), to black independence (John Vianney Minor Seminary). He did not mention his resistance to a political appointment in the Department of Education or the EEOC. ("If I ever went to work for the EEOC or did anything directly connected with blacks, my career would be ruined. The monkey would be on my back to prove that I didn't have the job because I am black.") Finally, he did not explain the reasons he stood for renomination for a position as the nation's chief of civil rights enforcement.

Understandably, Thomas was attempting to construct a stable, unified public identity, if not a coherent and unified self, to deal with the character question, to reassure the nation that he had derived middle-class values from a lifetime among individuals in small communities helping one another, without government intervention. In denying any fundamental spiritual or political transformation (in contrast to his account only four years earlier), he implied it was the values of a liberal society that had changed to require him to embrace race as a fundamental characteristic of identity, and to use his racial identification as the grounds of political affiliation. This acknowledgment of racism as an unavoidable aspect of contemporary American political culture then became a justification for his return to supporting a free enterprise society and a color-blind Constitution (Gilson, 1997).

As a spiritual conversion narrative, Thomas's account fails (Danforth, 1994). First, in African American autobiographies, from slave narratives to the autobiographies of Frederick Douglass and Booker T. Washington, the life of the individual is shown to be intimately bound up with the experiences of African Americans as a people. Their stories are personal stories of survival, but also testaments to their ancestors and to their successes as a people (Pinckney, 1995: 41–46; cf. Sollors, 1986: 1–39). In Thomas's narrative of self-help, however, it is as if he and his grandfather alone made history. There is no sense of community struggle nor any sense of group identification. When race is present in the story, it is something to overcome. If racism is pervasive, so are the values of the small capitalist who has no race. Whiteness is the norm and is normative, standing for everything and nothing in its representative power (Dyer, 1988: 44–64; Wright, 1991: 97). In this sense, the story of Clarence Thomas is indistinguishable from a rags-to-riches story of American liberalism. It takes the values of individualism—free enterprise, mobility, self-sufficiency—uncritically, blurring the boundaries between myth and reality. To talk about Thomas's erasure, then, is also to talk about the reracializing of American myths about political and economic virtue.

Second, Thomas's confirmation autobiography involved a conversion without rebirth or transformation, a necessary ingredient of salvation. A conversion narrative begins with original sin (or innocence) or a condition of natural slavery (or freedom). It moves from moral certainty to confusion and again to moral certainty. But a conversion narrative that has no original condition gives one no opportunity to transcend. In his origin story, Thomas carried his past of self-help, an internal place of solace or relief from the corruption of society, within himself. He did not confess that he had lost faith nor reveal he had lost his way, but insisted he had always remained on the "true course." He was regenerate from the start, in no need of spiritual or intellectual salvation. His retreat into a timeless past, removed from the contradictions of modern society, reflected his inability to gain critical purchase on the myth of a unregulated "free" market or the fantasy of cultural refuge through stories. His identification with private liberties, economic virtues, and the notion of an autonomous self unconnected to a people or community, positioned his primary identity as private, tied to economic activity; his secondary identity as racial. It is as if Thomas had no political or public self to display or defend, but merely transported his private self onto the public stage of the judiciary hearings and into the public sphere.

In one sense, then, his story is part of the genre of a liberal conversion narrative—from poverty to status. But within the Hegelian logic of identification with the liberal state, the process of forming an identity involves a two-stage process from a "secondary" affiliation (to a group such as tribe, race, or family) to a "primary" identification (to the nation or state). One did not progress from one identification to another; both identifications coexisted and, as Slavoj Zizek points out, are already mediated by the market and the state (1995: 1511–32; 1994: 1–33). The logic of Thomas's individuation, however, displaced the importance of (all) group affiliations as the basis of identification. Like the quintessential American liberal hero, Thomas presented himself as a subject already formed in isolation, apart from others; like the classical liberal, he was "born," not made. His identity was not contingent nor historical; it was natural, created independent of economic and political conditions. His reference to the judicial role as an impartial and objective lawgiver exemplified the degree to which he would remove himself from communities of both primary and secondary identifications, a guarantee he (and the senators) believed would protect liberal justice.

Fictionalizing the Self

If Thomas's Horatio Alger narrative fails as history and fails as spiritual or intellectual conversion story, it also runs directly counter to his identification with another American narrative, the story of another Thomas, Bigger Thomas (Efron, 1992: 28). Richard Wright changed the tradition of African American autobiography with his autobiography *Black Boy*, published four years after *Native Son* (Pinckney, 1995). After Wright, black authors wrote of the ruin of black institutions, the destruction of the black family, the schools and the church, their disgust with the South, and their desire to move away. If white racism corrupts, black culture corrupts absolutely. The new African American antihero, such as Eldridge Cleaver, was unregenerate; he sought vengeance on white society and its possessions (including its women), and even on his own culture.

Bigger Thomas was a representative of this new black hero. A native-born American, as the title indicates, Bigger is full of rage and resentment at black marginality and oppression. He is also profoundly isolated—not only from white society, where he is unable to make sense of the language of whites, and terrified even to look his future employer in the face—but also from the black community. He taunts his fellow gang members for their fears of getting caught in petty theft and forces them to play a game that "imitate[s] the ways and manners of white folks," in an exercise of self-loathing and race-envy (Wright, 1991: 18). Indeed, it is as if he inhabited another world. Yet Bigger takes every opportunity to exercise domination over those he considers weaker than himself—especially women (France, 1990; Mootry, 1984). In the first "rape" scene in the novel, Bigger "feminizes" Gus before the gang, forcing him to lick the knife he holds to his lips (Alan France, 1988: 416).

Wright's narrative has been interpreted as a graphic portrayal of the inhumanity of racism, but Bigger's indignation and sense of powerlessness are also a portrait of Friedrich Nietzsche's *ressentiment* (the rancor of a "slave morality"). With the misguided rage of the injured, he accidentally murders Mary Dalton, the daughter of his employer and landlord, hacks up her body and stuffs it in the furnace, and then frames another for his crime; he subsequently rapes and murders Bessie Mears, whom he drags along with him in fleeing the police, in an act of self-loathing. He persecutes those he tried to love but could not (thus showing the pathology of the colonized; Fanon, 1952).

The persecution of women is so pervasive and uncontrolled throughout the novel, Alan France argues, that it spins out of the control of Wright, as well as Bigger. Reading the text on the surface, France writes, *Native Son* can be seen as the struggle for freedom against white domination; reading it from beneath, it is the "story of a black man's rebellion against white male authority," in which the "rebellion takes the form of the ultimate appropriation of human beings; the rape-slaying, which is also the ultimate expropriation of patriarchal property, the total consumption of the commodified woman" (1988: 414). In murdering Mary, Bigger reaches sexual climax, linking economic exploitation (the possession of Mary as white property) with sexual violence. In raping and murdering Bessie, he subdues her as his own object or possession over which he had dominion, the woman who would not stand by him. In the text, Mary Dalton becomes an absence (Mary's murder is a mere means to Bigger's self-awareness), and Bessie becomes a mere incident to the crime. Thus while Bigger goes to his death racially isolated, his phallic power (sexual independence) is undiminished. In "How Bigger Was Born," Wright remarks that he is embarked on a novel (never realized) about "the status of women in modern American society," as if *Native Son* were not itself a statement on the subject (Johnson, 1988).

The gendered silences in France's own reading are instructive as well. As the murder of Mary becomes further removed in time, Bigger's memory of it changes, and he is no longer certain whether it was accidental. From a legal standpoint it makes no difference, for even Bigger realizes that his presence in her room will be interpreted as an act of rape. However, Mary Dalton does not merely represent her father's wealth or white property, nor is Bessie Mears merely Bigger's property to be disposed of at will. From one psychoanalytic perspective, they also represent the subversive power of women and threat of boundary breakdown—the constructed boundaries between public/private, culture/nature, pure/impure—operating in the social world. Mary's subversive power comes from her ignorance of black culture, her naive and reckless request that Bigger take her and her boyfriend to a restaurant in a black neighborhood. Bessie's power, despite her resignation and weekend drinking, comes from her first (and fatal) challenge to Bigger when she resists his flight from the police and then his sexual overtures. The relegation of both Mary and Bessie to the private, domestic, or propertied world is not an absence in the text so much as a political presence that makes visible the dependency of American racism on their suppression. White women's wealth (through their husbands or fathers) and their imagined sexual virtue justified white domination of black men (through lynching, for example) and the concomitant requirement that black women control (satisfy) their men. The stereotype of black women's sexual availability similarly justified white men's sexual violence against them and threatened black men's sexual privileges.

The silences in Thomas's own confirmation narratives with regard to women—the failure to credit his mother in his autobiography, the elision of his first marriage and divorce, and his overt contempt for women—as well as his derogation of his sister for receiving welfare, his admitted appetite for pornography while in Yale Law School (Danforth, 1994: 44), and his alleged sexual harassment and disregard of Anita Hill's testimony—mirror the hostility of Bigger Thomas toward women and the subversive power they represent. Indeed, Clarence Thomas recalled the psychological impact of *Native Son* on himself, identifying with the feelings that Bigger acted on, which Clarence had learned to "suppress."

Like Bigger, moreover, Clarence Thomas would not defend himself when required to in a tribunal. To an incredulous Senator Heflin, he claimed he did not even listen to Hill's testimony, although he did refute her charges in every instance. Instead, he attacked "the process" itself, as Bigger struck out at white and black society alike. "I am a victim of this process. . . . I have complied with the rules. . . . I have endured this ordeal for 103 days. . . . Enough is enough." He invoked the language of political loyalty and subversion: he accused the senators of witch-hunting. "This is not American. This is Kafka-esque. . . . We are destroying our country. We are destroying our institutions. . . . This is far more dangerous than McCarthyism" (U.S. Senate Judiciary Committee, 1991: 184). This likened the hearings to those of the House Un-American Activities Committee, a historical moment in which a committee of the Senate cannibalized itself, as senators accused one another of disloyalty, megalomania and fanaticism. The reference to McCarthyism thus carried a not-very-well concealed threat: in the senators' search for internal enemies, they would destroy themselves. If they brought him down, they would go down with him.

Even though Thomas denounced the process, he was willing to let that same process decide his innocence. He invoked the discourse of defamation or character assassination. "My name has been harmed, my integrity has been harmed, my character has been harmed, my family has been harmed, my friends have been harmed. There is nothing this committee, this body, this country can do to give me my good name back, nothing." His appeal was framed in terms of rights to privacy, a good reputation, and a "fundamental sense of fairness," terms that transcended racial divisions. "I am not going to allow myself to be further humiliated in order to be confirmed. . . . I will not allow this committee or anyone else to probe into my private life. This is not what America is all about" (U.S. Senate Judiciary Committee, 1991: 8–9).

Thomas went on to admit to paranoid fears of death and castration (Danforth, 1994). For him, the process had become "a high-tech lynching for uppity-blacks who in any way deign to think for themselves, to do for themselves, to have different ideas, and it is a message that, unless you kow-tow to an old order, this is what will happen to you, you will be lynched, destroyed, caricatured by a committee of the U.S. Senate, rather than hung from a tree" (U.S. Senate Judiciary Committee, 1991: 157–58). Despite the dubious historical accuracy of the lynching metaphor, Thomas used it to brilliant effect. While black men were rarely lynched for violence toward black women (Hall, 1983; Freedman, 1992), Thomas appealed to the senators in patriarchal references to castration fears and status anxieties. While Hill does appear in his story, it is not in her own voice, but as seen through the prism of his own anxieties. She was a threat to his political survival, indeed to his physical survival, and to his inheritance as a native son. As Senator Alan Simpson put it to Hill, "You could have killed him, but you didn't" (U.S. Senate Judiciary Committee, 1991). Attacking a black man's sexuality became equivalent to destruction of his physical body, indeed, his very life. Thomas as a black man in a white-dominated society saw his sexuality as integral to his identity in ways that white people might not understand. As Homi Bhabha (1992: 247) notes, "If the lynched body is black, its real color is its gender."

Conclusion

In order to attack a political process that permitted only certain stories to be told, Clarence Thomas crafted an autobiography that traded on a legitimating discourse. Rather than a far-flung attack from the margins, his defense was part of the liberal ethos that criticizes the state and reveals a suspicion of politics. When candidates run "against the system," populists emphasize grass-roots involvement rather than elite management, and progressives want to replace the political hack with the administrative expert. Yet, skepticism toward the political in such cases is often a way of emphasizing the private world, the world of market relations, as the realm of freedom. Thomas attacked the politics of the nomination process and, ironically, used it to make his confirmation a success.

If, as Garry Wills points out, the manner in which a nominee chooses to answer questions indicates a great deal about his judicial temperament and his openmindedness (1995: 42), Thomas's use of literary and folk stories and his demeanor at his confirmation hearings suggest an intolerance for voices and ideas outside of his own sense of history and political perspective. He appears to have taken, in almost Reaganite fashion, the story of Bigger Thomas as his own (Rogin, 1987). If Bigger acted out the "feelings that I had inside that you learn to suppress" in rape and murder, Clarence would act out Bigger's rage and rebellion in judicial opinions denying government redress of economic or racial inequality. Linking Bigger's story of rage and powerlessness with the Pinpoint story of overcoming adversity, Clarence Thomas created a therapeutic political autobiography, justifying his extreme and historically suspect jurisprudence.

Indeed after seven years on the Court, he has voted with Antonin Scalia a full 85 percent of the time, voting to deny prisoners the protections of the Eighth Amendment's ban on cruel and unusual punishment against the brutality of prison guards (*Hudson v. McMillan*), refusing to make it easier to prosecute traffic in child pornography (*United States v. X-Citement Video*), supporting cross-burning as a protected activity under the First Amendment (*R.A.V. v. St. Paul*), undercutting the inroads of the Voting Rights Act in enfranchising blacks by denying the role of race in redrawing district lines (*Shaw v. Reno*), and voting to strike down affirmative action plans as violative of the color-blind promise of the Constitution (*Adarand v. Pena*). Like Ronald Reagan, Clarence Thomas takes the world of fiction as real; the consequence seems to be a real-life judicial politics of racial resentment and revenge.

Part III
Identity Stories in Public Policy

7

Talking Straight: Narrating the Political Economy of Gay Rights

Jonathan Goldberg-Hiller

> Neither the State of Colorado, through any of its branches or departments, nor any of its agencies, political subdivisions, municipalities or school districts, shall enact, adopt or enforce any statute, regulation, ordinance or policy whereby homosexual, lesbian or bisexual orientation, conduct, practices or relationships shall constitute or otherwise be the basis of, or entitle any person or class of persons to have or claim any minority status, quota preferences, protected status or claim of discrimination. This Section of the Constitution shall be self-executing.
>
> —Amendment 2, Colorado State Constitution. Passed November, 1992

> When I was a homosexual, if a law had passed giving me special rights, I wouldn't be happily married today.
>
> —Paul Paulk, Newpaper Advertisement, 1995

Amid the structural threats posed to American social and political life by a newly global economy, postcommunist geostrategic hegemony, and an emerging postindustrial domestic landscape, the usual suspects are harder to blame. Increasingly, gay rights and gay activism have become the central axis for conservative claims of cultural and political implosion and the imperative of a politics of values. Stories about extensive gay and lesbian political agendas, outrageous queer direct action, poor hygiene and AIDS, pedophilia, and the threat of youth "recruitment"—a modern-day Sodom and Gomorrah—are commonly deployed to recapitulate the importance of "family" and "Christian" values, reinforce social hierarchies, and devalue diversity. When these "perversions" are said to be protected by "special rights" that further impede the function and efficiency of democratic government and social institutions, a fusion of voters into an outraged majority has been driven to the polls in the quest for political purification. Such was the case when Colorado voters in 1992 approved state constitutional Amendment 2 to ban antigay discrimination ordinances.

This chapter seeks to examine the ways such purification politics are materialized through narratives of "disidentification" (Patton, 1993) and how they respond to a changing political economy. The arguments I analyze are reconstructed from legal briefs submitted to the U.S. Supreme Court as it considered a challenge to constitutional Amendment 2. I pay more attention to the rhetoric of the amendment's defenders because their arguments repeatedly invoke narratives of disidentification in order to promote their majoritarian challenge to judge-based decision making. I assess the sovereignty-enhancing quality of this rhetoric below and conclude this analysis with some reflections on the implications for contemporary politics.

Disidentification in Law and Politics

It is important to note that neither identity stories nor the arguments of special rights are new in American politics. Similar vilifications have been applied to legal and illegal immigrants, unionists, African Americans, Mormons, and Jews, to name just a few. Apart from the change of characters, what remains unique to the morality tales I consider here is that—unlike these other American antagonists—gays, lesbians, bisexuals, queers, and the transgendered have not always been discrete groups located nationally, spatially, or historically, and thus have rarely threatened native conceptions of sovereignty over such constructions.

That began to change once sexual minorities successfully challenged the stigma of a medical psychopathology in the early 1970s, disturbing the associated forms of political surveillance and sovereign practices in immigration, military policy, and housing by which sexual minorities were socially "contained" (Fortin, 1995). Freed from a malignant classification and broadly mobilized, homosexuals began to develop social and political identities challenging, subverting, and borrowing from the dominant sovereign social codes of nation, space, and history (Melucci, 1989). Because "male and female homosexualities [are] still fuzzily defined, undercoded, or discursively dependent on more established forms" (De Lauretis quoted in Weeks, 1995: 109), it is not accidental that this politics privileges "coming out" (Blasius, 1992; not coming across, not coming into citizenship, but emerging already) from within suburban and urban life, family and workplace, church and organization. For some activists, this has been a conscious "project of cultural pedagogy aimed at exposing the range and variety of bounded spaces upon which heterosexual supremacy depends, [to] see and conquer places that present the danger of violence to gays and lesbians, to reterritorialize them" (Berlant and Freeman, 1993: 205). Such boundary challenge and subversion are fought by conservatives, often on the terrain of the law. Fearful of such loss of control over everyday sovereignty, one conservative antigay activist testified to his own concern at "granting . . . protected status to a group that has no identifiable characteristics" (Goldberg, 1994: 1072).

The claim of special rights, first articulated in debates over the 1964 Civil Rights Act, is an attempt at reasserting these boundaries and creating the legal definitions of such identifiable characteristics in order to cabin the threat of sexual minorities. But where this rhetoric was earlier intertwined with other sovereign discourses such as federalism to limit and contain an "excess" of civil rights demands in the 1960s (Marcosson, 1995; Schacter, 1994), its success today is dependent upon novel arguments and rhetorical positions that have repositioned sovereignty discourses. Because emerging sexual identities have borrowed from the legacy of antidiscrimination law (aligning themselves in the process with the pioneering civil rights and women's movements), the claims of "special rights" presses contemporary images of a homosexual movement into a policy response regulating access to justice. For the first time since the postwar civil rights revolution, denials of legal access have been voted upon by popular majorities, and states have publicly defended these new limits. Stories about the political and social challenge of sexual minorities have thus become deeply embedded in increasingly frequent official public discourse about the limits and capacities of government and the proper freedoms of civil society.

The narrative argument that gays ask not for civil rights but special rights designed to protect their distinctive behavior succeeds at the level of the popular imagination (despite its present lack of success at the legal level) because it performs two stock and legitimating operations. The first is that it provides a cultural focus for policy language advocating political retreat. Far from the regulation of sovereignty by strengthening national boundaries (as done by immigration legislation), by invocations of jurisdictional limits invoked by federalism, or by the preservation of the contours of social space—all of which demand an increase or valorization of governmental authority—this new regulation withdraws from formerly recognized public commitments. These limits on governmental authority deeply resonate with other common discourses of scarcity and exclusivity endemic to American liberalism, confusing in the process civil rights based in the values of a free and democratic society with entitlements that have always been qualified by the level of economic development. Second, by specifying the commitments preserved by such a reversal as traditional and conservative, these stories rename the threatened but culturally valued institutions as *the minority* interests to be protected *from* civil rights advances. This rhetorical position is clearly if not glaringly marked by the 1996 Defense of Marriage Act that permits states to deny recognition of same-sex marriages conducted in other states as though such unions were a direct imposition upon heterosexual marriage (read privilege). As Cindy Patton has forcefully argued, such tensions between new right and gay movements, both of which rely on civil rights discourses *performatively* to form and reshape political subjectivities and privileges, allow the promotion of "societal *dis*identification with the other: if neither group could reasonably hope to recruit many outsiders to its identity . . . disidentification produce[s] at least temporary allies" (1993: 145; italics added).

Such a tactical deployment of rights language has its genealogy in what Michel Foucault has called governmentality. Governmentality comprehends the changing forms of modern sovereignty, an "art to government" stemming from an introduction of economy into political practice beginning in the sixteenth century (Foucault, 1991: 92), which slowly changed a juridical sovereignty exercised on territory to a sovereignty exercised on the relationship between people and material, cultural, and social things.

This plurality of aims and identities has implications for the mechanisms of sovereignty. Where law and sovereignty were once inseparable (see Luhmann, 1990: 11–56), it increasingly became a matter of "employing tactics rather than laws, and even of using laws themselves as tactics—to arrange things in such a way that, through a certain number of means, such and such ends may be achieved" (Foucault, 1991: 95). I take from this understanding of governmentality not the eclipse of law and the juridical for sovereignty practices, but rather its regular return, its competition and collusion with alternative "tactics" and discourses, and its utility for ordering access to those material relations that make up a political economy. As Foucault has noted, "it is the tactics of government which make possible the continual definition and redefinition of what is within the competence of the state and what is not, the public versus the private, and so on; thus the state can only be understood in its survival and its limits on the basis of the general tactics of governmentality" (1991: 103).

Colin Gordon has observed that these are concerns about "liberalism as a form of knowledge calculated to limit power by persuading government of its own incapacity; [of] the notion of the rule of law as the architecture of a pluralist social space" (1991: 47). Seen in this light, stories about both gay behavior and the nature of civil rights are referenda on the model of law as a plastic and nearly unlimited source of liberties facilitating a universal participation in the social contract. In contrast to this liberal pluralism based on the imperatives of self-identity is a view privileging social institutions such as families, local schools, businesses, and churches, and with them their unassailable hierarchies and privileges. This argument for private privilege establishes an alternative allocation of values for constituting a political economy. Yet there is an undeniably public character to these concerns, as well, seen most clearly in the argument that democratic majorities are the sovereign bodies around which such "traditional" privileges should be maintained. It is this political argument about the democratic nature of sovereignty in opposition to its genesis in universal rights undiminished by public opinion that has turned conservatives against the courts, and against the rights claims and alternative sovereignty practices of gay social movements.

This tension between courts and publics is not absolute, however, and this has important ramifications for the tactical deployment of law. In a strategy designed to peel gay rights claims from those of African Americans, the new right has struggled over the meanings of family and political correctness to distinguish "illegitimate" claims to civil rights from those deserving protection (Patton, 1995). This partial valorization of the law is compounded by the complex logic of formal legal instruments designed to prevent excessive civil rights claims. Restrictions such as those found within Amendment 2 preventing gay, lesbian, and bisexual identities from gaining standing before the law for purposes of antidiscrimination litigation simultaneously recognize these same "orientation[s], conduct, practices or relationships" as constitutive of the identity languages Justice will remain blind to. Thus the law is the site at which some coding of identity is both enunciated and suppressed.

The importance of this fact is not that law is always central to this identity politics (just as law no longer completes sovereignty practices). Law remains only part of the social texture of everyday life. Nonetheless, social rights may signal inclusion into the liberal community, or provide the terrain, even in their negation, on which social communities can be reasserted (Bower, 1994; McClure, 1993; McCann, 1994). Indeed "queer" identities opposed to the assimilationism and separatism of some lesbian and gay politics (Hennessy, 1994) have been argued to be intentionally beyond or "against" the law, perhaps for solid strategic reasons in light of special rights rhetoric (Rohrer, 1996; Gamson, 1995).

The imbrication of law and politics means that while law remains important to issues of identity and community, formal decision making within the law is only one—and perhaps a minor—determinant of rhetorical outcomes. Much as in the abortion controversy (Luker, 1984), court decisions are themselves challenged in the name of democratic, cultural, and social powers, and higher legal and constitutional principles, recursively feeding the arguments and rhetoric that initiated legal challenges. My goal below is to examine law in this complexity as both a site and a "cite" of identity formation and contested sovereign boundary indicating the limits of community as illustrated in the arguments of Amendment 2 supporters.

Amendment 2

On November 3, 1993, Colorado voters approved Amendment 2 by a majority of 53.4 percent. Nine days later three Colorado cities with antidiscrimination legislation protecting sexual orientation, several individuals, and a school district filed to have the amendment declared unconstitutional and asked for a preliminary injunction. In a series of hearings and trials appealed to and remanded by the supreme court of Colorado, that injunction was made permanent, and the amendment was declared unconstitutional. This ruling has been sustained by the U.S. Supreme Court.

The state appellate courts were consistent in their rulings against the amendment's constitutionality. Amendment 2 does not pass constitutional scrutiny for several reasons. Foremost among these is that Amendment 2 infringes on a fundamental right to participate equally in the political process guaranteed by the equal protection clause of the fourteenth Amendment to the U.S. Constitution. By increasing the threshold of participation for an "identifiable class" of people who must first repeal a statewide constitutional provision before passing local legislation protecting their civil rights, Amendment 2

> alters the political process so that a targeted class is prohibited from obtaining legislative, executive, and judicial protection or redress from discrimination absent the consent of a majority of the electorate through the adoption of a constitutional amendment. Rather than attempting to withdraw antidiscrimination issues as a whole from state and local control, Amendment 2 singles out one form of discrimination and removes its redress from consideration by the normal political processes. (*Evans v. Romer*, 854 P.2d 1270, 1285 [Colo. 1993], argument supported by Justice Kennedy, *Romer v. Evans*, 94–1039, 5 and 8, [1996])

The Colorado high court ruled that such an obstruction to the "fundamental right to participate equally in the political process" required a "compelling state interest," invoking the highest standard of court review in antidiscrimination doctrine—"strict scrutiny"—even though gays, lesbians, and bisexuals would not be added to the list of traditional "suspect classes." This holding set up the framework for the defendants' case: they would need to show how Amendment 2 was tailored to advance at least one compelling interest in order to preserve its constitutionality, or show that the level of scrutiny was inappropriate, and hence argue that the threshold for allowable state action was incorrectly held too high. Despite their failure to achieve either option, it is this language that most interests me here.

If antidiscrimination law is best (because originally) conceived as protection for "discrete and insular minorities" (*United States v. Carolene Products*, 1938; Ely, 1980: 76ff), then the state of Colorado argued first that gays, lesbians, and bisexuals are neither. Because this "group" that was given legal if not social coherence by the antidiscrimination statutes they had successfully sought in Denver, Boulder, and Aspen had thereby revealed their political power (despite being outspent 17 to 1), they could not be compared to those groups with a demonstrable history of prejudice and the status indicators that signified their disadvantage. This argument minimizes the importance of social facts of discrimination at the same time as it establishes an impossible catch-22: any group able to protect itself through antidiscrimination statutes did not need the law after all. Bolstering this paradoxical reading, the state implied that local ordinances designed to protect jobs, housing, and the like were tantamount to property interests in the state, a perversion of republican principles that would reverse traditional state-society relations as well as corrode the worth and integrity of the group that depended upon such legal language. Although the state's arguments did not make this latter consequence explicit, the conservative Pacific Legal Foundation did in its supporting brief.

> The civil rights struggle of the 1950s and 1960s secured the political rights and basic opportunities necessary for black Americans to fully enjoy the fruits of citizenship. Since then, however, the civil rights "movement" has been transformed into an establishment dedicated to perpetuating itself and expanding its power. The traditional civil rights movement derived its moral legitimacy from the universality of the rights it sought to establish. The modern civil rights establishment has abandoned this moral claim by transforming the meaning of civil rights from those fundamental rights all Americans share equally into special benefits for some and burdens for others. . . . There is no reason to believe that new politically active groups who choose to identify themselves in some manner will not also seek to parlay nondiscrimination into affirmative duties. (Brief of the Pacific Legal Foundation, 1995)

Since legal protection granted undue "affirmative duties" that inflated the power already signaled by the emplacement of local antidiscrimination statutes, the state argued it was entitled to reassert a threatened sovereignty. In this manner, the state reconceptualized Amendment 2 as a bulwark against a group's "ability to define the agendas of all levels of government" (Brief of the Attorney General of the State of Colorado, 12), effectively making state authority a minority interest to be protected. In this manner, the state's vulnerability models a valid minority position intentionally in contrast to a manner that gays and lesbians cannot muster. Rather than discrimination from this vantage, "the intent and effect of Amendment 2 is to withdraw a deeply divisive social and political issue from elected representatives and place its resolution squarely in the hands of the people" (12), a matter that "goes to the heart of state sovereignty" (14). This democratic sovereignty includes those of every sexual orientation for no one is "fenced out" in ways traditionally thought to apply to discriminated minorities. Sexual minorities are not powerless, denied the right to vote or organize, nor subject to reapportionment to dilute their political effectiveness; "they continue to have precisely the same rights as anyone else who has lost an election" (20). It is not the minorities who are denied political representation by Amendment 2, but the people whose rights were trampled by the Court's improper injunction: "The right to vote can be infringed just as effectively by nullifying votes as by preventing them from being cast in the first place" (20).

In this argument, state sovereignty must be used to limit social identities—or "fundamental group rights" unprotected by suspect class status in the language of the Colorado supreme court—because there are no reasonable limitations to which groups might qualify for "preferential treatment"; "any conceivable group, from a boy scout troop to a group of tax protesters fits the definition" (Brief of the Attorney General of the State of Colorado, 24). As a consequence of this legal activism—what the Colorado brief derisively named "substantive equal protection" (21) in an allusion to *Lochner v. New York* (1905) and the eponymous era of extreme judicial activism—states must inoculate themselves against an imminent "political chaos" (22) and gain a secure foothold on the "slippery slope" toward federal legal oversight of traditional state concerns (U.S. Supreme Court oral arguments, transcript, 13). Amendment 2 properly answers these mixed metaphorical dangers in this argument by rationally (though admittedly not neatly) advancing three basic interests that the state must maintain to preserve a precarious sovereignty: protection of limited resources by limiting antidiscrimination enforcement to those "particularly deserving of special protection" (13); furthering efficient law enforcement; and protecting "prevailing preferences of the State's population," particularly property and religious rights.

In support of this last claim, the state marshaled evidence of private institutional vulnerability to gay acceptance, in support of which Justice Antonin Scalia agreed that "Coloradans are . . . entitled to be hostile toward homosexual conduct" (*Romer v. Evans* 94–1039, Dissent, Slip at 9). This "right to prejudice," secured by a bare majority in the *Bowers v. Hardwick* (1986) antisodomy case, is a crumbling legal edifice, as well as blatantly mean. What provides this argument with its legitimacy and its power for the tactical purposes of disidentification, I argue below, is the economic claims that anchor it.

Downsizing Rights: The Politics of Scarcity

"The supporters of Amendment 2 were acutely aware that laws and policies designed to benefit homosexuals and bisexuals could have an adverse effect on the ability of state and local governments to combat discrimination against suspect classes" (Brief of Attorney General of the State of Colorado, 27). If the argument of a precarious state sovereignty is marshaled to deny the priority of the state's duties to combat discrimination against gays and lesbians, then the claim that Colorado is subject to constitutional fiscal constraints in its enforcement of civil rights plays two supporting roles. The first is to distinguish "deserving" minorities from those with whom the majority should not identify, preserving the state's commitments to "suspect classes" at the expense of "a politically powerful and relatively privileged special interest group" (28). Such a rhetorical move supports public testimony that it will be blacks and women who will be most harmed by the extension of antidiscrimination protection (see evidence presented in Goldberg, 1994: 1076–77). Whether this is designed to build allies with other civil rights groups is perhaps less important than the simulation of a universality of concern (a recognition of pro-"true"-civil rights) and the reestablishment of boundaries through a reasoned response to what Judy Rohrer has called the "politics of scarcity" (1996: 50) exemplifying this new language.

A second role of this scarcity rhetoric is to transform the images of sovereignty of the liberal state away from the foundational Lockean idea of a limited government whose "contracted" authority rests upon protection of basic rights to liberty. These classical liberties are often understood as negative in that they establish formal inhibitions on official power and prerogative. In a strange inversion of this social contract imagery, it is not rights that are central to liberty, but liberty that is central to rights, a positive conception of rights which works as a reflexive limit upholding democratic sovereignty. The state's legitimacy is now seen to stem from a recognition of its own promiscuity on behalf of personal freedoms, an Odysseus bound at the mast against the sirens of social and sexual need in the quest of its own sovereign destiny. Such erotic allusions mirror and, in fact, help construct the sexual economy by which a majority understands and privileges itself while vilifying those gays, lesbians, and bisexuals that it opposes.

While the limited state that must "draw the line" at rights for sexual minorities is one frame by which support for constitutional limits is constructed, the other is the inversion of majority and minority positions through rhetorical reversals. One way in which this is done is to argue along the lines of the politics of scarcity, demonstrating the zero-sum character of fundamental rights doctrine and promoting a politics of disidentification. Robert Bork argued in opposition to the Colorado supreme court that it was not just the sovereign majority whose rights were infringed by nullification, but those equivalential yet more deserving groups who lobbied for the amendment. Protecting groups through "fundamental rights" doctrine "infringe[s] the 'fundamental political rights' of those groups, such as Colorado for Family Values, that disagree with 'independently identifiable groups' such as respondents" making the disidentification coalition the real victims of "disenfranchise[ment]" (Brief of Robert Bork, 1995).

This and similar economic arguments infuse the claims that rights endanger traditional institutions, values, and their champions at the same time that rights are upheld as integral to the authentic expression of groups whose goal is the conservation of a proper sovereignty. Here governmentality integrates the economic and the legal as separate but reinforcing tactics. Where rights promote inroads into democratic authority, economic rhetoric tames the excess while transmuting antagonism into a defense of the political commons. The difference between patriots and perverts is made all the more palatable, thereby allowing the connection between economic and moral authority to be reinscribed.

The Efficiency of Rights

The alleged rationality of Amendment 2 is also based on its contribution to political uniformity. Elimination of city anti-discrimination ordinances protecting gays, lesbians, and bisexuals is argued to promote efficient enforcement, maximize individual liberty, preserve traditional social norms, enhance economic and legal predictability for employers, and ensure "that the deeply divisive issue of homosexuality does not serve to seriously fragment Colorado's body politic" (30). This argument seems awkward at first glance because the political fight for Amendment 2 provided the spectacle of just what it was designated to cure, and because the utility of the fear of fragmentation and factionalism is so deeply implicated in the earlier arguments necessitating the amendment. Yet it also reemphasizes the urge toward a seamless sovereign, one whose own body remains unblemished through the exfoliation of those whose bodily practices do not conform to a sanctioned norm and thereby mark selected groups for disidentification.

What is interesting about this argument is its subtle rearrangement of the foundational ideas of political authority and its subversive meaning of the metaphor of body politic. The locus classicus for this metaphor is Thomas Hobbes's *Leviathan* where the frightening image of a state of nature in which the solitary, poor, nasty, brutish, and short life devoid of political agreement is contrasted with an artificial image of the self in which sovereignty is to be alienated.

> For by Art is created that great LEVIATHAN called a COMMON-WEALTH, or STATE . . . which is but an Artificiall Man; though of greater stature and strength than the Naturall, for whose protection and defence it was intended; and in which, the Soveraignty is an Artificiall Soul, as giving life and motion to the whole body . . . by which the parts of this Body Politique were at first made, set together and united, resemble that Fiat, or the Let us make man, pronounced by God in the Creation. (Hobbes, 1968: 81–82)

As God creates man, so man creates the state through a convention constituting the sovereign body politic. This convention privileges the rational. In Bryan Turner's words,

> The Hobbesian problem of order was historically based on a unitary concept of the body. The social contract was between men who, out of an interest in self-preservation, surrendered individual rights to the state, which existed to enforce social peace. However, the regime of political society also requires a regimen of bodies and in particular a government of bodies which are defined by their multiplicity and diversity. The Hobbesian problem is overtly an analysis of the proper relationship between desire and reason, or more precisely between sexuality and instrumental rationality. This problem in turn can be restated as the proper relationship between men as bearers of public reason and women as embodiments of private emotion. (1984: 113–14)

In the democratic—as opposed to Hobbesian absolutist—state, this tension between reason and desire continues, but not precisely in its gendered form identified by Turner. Civil rights to difference shift the boundaries of legal application, but by a similar logic new rights will only be protected where reason can dictate an expansion. It was reason that brought men together and legitimated the body politic through a social contract, and it is reason that can breach the divide between men and women, expunging desire from reason in the equivalent of contract renegotiations. Women retain an uncertain status for many groups today promoting traditional families, but race provides a better handle for their argument. As the Colorado attorney general argued before the state supreme court, "[gay rights are] different from all other civil rights issues discussed in all of the precedents before us today. In racial matters . . . there have been conflicts, but the moral consensus was decided for all time in the Civil War."

In a civil war, desire and aggression annihilate themselves, much as the state of nature is recognized in the relations between the races, and what remains is consensus or reason around which civil rights protections can be legitimated. Unlike civil rights protections for race, gay rights remain too volatile, too filled with aggression and passion to be included in the body politic; gays, lesbians, and bisexuals remain within a state of nature, beings defined by their desires. As Amendment 2 protects private forms of discrimination and aggression, it thus revalues the state of nature, asserting a sovereignty denying to the state its right to extend civil rights protections that now must be *reigned* in. As members of the body politic in this logic, we have less to fear from each other than from those marked by a desire that cannot appropriately be and—as the case against gay marriage makes clear—will not be allowed to be domesticated in common institutions.

Instead, aggression and violence play their part in acts of sovereignty that reimagine the violence of the state of nature.

Conclusion

The changing sovereign discourses of modern governmentality have increasingly become mediated by the politics of gay, lesbian, and bisexual identities, and the legal rights around which these identities have maneuvered. The latest act in this drama is the regulation of access to the law via stories that recapitulate traditional liberal tensions between state and civil society, economic and political interests, reason and passionate character. The central theme is a refutation of the model of social rights that emerged during Franklin Roosevelt's New Deal. The links that were forged then between individual and collective liberties and economic growth, and that sustained the identity and social justice claims of postwar social movements, have now come under sustained attack. No longer seen to be a universal premise of sovereignty, civil rights are frequently depicted as a cultural and economic drag on the promises of the social contract, and identified with what has always been weak and scarce in the American political landscape: economic rights to the commons. Stories about gays and about rights have been tactically deployed to fuel a growing realm of public opinion that asserts that legal rights and legal identities are best determined by democratic majorities rather than by courts and legal obfuscations.

Consider the following advertisement run to urge Hawaii legislators to thwart court extension of antidiscrimination law to homosexual marriage.

> *Constitutional Amendment or Same Sex Marriage? The Choice Should Be Yours*
> Over 70% of the people are against same sex marriage. But without a constitutional amendment, the courts will force same sex marriage on the people of Hawai'i this summer.
>
> A constitutional amendment bill has already passed the House. Now the Senate must act. They must make a simple decision—same sex marriage or a constitutional amendment. Incredibly, some senators don't even want voters to know where they stand on this issue.
>
> It's time for accountability. It's time to put the people first. That's what the democratic process is all about. (The Honolulu *Advertiser*, March 27, 1996: A8)

Significantly, the image of "the people" who must be put "first" before, presumably, sexual minorities is unlimited; there are no bounds to "the people" and no basis for self-knowledge and reflection absent a formal political dominance. Sovereignty therefore becomes powerfully reasserted. There is, in this tautologous reflection, no possibility that majorities can be wrong, in large part because gays and lesbians do not figure in this account.

Or do they? In a very tangible manner, it is the stories of gay and lesbian power, their political agendas, and the minority-like vulnerability of nongays that constitutes the antagonists around which these staggering majorities are formed. As a form of disidentification, public opinion thus serves less as a public sphere in which reason infuses democratic sovereignty (Habermas, 1989) than as a realm of unreason. In such a situation, moral languages such as justice and equality are harder to hear, and compromise is difficult to establish.

If moral languages are mute, moral positions are nonetheless manufactured through the tactics of economic argumentation and disidentification. A letter to the editor of a Honolulu newspaper in the midst of the highly charged debate over gay marriage makes clear the force of these tactics. "What is at issue," the author writes, "is the governmental validation and promotion of homosexuality and the granting of special government privileges and preferences without any evidence of reciprocal contributions to the society that will bear the costs of such privileges" (*The Honolulu Advertiser*, May 10, 1996: A18). The impossibility of such a balance sheet without a recourse to moral languages only creates the impression that these are excessive demands, thereby crafting their own pseudomoral imperative.

A political environment stripped of an acceptable normative language makes the pursuit of rights less tactically advantageous for sexual minorities. But it does not diminish the likelihood of its continuation. As public opinion today demands that states withdraw from previous positive assertions of sovereignty, the politics of sexuality that is the medium of this expression has begun to infuse all aspects of sovereign practices. No longer located in an expanding public space but increasingly in sexuality, sovereignty practices have become loaded with all the prejudices and antagonisms that a politics of scarcity and disidentification can apply. Such a public retreat marks novel boundaries of the state. Thus it is that issues often far from the central justice agendas of social movements and conservative groups—issues such as gay marriage, gays in the military, and gay parenting—will likely continue to emerge as central concerns of public policy.

8

"It's Not Just Naked Women"—Regulating Transgressive Identities in Cyberspace

R. Scott Daniels

> With the proliferation of choice, difference is disappeared. The choices mask the impossibility of deviance if that deviance threatens to disorder or re-place dominant constructs of pleasure and power.
>
> —Sandra Buckley, "Penguin in Bondage" (1991)

The debate over regulating the transmission and access to pornography through cyberspace has been a heated one. Although it has been couched in terms of morality and a problem of protecting children from exposure to adult materials, there is more going on in the debate than just legitimate concerns regarding availability of pornography to children. If that were the concern, one would think that existing laws would address the problem. Instead, other issues are at work. Instead of concentrating on free speech—ostensibly the center of the debate—this chapter concentrates on an aspect of the debate that has not yet received much attention. Confronting us is a new space popularly referred to in a quintessentially American vocabulary as a "frontier," and as such regulatory concerns have arisen with great intensity. Regulation and the frontier invoke each other, and in some cases this becomes personified, as in the Marlon Brando character of the Regulator in the Arthur Penn western *Missouri Breaks.* Involved here is the more impersonal regulation and containment of transgressive identities and the representation of self in cyberspace and elsewhere. I argue it is this issue that influences the current policy debate. Toward this end it is important to understand that I conceive of cyberspace as a "heterotopia," a space that serves as a countersite, "a kind of effectively enacted utopia in which the real sites, all the other real sites that can be found within the culture, are simultaneously represented, contested, and inverted." A place that is "outside of all places, even though it may be possible to indicate" its location in reality (Foucault, 1986: 24). Thus the space of cyberspace is not unreal, nor are the identities that are contained within it, although their reality may be also something that is not entirely given.

Cyberspace and the identities within can be considered as simulations in the way that Jean Baudrillard talks of simulations. Just because they are simulations, however, does not mean they can be disregarded or taken lightly. As Baudrillard argues, a "postmodern" war like the Persian Gulf War is a simulation fought through computer graphics and video-mediated targets. Yet that does not make the war any less deadly nor the casualties any less dead (Baudrillard, 1994a: 37). Furthermore, simulations are no less dangerous to authority because they always leave "open to supposition that, above and beyond its object, *law and order themselves might be nothing but simulation*" (Baudrillard, 1994a: 20). In the same way the simulations in cyberspace help to show the ways that the "real" has become progressively open to interpretation. This is especially highlighted in the debate over cyberporn and how its policy discourse's implied narrative takes simulated identity as the constitutive object of its concern.

The Debate

In 1995 Senator James Exon (D-Nebraska) proposed the Communications Decency Act, a law that makes it a criminal act to engage in the creation and dissemination of "obscene" materials through the Internet and other networks readily accessible by computer. The law also makes it a crime to send such communications to friends by e-mail. Although the full text of this law never made it past the Senate, another version of it was passed as an amendment to a larger communications law. What is ostensibly the purpose of the law is to contain the rapid distribution of pornography on electronic networks so that children are not exposed to the images. Children, it has been argued, are protected from print forms of pornography, but in cyberspace anyone has access to these works. Disregarding the enforceability of such a law, the fact that a group of senators would believe that the issue was of such importance as to warrant a significant amount of the government's time and money in order to deal with it signifies the threat that such forms of communications are seen to pose. That it has been seen as a significant enough debate to warrant various academic studies and significant space in newspapers and magazines also is a sign of the fear and threat felt on both sides of the issue. But the question remains, what is at issue? Pornography is readily available through a variety of means. It had become a regular part of this society before the advent of "the ghost in the machine." And yet the regulation that is being attempted is not the regulation of pornography in general, just the regulation of what can be obtained through electronic means. The electronic has become more of a "real" threat than the physical, and here lies the opening to larger anxieties about identity in cyberspace.

Inconsistencies in the Debate

As pointed out above, the debate is not just about pornography, it is about its distribution in cyberspace. The Communications Decency Act is not an attempt to stop pornography, nor is it an attempt to contain the symbols of power that are so repugnant about pornography. The symbols of power would be allowed to exist in another form within, and without, the electronic community. Sandra Buckley shows that the elimination of explicit graphics and texts does little to eliminate the symbols of power that are contained within them (1991: 163–95). Far from removing the symbols of dominance, the symbols are instead allowed to "transform the subjects, objects, and experience of the everyday into eroticized fantasy objects" (184). The symbols of pornography are allowed to exist and proliferate throughout society and thereby serve to further reinscribe and maintain existing constructs of power.

Since it is not these symbols that are under attack, since these symbols would, by default, be allowed to detach themselves and exist through other means, then it becomes questionable as to the moral character of the legislation and whose interests are most promoted by it. It also calls into question what it is that is being regulated.

The argument concerning children is even more problematic. Calls for the protection of children from pornographic images have been with us since the eighteenth century at least (Hunt, 1993a). While not new, this argument still contains a resonance that people hear. The problem is that no one can exactly tell us what it is that we are supposedly protecting children from. Again, the symbols of domination against women exist far beyond the explicit words and images of pornography. These symbols inform the advertisements that assault us daily. They also inform our news broadcasts and popular forms of entertainment. So again, the bill is not trying to protect children from what makes pornography so repugnant. Further, the threat from cyberspace is supposed to be one of accessibility; however, the threat, in order to be realized, has to assume a child with computing abilities greater than that of adults.

Senator Dan Coats (R-Indiana) stated: "We face a unique, disturbing and urgent circumstance, because it is children who are the computer experts in our nation's families" (Elmer-Dewitt, 1995: 40). One is left to wonder, if it is the children who are the computer experts in the family, then who exactly are the distributors and consumers of pornography? Realistically it is unlikely that children younger than thirteen have the computing skills to do everything that is required to download, decode, and view these images.

Furthermore most sites are private and require proof of age before one can join. Lastly, if the children we are concerned about are those with the computing skills to view these pictures, namely teenagers, then why worry just about electronic forms of distribution? The accessibility of pornography to teenagers (and younger) in our society is such a given that it has become a regular part of our popular culture. The perceived threat is more than that children stand to be exposed to "filth."

The Threat of the Transgressor

The main consequence of this law is not so much in the ways that it limits free speech through its attack on pornography, but in the ways that it limits the alternative constructions of self that are provided by the identity of the cyberpornographer and the images (and texts) s/he distributes.

In the *Time* magazine article concerned with cyberporn, the authors made it a point to explain that the problem with cyberporn is that "it's not just naked women," and that the "market seems to be driven largely by a demand for images that can't be found in the average magazine rack" (Elmer-Dewitt, 1995: 40). Clearly part of what is threatening is the type of images that are available. The *Time* report leaves one to think that if the images were confined to the "typical" images of naked women, that would be okay.

What makes these other images so threatening is that they help to reinscribe sexuality, and that is threatening in the same way that it was threatening before the French Revolution (Hunt, 1993b). The reinscription of sexuality calls into question the morals that sexuality is based upon. In doing so, it also calls into question the current forms of social hierarchy. What becomes worrisome is precisely the fact that the materials are not just naked women. Sexuality is expanded to include forms that are considered deviant. With the easy transmission and creation of identities beyond that which is acceptable, people are able to safely engage in other kinds of sexuality, which causes a questioning of the deviancy of the act in the first place. Because the controls on sexuality come into question, the power relations that rely upon those controls to maintain themselves also come into question. Thus the freewheeling sexuality of these images are threatening not because these pictures are offensive, but because they are appealing. There exists within cyberspace uncontrollable, transgressive identities that disrupt conventional understandings of morality and power. Since the arguments of these transgressive identities are seductive and compelling, they become threatening because their very seductiveness undermines our conceptions of what it is we are and, as a result, how it is we should be governed.

A second concern stems from the identity of the cyberpornographer. The cyberpornographer is different from print pornographers such as *Playboy*'s Hugh Hefner because the identity does not necessarily relate back to a body. The identity created by the cyberpornographer is one that is not necessarily based upon the experiences of the physical body that created it. As a result, the constructed pornographer identity does not connect back to a body and can, in fact, become a persona adopted by several people. The identity can exist exclusively in cyberspace without appearing in physical space. Since the identity does not relate back to a body, the regular means of control are disrupted. Laws, for example, are based upon bodies. One controls transgressiveness through threatening physical pain or incarceration. What is unique about the cyberidentity is that there is nothing to punish. The Communications Decency Act proposes to embody these identities. If you distribute material deemed offensive, then you are a pornographer, regardless of what other activities you may be engaged in. The transgressive identity threatens standing power relations enough that it takes precedence over all other representations of the self.

The clearest example of the difference between the print pornographer and the disembodied nature of the cyberpornographer is available from the vast public network known as the Internet. The postings on the Internet do not bring in a profit to the poster, who posts for reasons different from the print pornographer, partly perhaps for the thrill of the transgressiveness involved in posting. Furthermore, no one controls the group to which he/she/it posts. Accountability is lost. Ostensibly, then, identity is implicated in the regulation of pornography, and the potential anonymity of cyberspace threatens this regulation. A distinctive chiasmus is put at risk: we seek to identify pornographers so we can regulate their activities, just as we seek to regulate activities so we can "identify" (produce and regulate the identity of) pornographers (and others). Cyberspace threatens both.

However, is it necessary to label those who do post as pornographers? I may post a picture of a naked body because others might like it and so that I might become part of a community interested in nude bodies or alternative forms of sexuality. As with all postings, I create an identity to post it precisely because I am not a pornographer, but to post the picture requires that I step over lines of acceptable action in the physical world. It would not be considered acceptable if I were to post a pornographic picture on a plywood wall. Doing so could get me arrested. Therefore I create an identity that posts these pictures in cyberspace (like a poster on a wall only if that poster is enclosed in several envelopes, each envelope requiring a complex series of manipulations to open if one wants to see the picture, with the only indicator of what might be inside being maybe a line of text that says "gorgeous blond male").

This identity in cyberspace does not, however, constitute the limits of my being. This identity can conduct its business, talk to its friends, and never come in contact with my other identities in cyberspace. Alternatively, it can come into contact with another of my identities and argue the pros and cons of a particular issue. Identities remain true to themselves, not to the bodies that create them.

A classic example is the case of Julie (Stone, 1991: 82–84; Stone, 1995; Van Gelder, 1985). Julie, confined to a wheelchair, entered into an on-line chat room one day and became the center of the community. People frequently asked her advice and the advice she offered helped to transform their lives. No one had ever met Julie physically, but there was no doubt as to her esteemed presence in the community. Julie was not only instrumental in helping people with their personal problems, she was also instrumental in creating and organizing a woman's Special Interest Group (SIG) within the electronic community where she existed (Van Gelder, 1985: 101; Stone, 1995: 72). She was also relentless in ferreting out "impostors," once again highlighting the transgressiveness and instability of the electronic identity. After many years of involvement with the community, Julie was discovered to be what we would call a middle-aged, able-bodied, male psychologist. When Julie's physical identity was exposed, there were a variety of reactions among the community where she existed. Many felt betrayed and some said they felt raped. Most were not pleased. But the question remains, who is Julie? If she is not "real," then why the extreme reactions by those who had been "fooled"?

Julie calls into question not only the reality of herself, but also the reality of all constructions of self, both electronic and physical. Part of the reaction against Julie is that she calls into question those aspects of ourselves that we consider fundamental; part is that the constructions of male and female are based upon more than an ability to adapt to the social constructions of male and female. Interestingly enough, Julie was "discovered" not on the basis of her gender inconsistencies, but on the inconsistencies of her identity as a handicapped person. That is, the "story" frayed at a point different from what one would consider a basic construction of self. Lastly, the doctor who created Julie continued to be a part of the community, but the identity he used was markedly different from that of Julie's. There were some who tried to elicit Julie from him, but were unable to: Julie is a different person.

What matters most in cyberspace is not the physical markings that make you male/female, white/nonwhite, adult/child, but your ability to handle the discourses that mark one as male or female, etc. The cyberpornographer raises these same issues, although the issue at stake is not one that is based on biology, but one that is based on what is considered a basic and valid morality. Like Julie, the identity of the cyberpornographer threatens those constructions we hold to be legitimate and unassailable, and the identity need not relate back to the beliefs of the physical body. The identity is able to exist on its own terms. What too often happens is that the identity gets confused with the body and thus the efforts to somehow relate those identities back to a body, back to something "factual."

Why Me? Why You? Why It?

A reason for the concentrated effort on controlling the identity of the cyberpornographer is that it is such a banal and easy identity to restrict. No one sees much use in preserving such an identity. Furthermore, it is an easier identity to attach a threat to than most other identities. Hackers, for example, constitute another threatening identity. The problem, though, is that the threat the hacker presents is so diffuse that it makes it difficult to get the backing to attempt eliminating it entirely. The cyberpornographer, on the other hand, constitutes an immediate threat to morals, children, and women. The threat of the cyberpornographer, unlike the threat of the hacker, can be made to take a physical form (e.g., the Blue Book, a collection of images taken from the networks and collected in a blue binder used by Senator Exon to pass the CDA); this physical form represents an immediacy that is not contained in other identities. Additionally, other identities have their supporters while the cyberpornographer has only tenuous support at best. Debates settle around First Amendment issues, not about the hyped-up threat of the particular identity, thus allowing the discourse concerning representations of self to be neglected and informed through preexisting power structures. This conveniently ignores the political nature of the threatened identity by pushing off the issue as something else. As the cover of *Time* presented it: "Can we protect our kids—and free speech?" The answer becomes one of what constitutes free speech, not one that allows children or ourselves access to potential alternative understandings of legitimacy.

The importance of the cyberpornographer, therefore, lies precisely in its banality. It is an easy identity to adopt, thus it can serve as an introduction into transgressiveness. Furthermore, it serves as a protective barrier for other transgressive identities that exist within and without cyberspace, identities that have the ability to speak to and question power more directly.

A successfully waged campaign against the pornographic identity, as it stands now, would merely eliminate one configuration of identity with little in return. Nonetheless, this identity, although insipid, still causes problems for the political assumptions of power. Not easily punished or tracked, it is able to highlight the way that power operates at times, especially when it calls into question certain moral codes that do little more than support existing power relations.

The major problem with the elimination of the pornographic identity is that all transgressive identities are made more vulnerable. First the (virtual) burning of flags is banned; then (virtual) criticisms of military intervention are censored. Already there are moves toward limiting the ways that one can represent oneself in cyberspace. Speaker of the House Newt Gingrich (R-Georgia) has weighed in on the debate. Although against the

Communications Decency Act, he is for a more direct attack upon the ways in which we represent ourselves. In an interview with *Wired* he stated that his "bias is against trying to censor the Net and in favor of going after people," that the best approach is not "to go after the Net; it's to go after the behavior" (Dyson, 1995: 109).

Such a position makes it explicit that there is to be a privileged identity that engages in nondisruptive behavior, and this identity does not engage in cyberporn, or at least the cyberporn that is more than just naked women. But more important is the idea that the problem is not multiple identities, but that of bad behavior. Alternative identities are discounted as such, they are instead reinscribed as indicators of good and bad behavior. It is important that all identities within cyberspace be reattached to bodies. The idea is not to mess with the discourses of self, but to concentrate them so that all identities relate back to a single body. The position is that there is room for identities to exist as long as they behave. Thus disruptive identities are controlled or eliminated by reinscribing the transgressiveness contained within them as disruptive behavior.

A major problem with such a position is that there is little toleration for women. While concentrating on blatant and banal transgressive identities, the support for all transgressive identities is undermined, including that of women. Women in cyberspace and society have been constructed as Other, as transgressive. Carole Pateman shows that throughout the modern liberal tradition, women have been placed in a position where action from them was constituted as disruptive. She points out that Jean-Jacques Rousseau's, Sigmund Freud's, and G. W. F. Hegel's conception of women in the public sphere was one of deadly "disorder" (Pateman, 1989: 17–32), that the incorporation of women into the public sphere is so different from that of men that women end up symbolizing everything opposed to public order (1989: 4). However, the transgressiveness of women extends beyond their participation in a patriarchal public sphere. Jacques Lacan points out that Woman serves as a building point for the male identity, that the identity of Woman is fixed by the subjective identity of the male so that the male can distinguish himself as a separate subject. If the woman is allowed to become a subject also, this undermines the positioning of the male identity construction. Therefore it becomes imperative for the male identity to maintain Woman as a fixed point from which he can distinguish himself as a distinct identity (Brennan, 1993: 108–9).

So Woman is clearly a transgressive identity in physical space, but how does this translate into cyberspace? Here Katherine Hayles's (1993) contrast of presence/absence with pattern/randomness is useful. If the woman in physical space serves as a fixed point from which the male subject distinguishes himself, then cyberspace might free her from the status of a fixed point. What happens instead is that Woman becomes randomness. She becomes a lack of pattern, the background from which men once again emerge as distinct entities. In cyberspace one is recognized by the patterns that one presents. To distinguish yourself, you create a stable pattern, which serves as your identity. One can argue that this is what the government regulations are attempting to do, to stabilize patterns and reduce the randomness that causes disruptions. They are trying to reduce the number of transgressive, nonstable patterns so that individuals can be quickly identified and governed. The creation of the citizen-subject is not to be dramatically different in cyberspace from that of the physical citizen-subject. However, women still constitute a problem since they form the randomness from which the patterned self distinguishes itself. This is not to say that there cannot be a patterning for Woman, but that her patterning comes from the man's patterning of her. She does not create who she is, she is created by how she serves his creation. However, this must remain absolutely so, otherwise randomness takes over and all becomes illegible. Adopting the male patterning reserved for her only heightens the distrust that one has for Woman; maintaining a pattern only increases the fear of infection from the randomness that is inherent to her.

I Seem to Have Caught a Computer Virus

Attacks on transgressiveness are an attempt to maintain a current order upon an otherwise "unruly" sphere. More importantly, they are an attempt to contain the infections of randomness that exist in cyberspace from entering into physical world relations. These infections occur through the fact that bodies are not primarily physical. Bodies are a mixture of discursive practices and of physicality. For the most part they are discursive, as is witnessed by the method by which one becomes a citizen. Citizens are not merely the physical manifestations that exist within a particular boundary region, they are a set of discursive practices that determine their citizenry. Typically these discursive practices are placed upon a physical body, but the physical body is the least important aspect of defining what it means to be a citizen. What becomes of primary importance are the discursive practices.

Similarly, an identity in cyberspace is a discursive practice. Here the creation of an identity is free of the physical body entirely. One's ability to be someone is based upon one's ability to maintain a particular set of discursive practices. Thus the distinctions between male/female, machine/human/animal, white/nonwhite, child/adult are freed from physical markers. Yet engaging in discursive practices contrary to what you "are" causes a reevaluation of how you are. Similarly, it causes the same reevaluation in others.

One can look at the reactions to Julie's "true" identity as an example of this. Another example comes from the community where Legba "lives." Legba is gender neutral. Its gender is unspecified and that is how it is treated. Legba is an intelligent member of the community and engages in many abstract and theoretical debates. One day Legba and a man get into a debate and begin to establish a friendship. This goes on for several months with the Man becoming more impressed with both Legba's intellect and its deep commitment to their friendship. The Man falls in love. In an ideal world, this would be the end of the story, except that the Man cannot accept Legba's gender (or lack thereof). Because of Legba's intellect and style of speech, the Man is convinced that Legba's physical manifestation is male. However, if this is so, then his love for Legba calls into question his assumed heterosexual identity. The Man is in a quandary, either Legba is a female that is not "really" a female, or he is not "really" a heterosexual. The quandary before the Man lasted for several months and almost ended in the dissolution of his marriage.

Since the discursive practices in cyberspace cause reevaluations in the constructed identity of the physical body, it begins to highlight many of the discursive practices of the physical body. One's identity becomes destabilized and ambiguous. However, this messes up governance. The problem is not so much that people adopt new discursive practices constantly, but that the discursive practices shift more frequently, thereby allowing ambiguities to enter. The goal of governance is to clear up these ambiguities, to make all manifestations relate back to a body, and we are complicit in this in that we are uncomfortable when we are "fooled" or do not know whom we are dealing with; we want to make sure that people are who they say they are. Julie is hated because she turns out to show that what and who we are is not necessarily what we physically are. We turn out to be who (and how) we say we are. Reality begins to become a story. Or rather we begin to understand that reality is a set of competing stories. What the Internet does is upset our understanding of "true" or "real" stories and begins to allow alternative stories of who and how we are to come into consideration. What the Communications Decency Act attempts to do is control and limit the creation of alternative reality stories.

If discursive practices are what is most important in how it is that we are understood, then it becomes the prerogative of power to maintain a set of controls on the ways that those discursive practices manifest themselves. If one is able to engage in discursive practices that can in some measure rewrite the ways that one is identified as a citizen, if one is able to engage in discursive practices in a way so that one realizes that who one is is mostly dependent upon how one is, then one is left with a means to contest power that writes oneself in a particular way over other ways of being. Governance has a stake in the types of identities and representations that are allowed to occur. Limiting representations makes its job easier while maintaining current conceptions of reality. And we make its job easier in the process by treating the electronic representations of self as a game, as something not related to the "real" us. As a result we lose the ability to affect the discourse that constitutes us as governed entities. Meanwhile the various representations of self, electronic and otherwise, persist as the primary way by which we are understood for governing purposes. The debate in Congress over the Communications Decency Act is an indicator as to how real some take these representations to be and the need to regulate them.

On Pornographers and Censors

There still is the issue concerning the symbols of power and dominance that exist within pornography. Not all pornography engages in the transgression and deviancy that I have been arguing are important to maintain alternatives to current power relations. However, a blanket attack on all forms, I argue, does little while losing much. The same can be said of cyberpornographers. Most engage in a transmission of symbols that only help to reinscribe current relations within society. However, there are many that offer alternatives to those constructions. Any debate concerned with limiting pornography has to take into account that both pornography engaged in maintaining current power relations and "censorship share the same function of foreclosing potential sites of alternative identifications. They both order and organ-ize bodies" (Buckley, 1991: 191). Both are engaged in the practice of halting the alternative identity constructions that allow a questioning of power, that allow transgressions to occur. Both are instrumental in maintaining Woman as the fixed point from which the male can distinguish himself as distinct, and in maintaining the "nonnormal" as sights of danger. Both are instrumental in essentializing constructions of male and female.

Conclusion

Therefore, even, or especially, as the previous examples indicate, the attempts to impose or uphold moral standards in cyberspace do more than regulate the flow of images and texts. The regulatory impulses coursing through the Internet today also are operating to constrain the flow of alternative identities that can be used to question the prevailing systems of power. While Congress argues that it has the interests of our children at stake, it ends up conceivably having greater effect in maintaining the boundaries of discursive and interpretive practices. And it does so by way of constructing narratives of danger that limit considerations of alternative practices. By failing to distinguish between the types of pornography that exist and the types of narratives they engender, we help to maintain otherboundaries, and in the process, limit the possibilities for our own explorations of difference.

9

Welfare Queens: Policing by the Numbers

Barbara Cruikshank

Welfare recipients are obviously intimidated and dominated by state power, excluded from political self-representation and participation. Yet media representations of the welfare queen, especially the figure of the black welfare cheat, assign her sovereignty over the system of welfare. She is both sovereign and subject. As such, she is in many ways a typical liberal democratic subject (Foucault, 1983; Rose, 1990; Gordon, 1991).

The sovereign status of the welfare queen is often taken to be an effect of illiberal ideology and racism, not an effect of liberal welfare state practices (see Fraser and Gordon, 1994; Lubiano, 1992; Piven, 1990). As the subject of ideology and racism, the myth of the welfare queen is used to explain the excessive and punitive police practices of the welfare state (L. White, 1990: 37).

In what follows, I reverse the terms of that explanation: excessive, punitive, and "productive" police practices produce the myth of the stereotypical welfare cheat. The stereotype does not justify practices; rather, practices justify stereotypes. I want to demonstrate how the material practices of the state make credible and sustain the welfare queen narrative and its power to delegitimate the receipt of public assistance.

The reason for my reversal of the relationship of punitive practices to stereotypical narratives is strategic. The welfare rights movement and its strategists have historically sought to combat the racist and ideological representation of the welfare queen by calling upon her to represent herself, to act in her own interests with others of her kind (Piven and Cloward, 1979; Funiciello, 1990). Yet these critics seek to mobilize the very mythical queens they seek to debunk. To argue for the inclusion of excluded poor women's voices in debates over welfare reform is already to take the welfare queen for granted, to take her for "real."

Yet how do we account for the factual existence of this mythical queen? The short answer is, by the practices of accounting. Numbers quite literally constitute the body of the mythical queen; the anonymity of numbers allows the variable inscription of her body by race, class, will, and gender. I argue that it is crucial to study the governmental practices that make for her embodiment in rhetoric more so than to account for what effect rhetoric has on her body.

If we were to end our critique with the claim that welfare cheats are excluded from democratic politics and stereotyped in the media, we would fail to see that the terms and the subject of our critique—welfare fraud and welfare queens—are produced by power. Judith Butler notes a dual relation of the subject to power in her analysis of gender and feminist politics: "It is not enough to inquire into how women might become more fully represented in language and politics. Feminist critique ought also to understand how the category of 'women,' the subject of feminism, is produced and restrained by the very structures of power through which emancipation is sought" (1990: 2). I argue here that a critique of welfare cannot simply call for more participation on the part of or in the name of welfare recipients in the definition and provision of their own needs, i.e., through "the politics of need interpretation" (Fraser, 1990). Before calling upon welfare recipients to act in their own interests, to represent themselves politically as recipients, to paraphrase Butler, it is necessary to examine how the category "welfare recipient," the subject of welfare, is both produced and restrained by the relations of rule we call "welfare" (Mohanty, 1991).

The Subject of Welfare

A welfare fraud suspect is a subject of welfare rather than a subject of the state, a subject of eligibility criteria in a means-tested program, a subject of administrative procedure rather than constitutional due process, a subject of error rates rather than personal goals and intentions. She does not break the law, but she receives a grant for which she is "ineligible." Techniques of welfare fraud administration—statistics, accounting, data matching, welfare fraud hotlines, calculations of cost and benefit—provide the political rationality governing poor women's citizenship in terms of a crisis of "waste, fraud, abuse, and error."

Unlike self-governing citizens, a recipient's *freedom* is not the condition of her subjection, it is her *eligibility* to receive public assistance, which is quantifiable and calculable (on freedom and liberal citizenship see Dumm, 1996; Rose, 1990). This is not to say that freedom cannot be quantified or calculated, only less obviously so. Eligibility criteria (whether that of Aid to Families with Dependent Children—AFDC—or its 1996 replacement, Temporary Assistance to Needy Families—TANF) set the terms of welfare and confer a unity on welfare recipients so that then, and only then, is it possible to govern welfare recipients according to those criteria. However, that unity is purely the product of numbers. The numbers do not represent the realities of poor women's lives or their solidarity, but constitute that reality. Lucie White describes the life of Mrs. G., a welfare recipient accused of welfare fraud: "In order to participate in AFDC, Mrs. G had no choice but to conform her life to the conditions the program imposed" (1990: 43). Mrs. G was "compelled to assent" to the terms of welfare. Welfare, like liberal democratic government in general, is both voluntary and coercive.

Beginning with the "voluntary" subjection of the welfare applicant to administrative rules in return for money, vouchers and services, she is immediately subject to a whole series of double-binds that circumscribe her choices, not least of which has her trade her constitutional rights for a welfare check. Administrative laws and procedures determine not only her political and public behavior, but also the terms on which she can discuss and handle the basic and mundane aspects of her everyday life—where she can live and with whom, what she can buy and where, who she can trust.

First, unlike most felony crimes, the investigation and prosecution of welfare fraud is only rarely carried out in criminal courts and governed by the rules of due process (Collin and Hemmons, 1987). The presumption of guilt is endemic—recipients must prove that they are *not* guilty in administrative hearings. Everyone knows that families could not survive on welfare grants that rarely approach 70 percent of the federal poverty level. The first premise of welfare fraud investigations, therefore, is that anyone living in relative stability must be cheating the system somehow. Second, investigations usually take place in administrative settings, having moved out from an overcrowded criminal justice system. In administrative hearings, one has no right to legal counsel, neither the rules of evidence nor the final authority is clearly determined, and cases can be turned over to county prosecutors at any time. Third, anyone and any number of agencies can initiate a fraud investigation in most states: a disgruntled lover, the landlord, a father attempting to evade child support payments, or a postal worker can call a state welfare fraud hotline anonymously; a computer match from another bureaucracy spits out a notice to attend an eligibility hearing; a child protective services worker can threaten an investigation in order to achieve anything from getting a woman to agree to therapy or taking her children away. The penalties of welfare fraud are constantly repeated to recipients in standard eligibility meetings and subsequent verification actions. Fraud hotline posters are often conspicuous in waiting rooms. Finally, investigations can be conducted on the agency, city, county, state, and federal levels, even by private investigators under county contract who earn a percentage of the amount recouped in fraud convictions and overpayment designations. Even if you want to trace the lines of authority for the systematic

State of California
Pete Wilson, Governor

Health and Welfare Agency
Department of Social Services

Do You Know Someone On Welfare (or Food Stamps) Who:

- Is working and not reporting it?
- Has an unreported person in the home ?
- Has unreported bank accounts or other assets ?
- Is drawing welfare or food stamps for a child who is not in the home ?
- Is drawing welfare or food stamps in more than one county at the same time ?

If so, you may call the

WELFARE FRAUD HOTLINE

1-800-344-TIPS

Remember. Welfare Fraud is a Crime !
All calls will be acted upon.

PUB 109 (1/91)

Figure 9.1 Materializing the Welfare Queen.

harassment of welfare recipients, the location of power in the case of welfare fraud is extremely difficult to determine because power is exercised in innumerable locations.

Welfare fraud does not link women in poverty to the state so much as link data bases for computer cross-matches among agencies such as the Internal Revenue Service, Social Security Administration, Department of Labor, welfare agencies and even state lotteries, in a vision of "system integrity." Welfare fraud administration is a strategy to clean up, police, account, and discipline an unruly welfare program, not to discipline recipients. However, the policing of numbers and strategies for ferreting out "waste, fraud, abuse, and error" have a decisive, disciplinary, and productive effect on welfare recipients. Welfare recipients are substantiated by eligibility criteria and then, as eligible recipients, subject to the terms of welfare. Rather than merely excluding welfare recipients from citizenship and democratic participation, eligibility criteria expand the scope of the political and strategically mobilize the queen's body.

The Mythical Body of the Queen

If the terms of welfare substantiate welfare recipients in general, how is it that welfare recipients and especially "welfare cheats" are so often stereotyped as black? How are the terms of welfare inscribed onto the body of "the black welfare queen?" Why is the racist and sexist narrative of the black welfare queen repeated so often? Not one of the professional and governmental publications on welfare fraud that I have read specifically mentions the mythical black welfare queen and not one accounting innovation specifically targets or counts "welfare cheats" by race.

The allusions and allegations made by Ronald Reagan are legendary for legitimating the allegedly popular stereotypes that equated welfare and race. Proudly illiberal, Reagan charged that welfare was not a solution to the inequality that flowed from capitalism; rather, welfare was the cause of inequality. The narrative Reagan spun on the welfare queen took on the quality, first, of an explanation for the "welfare mess" and, second, of a clarion call to taxpayers to clean up that mess.

As Wahneema Lubiano notes, Reagan's vituperative narrative made all recipients black and all guilty of fraud. Lubiano points out that the "real" facts of welfare and race matter very little, because the myths narrated by Reagan took on the appearance of reality: "And it does not matter that all such children needing state care are not black, or that poverty and unemployment are reasons that they need state care; what matters, what resonates in the national mind's eye, is the constant media-reinforced picture of the welfare queen—always black" (1992: 340). The black welfare queen is never fully embodied; she remains a fiction or, rather, she is embodied as a fiction. The media representation of the queen is a myth, but where does that leave us strategically? Lubiano's explanation leaves us only with facts set against myth. But as her own argument demonstrates, in the politics of representation, the facts don't matter.

It is therefore more crucial to study the terms of the welfare queen's embodiment than the body of the queen. The welfare queen is not only an ideological scapegoat and fictive character, a racial formation; but perhaps more importantly, she is an administered reality constituted through the counting procedures of government agencies. The welfare queen's race and gender embodiment is the product of fictional narratives, but the fact that she has a body is an effect of numbers that specify the targeted population. Numbers are methods of inscribing the lives of welfare recipients and rendering them actionable. As Nikolas Rose writes, "numbers do not merely inscribe a pre-existing reality. They constitute it" (1991: 676). This is to say that administrative decisions based on numbers do not simply mask the expansion of power to legitimate stereotypes. Rather, administrative practices constitute the very "realities" they supposedly count. Thus, for strategic reasons, because I agree with Lubiano that the strategy of discounting myths with facts is fruitless, I want to present another narrative account of the mythical queen's origin.

The policies that set the terms of welfare predate Reagan's rhetoric. For all his hate-mongering, Reagan was not the source of the myth, nor were the media. Rather than an explicit attack on poor black women, the terms of welfare were set to attack "waste, fraud, abuse, and error" in the name of "system integrity." The myth of the welfare queen began to directly govern the lives of welfare recipients only after a series of crises were declared to threaten the welfare state and democratic government. Following the 1960s' surge in the numbers of AFDC recipients, in 1972 the Subcommittee on Fiscal Policy of Congress's Joint Economic Committee declared a "crisis in public welfare." The subcommittee called the welfare system "an administrative nightmare" resulting in "confusion, inefficiency, and lawlessness" (cited in Brodkin, 1986: 25). The crisis was discovered under the Nixon Administration, where the strategy of quality control (QC) was devised. Evelyn Brodkin (1986) and Michael Lipsky (1984) have pointed out the ways in which QC was used as a means to get the numbers under control, especially error rates in eligibility determinations, and to indirectly reduce the numbers of people on welfare.

Policies to "enhance system integrity" continued under President Jimmy Carter, who linked the cleanup to a second crisis, the "crisis of democracy" (quoted in Gardiner and Lyman, 1984: 2). The crisis of democracy was a political crisis, as Carter pointed out, and had only an indirect relation to welfare. Carter stated: "As a known or suspected part of the total federal budget, losses through fraud, abuse and error may be small. But compared to the tax bill of the average American, those losses are huge—and demoralizing" (10). Thus Carter transformed the political crisis of democracy into a crisis of numbers, the numbers of tax dollars lost to waste, fraud, abuse, and error, the rising number of AFDC recipients, and the rising number of taxpayers in revolt. To govern a democracy meant to discipline systems, not people, to govern at a distance provided by certain auditing techniques (Rose and Miller, 1992).

Under the direction of Carter's secretary of Health, Education, and Welfare, Joseph Califano, reforms were intended to document the fact that there were very few recipients committing welfare fraud, that there was, so to speak, no real crisis. Yet, in order to prove the integrity of welfare administration, Califano introduced even more ways to make welfare recipients calculable. At the end of a ten-year period of QC innovations, new verification requirements for AFDC eligibility could include photo identification, sometimes fingerprints, two proofs of residency, verification of Social Security number for every family member, even infants, birth certificates, proof of school attendance, and so forth (see Lipsky, 1984; Brodkin, 1986). Lipsky sums up the net effect of QC measures as "bureaucratic disentitlement."

Indeed, these strategies of welfare fraud prevention—strategies that changed the terms of welfare—made Reagan's attack possible, made the "welfare cheat" real. The new terms of welfare included random QC checks, pre-eligibility screening for welfare fraud and errors, and a shift in emphasis from criminal to administrative prosecutions for welfare fraud. Rather than jury trials and jail time for fraud, recipients today are more likely to pay back any "overpayments" they receive from welfare agencies, perhaps with fines attached, without any proof whatsoever that they intended to commit fraud (see L. White, 1990). In other words, recipients pay the price for agency errors much as if they are guilty of fraud.

By transforming the political crisis into a crisis of numbers, by transferring the crisis from the political to the administrative realm, Brodkin (1986) argues, welfare officials succeeded in "depoliticizing" the crisis by steering a question of policy out of the Congress and into the hands of accountants and managers. However, the concentration on numbers rather than on votes does not necessarily indicate a shift away from politics, conflict, or domination. Rose (1991: 678–79) relates numbers to democratic politics: "Numbers are not just 'used' in politics, they help to configure the respective boundaries of the political and the technical. . . ." Rather than "depoliticize" the exercise of power, then, welfare fraud strategies give scope and method to the productivity of power.

According to Sheldon Wolin (1987: 477), there is a distinctively political motive for transforming a public and contested issue into the realm of administration and bureaucracy. "In brief, the variability of welfare programs means that at any political moment they can be expanded, sharply modified, reversed, even revoked altogether. Variability is the condition that makes possible two complimentary phenomena: a certain kind of flexible power and a certain kind of pliable citizen." This is another way to say that discretion is introduced through the extension of bureaucracy. But even more important, this "flexible power," as Wolin calls it (or micro-power, as Michel Foucault would call it), can be mobilized because welfare is rooted in administrative rather than constitutional law, and administrative jurisdictions are discretionary. Rather than a "depoliticizing" move, the expansion of administrative domains served to expand the reach of power, a particularly productive kind of power. A domain was established by reforms in which investigators determine the terms of a "fair" investigation, "fair" evidence, and so on. As an arena of power, this domain has fluid rather than fixed boundaries.

"Pliable citizens," (or as Foucault said, "docile bodies") are citizens whose bodies can be mobilized, whose race, class, and gender are useful, whose status is never fixed, and those who are never sure of their standing. Variable and flexible methods of welfare fraud administration are for "acting at a distance" upon welfare recipients (Latour, 1986). Again, far from being rationalized systems of social domination and control, the methods of welfare fraud investigation and administration are for policing numbers, not people. Far from being illiberal strategies or cynical and conspiratory efforts to disenfranchise certain citizens, welfare fraud administration is distinctively liberal. The terms of poor women's citizenship, to which I turn now, are the liberal terms of rights and responsibilities, the terms of a contract between citizen and state.

The Terms of Poor Women's Citizenship: Rights, Responsibilities, and Relationships

On the back of a typical application for welfare, food stamps, or general assistance, the terms of welfare are listed. Very often, a social worker will ask if you have understood these terms, and if so, the welfare worker will sign the form as evidence that you read and understood the terms of welfare. At this time, recipients are reminded of the penalties for welfare fraud. The terms listed lay out a whole series of double-binds to which the recipient "consents." The terms are listed in three parts: rights, responsibilities, and appeals. Rights include, for example, the right to apply for public assistance, the right to privacy, the right to have the application explained to you, and so on. The responsibilities include informing your case worker of any changes in the data provided on the form:

> If you give facts that are not true, or do not report a change, you may be charged with fraud. Any facts that you give may be checked by the county office. Facts that deal with your case can be gotten from other sources only if

> you agree in writing. However, if you do not give your written consent for us to check with other sources or provide us with other proof of your facts, your application may be denied or your grant stopped.

The forms I am using here are published by the Minnesota Department of Human Services, for example, DHS-1842 (3-87) PZ-01842-05.

A double-bind is presented here. If you choose to exercise your right to privacy, you forfeit your right to assistance. The groups that exchange information with the welfare department include the Social Security Administration, Internal Revenue Service, Department of Jobs and Training, Child Support Enforcement, unemployment agencies, medical assistance agencies, Department of Agriculture, mental health centers, state hospitals, nursing homes, insurance companies, Department of Public Safety, collection agencies, anyone under contract with the Department of Health and Services, and social service agencies.

Reasons listed for obtaining information include the need to decide "if you or your family needs protective services." In other words, the information can be used against you in a juvenile court if a case is initiated by protective services. Information gathered is to be used in a punitive system of "protection." After this double-bind is a more serious one that claims that QC may choose your case randomly to verify your facts against third parties. "Even if you do not want the contact made, and you do not give your written consent, the reviewer may still make the contact after telling you." Cooperation is, of course, compulsory. This section does several things. First, it clarifies that even a county official is not the final arbiter of one's eligibility. The final determination of eligibility is always deferred, never settled, and usually discretionary. No one is in charge here; there is no ultimate authority in rules or in the adjudication of the rules. In the case of Mrs. G (L. White, 1990: 32), an administrative judge decided against her; then, after she filed an appeal, the county welfare director called her lawyer to say that "the county had decided that it wouldn't be 'fair' to make Mrs. G pay the money back." No explanation was given.

Second, the process establishes that quality control and welfare fraud investigation are the same thing. Errors can be caused by clients or workers, but the recipient pays in either case. The terror of random sampling is duplicated by the initiation of toll-free welfare fraud hotlines. Anyone can report suspicions about a recipient and some states guarantee an investigation. The most common callers are postal workers, disgruntled lovers, and ex-husbands. Third, one's consent is absolutely meaningless, but absolutely necessary. You must comply with the verification process in order to be eligible for AFDC, and you must consent to the invasion of privacy, the assumption of guilt before the law, but if you do not consent, you will be investigated anyway.

The appeals process, if you object to any of the above or the determinations of eligibility based on them, is extremely risky to pursue. Most significantly, if a recipient loses an appeal, "any overpayment you get between the effective date of the action and the appeal decision must be refunded to the county office." The appeals process, of course, does not establish precedents for future decisions (Lipsky, 1984: 15).

To provide an incentive to states and counties to actively pursue welfare fraud investigations and audits, the federal government fines states for error rates that are too high. In my own experience, fraud investigators are sometimes the heroes of media spots, but in state legislatures and Human Services Departments, they are routinely despised. There is an occasional plea sent out to welfare recipients to turn in their own kind in order to legitimate the unpopular AFDC program, an attempt to enlist the participation of recipients further in their own subjection, but it has to my knowledge enlisted no great numbers. With no constituency and no clear lines of authority, how is it possible to account for an exercise of power that has such pervasive effects upon women's citizenship? With so many lines of possible action, how is it possible to understand, let alone resist, the actions that are taken?

Conclusion: Locating Power and the Political

The actions that count as political resistance in critical studies of administrative reform and practice are laced with one central and foundational strain of argument. That is, the argument that bureaucracy and administrative practices function chiefly to "depoliticize" power relationships (see Brodkin, 1986; Fraser, 1990; Keane, 1984; Offe, 1985). The general argument is that when issues leave the arena of the state, they no longer produce conflict because the exercise of power is masked; issues disappear, as it were, from public consciousness and public debate. Against this, I have argued that the "regulation," "professionalization," or "depoliticization" of social life is better understood to be an expansion of the political and an extension of power's reach. In the field of welfare fraud administration, I have argued that transforming political problems into administrative ones does not "depoliticize" an issue so much as make it actionable. Government by numbers indicates an extension of power's reach rather than its concealment.

Critical theories of depoliticization are limited in their potential to imagine new forms of resistance because they fail to account for political power beyond the state, as Nikolas Rose and Peter Miller (1992) put it. Rather than relocate the analysis of politics itself, critical theorists equate politicization with relocating issues to the political by removing them from the arenas of administration, family protection, and so on.

Nancy Fraser (1990), whose work exemplifies the best in critical theories of the welfare state, lists four kinds of client resistance. These include individual resistance aimed, for example, at extending the administrative jurisdiction of an agency to include the needs of the client; second, informal organizations of groups such as the domestic kin networks documented by Carol Stack (1974); and third, clients who insist upon their own subjective narratives against the therapeutic narratives asserted by the experts. However, none of these forms of resistance is deemed "political" in Fraser's account. She reserves the designation "political" for a very specific fourth form of resistance, that of organizing as welfare recipients:

> In addition to informal, ad hoc, strategic, and/or cultural forms of resistance, there are also more formally organized, explicitly political, organized kinds. Clients of social welfare programs may join together *as clients* to challenge administrative interpretations of their needs. They may take hold of the passive, normalized, individualized or familialized identities fashioned for them in expert discourses and transform them into a basis for collective political action. (Fraser, 1990: 219)

Fraser fixes political resistance at the level of identity, a level that then sets resistance upon the state. In Fraser's account, it is only when we already embody the terms of welfare that we are acting politically. Her account rules out much of what I take to be crucial and political forms of resistance, those forms of resistance that target the terms of welfare that constitute the embodied and "identified" welfare recipient. The explicitly political subjectivity of welfare recipients is rendered, in Fraser's formulation, a mere organizational and ontological effect of the organization of state power, a frozen embodiment of power.

By pointing out the limitations of aligning the terms of resistance with the terms of embodiment and the terms of welfare, I seek to expand critical debate to encompass the constitutive terms of welfare. Practices of ruling and policing are not restricted to "the political" or to one domain of power. What we take to be *real* political issues, or identities that are authentically political, have bound us to forms of resistance that are not effective. This is nowhere more clear than in attempts by welfare rights activists to drag the "real" fraud into the political limelight by suggesting that the *real* political issues are the waste and corruption committed by corporate contractors throughout the public sector (Piven and Cloward, 1982).

Welfare rights activists have long understood "the welfare queen" to be an ideological ruse or political scapegoat to cover up the "real" abuses of power at higher levels of government (see Milwaukee County Welfare Rights Organization, 1972). The counterattack by welfare rights organizations and advocates aims to expose the "real" fraud committed by the rich and powerful, to unmask the irrationality of political leaders for whom welfare bashing is a political meal ticket. But despite the facts, despite the "real," and no matter how many people know about it, making an issue public is not necessarily an effective mode of resistance.

Resistance can also take the form of refusing to act as a recipient, a refusal to be what our relations to the state have made us. To treat the political subjectivity of poor women as the mere effect of power, then, does very little to explain the terms of welfare that determine her subjection. To hold the productive aspects of power politically accountable we must imagine a way to politically manage the fact that there is such a thing as the social construction of citizenship. Then the terms of that production can be democratized and made part of our political landscape.

10

Tales of Black Criminality: Racial Determinism and Fatal Narratives

Gerard Fergerson

> America is now home to thickening ranks of juvenile "super-predators."
>
> —William J. Bennett, John J. DiIulio Jr., and John P. Walters, *Body Count* (1996)

> One sees that the power relation that underlies the exercise of punishment begins to be duplicated by an object relation in which not only the crime as a fact is to be established according to common norms, but the criminal as an individual is to be known according to specific criteria.
>
> —Michel Foucault, *Discipline and Punish* (1977)

In November 1993, I was serving as a Milbank Memorial Fund fellow in health policy with the congressional Office of Technology Assessment (OTA). I was asked to comment on a draft congressional report addressing the link between the incidence of substance abuse and violence among youth in the United States (U.S. Congress, 1994). I was struck by the deterministic tone of comments by an outside research contractor that staff at OTA eventually felt had to be removed from the report. One particular paragraph jumped out at me in a section on alternative interventions to stem the incidence of addiction. The sentence that attracted my attention questioned whether federal support for public service announcements through preventive programs in the departments of Education, Justice, and Housing and Urban Development might work to discourage substance use and abuse among African Americans. The fatalistic tone implied that advertising and public service announcements would fail as public policy largely because social science had already proved that the causes of interpersonal violence and other "pathologies" found today in the inner city were so deeply embedded that "black men don't heed public service announcements."

In this case, public policy inaction was premised on unsubstaniated rumors that were themselves legitimated by referencing social science. In what follows, I examine how this social science has implied a racial determinism that increasingly in recent years has been used to explain the causes of increased inner-city violence, crime, and substance abuse in terms of an "urban underclass." The major consequence of this new racial determinism is that racial prejudice simultaneously has gained credibility and influence by way of the respatialization of identity—i.e., race is being reinscribed as the major explanatory factor for crime, this time by locating it in narratives that point toward contemporary urban legends about the neighbhorhoods of the urban underclass (see Gans, 1995; National Health Policy Forum, 1997).

This respatialized racial determinism has increasingly been appropriated by many scientists and policy makers for suggesting strategies to manage crime and violence (Edelman and Satcher, 1993; Office of National Drug Control Policy, 1994; and U.S. Senate, Committee on the Judiciary, 1993). This discourse evinces a consistent reliance on reductionist, static definitions: a new racial determinism that offers a story of a racialized urban environment, i.e., the underclass neighborhood—as the primarily immutable factor causing violence, crime, and substance abuse. While the older racial determinisms stressed the race of individuals or the culture of groups (Lewontin, Rose, and Kamin, 1984), the new racial determinism still tells stories of race and culture but now ties these to the urban environment—most often the underclass neighborhood (for examples, see Wilson and Herrnstein, 1985; Hawkins and Thomas, 1991; Tolnay and Beck, 1995; Dash, 1996).

Fatalistic Narratives of the Immutability of Crime: Biological, Cultural, Environmental

Recent scholarship on this alleged urban underclass in fact provides a poignant example of how biological, genetic, and cultural formulations are still popular but now are increasingly encoded, if then hidden, in narratives of the urban environment. Just as "welfare" has become an encoded racialized term that erases its reference to race even as it reinscribes it, the same is true for the "urban underclass." Therefore, race and culture get to operate in the urban underclass as deterministic explanatory factors even as the urban environment is what is foregrounded.

Several authors recently conclude, for example, that patterns of urban violence derive primarily from the influence of "criminogenic communities—places where the social forces that create predatory criminals are far more numerous and stronger than the social forces that create decent, law-abiding citizens" (Bennett, DiIulio, and Walters, 1996: 28). In such narratives, "criminogenic communities" operate as the urban equivalents of biological and cultural determinants of crime. Each factor, whether it is biological, cultural, or environmental, is narrated as essentially unchangeable. Though violence researchers are deeply divided on the constellation of biological, biophysical, and cultural properties that exert influences in models of causality in violence and to what extent different factors are mutable, the hallmark of the new racial determinism is a fatalism about the immutability of factors associated with urban neighborhoods and communities.

Visibility for deterministic tales of race and violence in the city is therefore not surprisingly bolstered by the growing salience of a "new biology of violence" (Marshall, 1993; Stevenson, 1995; Reiss, Miczek and Roth, 1994). For instance, even a 1994 National Institutes of Health (NIH) report that went on to recommend more interdisciplinary social and cultural contextualization of violence still nonetheless suggested that "there is evidence that African American boys are naturally more active. . . . Thus, research to separate out these cultural contributors to violent behavior may be enlightening." "Such studies should consider," the report further states, "how cultural factors are protective and predisposing." During a time when prevention initiatives are under assault as a policy option to reduce incidence in urban communities, biological and genetic explanations for human aggression and violence are prominent among researchers at the federal NIH.

And elsewhere too. "Are some people biologically or genetically predisposed to violence?" asked the Los Angeles *Times* in 1993 (1). "Could traditional medicine hold clues," the article continued, "even tiny ones, to making streets safe again?" The persistent employment of race as an epidemiological variable with a high predictive value, for example, has strengthened the imputation of biological and cultural deterministic views in violence research in particular. Narratives on violence increasingly read as if the genetic bases for aggressive behavior have been established through the sequencing of the human genome (Mestel, 1994).

Despite conclusions from three decades of interdisciplinary social and biological research debunking the usefulness of race as a valid scientific category, the media and scientific researchers continue to employ race as an effective predictor of and explanation for human aggression and crime (see DiIulio, 1994 for an example and Duster, 1990 for a critique). These tales of criminality reinforce conservative calls to reduce state intervention in social environments to promote violence reduction because both social science and popular press stress the immutable causes of crime. In turn, this causal framework reinforces calls for greater individual responsibility and stricter punishment.

Yet the growing authority of narrow cultural and biologic tales of criminality obscures what is ultimately a complex social phenomenon and cultural construct. Today's tales of criminality are then acts of oversimplification about violence; however, they are more than that for they also are critically constitutive oversimplifying narratives that exemplify the political implications of how the reporting and naming of violent events, the formulation of policy strategies, and the evaluation of existing initiatives are all framed by ongoing processes of social stratification. The system of social stratification promotes some oversimplifying stories over others. People in positions of privilege and power continue to prefer explanations of violence that suggest there is little the state can do to combat the biological and cultural causes of crime that allegedly help build the "criminogenic" moral landscape among an American "underclass."

It is also worth stressing that the authority of such explanations for urban violence is firmly supported by media that ignore their own role in the formation and dissemination of racialized policy narratives of crime (see for examples *New York Times*, 1995, 1996). The prominence of meditations on "black crime" (a frequent reification) in the popular press provides evidence of how the framing of violence solely as an "urban" public policy issue reinforces a process of racial formation that disproportionately focuses on incidence in minority communities. The media also fail to address how the criminal justice system's treatment of people helps reinforce racialized understanding of crime. Moreover, the media fail to effectively make visible alternative explanations for inner-city crime, including poverty, inequality, and racial discrimination. As a result, tales of criminality that stress narrow biological and cultural explanations remain ascendent, if now more than ever tied to the urban environment and located in the underclass neighborhood.

The Deconstruction of "Black Crime"

In a recent work on "black crime" in urban neighborhoods, Glenn Loury, a conservative black economist, has argued that "liberal representatives of these crime ridden areas are placing ideology above the safety of their constituents when they call for preventive programs instead of more prisons" (1994). He argues that policy leaders must act on a "willingness to view with contempt and disdain the urban black cultural milieu from which these violent predators arise" (35). William J. Bennett, John J. DiIulio Jr., and John P. Walters (1996) have echoed Loury's pronouncements with their own declaration that rates of violence among black men and women who live in underclass neighborhoods provide proof that "America is now home to thickening ranks of juvenile 'super-predators.' " The core of their argument is that "moral poverty," and not the failure of such public policies as gun control, is largely to blame for interpersonal violence. Urban minority communities that "breed crime," they contend, reflect "the dire criminogenic consequences of moral poverty in America."

This respatialized tale of "black crime" outlined by Loury and the others fuels white fears that all or most blacks are potential criminals or, at the very least, that the urban black "underclass" is predisposed to commit crime—violent or otherwise. Also, much like the comments from the NIH review committee, the assertion that one can discern a fixed cultural landscape among African American youth emanates from an impulse to circumscribe explanations of violence within a model focused on predictive behavior or individual culpability. The reductionist and racialized assertion by Bennett, DiIulio, and Walters that "moral poverty. . . . is what marks some disadvantaged youngsters for a life of drugs and crime while passing over others in equal or greater material distress" codifies a belief that black youth and white youth differ significantly in predictive ways in their fundamental inclinations and strategies to deal with interpersonal violence (also see Tardiff et al., 1995). "The point," they emphasize, "is that racism does not even begin to explain racial disproportionalities in the system: real differences in crime rates do" (1996: 56, 45).

They recommend, along with a growing number of other analysts, an increased emphasis on punishment through stiffer sentences with the results being increased incarceration and prison construction rates. Yet the policy agenda of today's respatialized racial determinism is based on the very selective social science it uses to legitimate its narratives, ignoring contravening research in three important areas: incarceration as a deterrence mechanism, the historical context of violence trends and causal explanations, and the impact of violence prevention and early intervention (Gans, 1995). The evolving body of social science evidence that incarceration is an effective deterrence mechanism provides much-needed context to frequent declarations that stiffer prison sentences and the prosecution of youth as adults will help to reduce violent crime rates. Yet this evidence continues to be effectively challenged by a variety of studies, including a Rand Corporation study that found there are higher recidivism rates and more serious crimes committed by youth who are prosecuted as adults in comparison to those sent to juvenile institutions (see Prothrow-Stith, 1991; O'Donnell, Cohen, and Hausman, 1990; Reiss and Roth, 1993; *New York Times*, 1996). Deterministic statements by conservatives are particularly egregious on this point. For instance, it is often asserted that millions of taxpayer dollars are expended needlessly to support school-based peer mediation and conflict resolution programs that could not possibly alter negative social influences that can only definitively be transformed in prison (for a review and critique of these arguments see Prothrow-Stith, 1991; Roper, 1991; Reiss and Roth, 1993; Reiss, Miczek, and Roth, 1994; National Association of Secondary School Principals, 1996).

Sadly, then, the obsessive and problematic focus on prison construction as a dominant policy response, as well as an inattention to social historical variables, commonly obscure the ways in which social and public health interventions have had an impact on communities that have been deemed impervious to change. This is particularly and strikingly the case with public discourse on the national decline of violent crime rates. Although scholars and the media have often exhibited zeal when it comes to a profile of prominent national declines in rates of homicide, not enough is mentioned about the declines in teenage homicide rates in various urban, mostly minority communities across the country. Instead, magazines such as *The New Republic* (1996) have chosen to profile the work of researchers who are driven by an ideological emphasis on the deterioration of moral values in American society. But this is rarely a focus on the deterioration of a moral imperative among the nonpoor to assist the poor or youth. More often than not, the tone is one in which there is a progressively deterministic claim about the poor and youth themselves along the lines that "the problem is that today's bad boys are far worse than yesteryear's, and tomorrow's will be even worse than today's." Such statements simultaneously ignore the potential impact of violence prevention and reduction programs with track records, as well as many other alternatives responses including an appreciation of the historical fluctuations in the naming of violence. (Is contemporary American society really more violent than the America of the early twentieth century, when lynchings were public spectacles in a great many places?)

Not all of the press has succumbed to the new racial determinism. The *New York Times*, which is usually more guarded and reticent on matters of race and racism in public policy, authored the following challenge to reductionist and racist characterizations of alternatives to prison in urban violence discussions in a 1992 editorial entitled "Young Black Men": "There's nothing inherently criminal in young black men of the 1990's any more than there was in young immigrant men of the 1890's. What is criminal is to write them off, fearfully, blind to the knowledge that thousands can be saved, from lives of crime and for lives of dignity" (A26).

Race and the Medicalization of Violence

The *New York Times'* attention to historical constructions of race, criminality, and violence suggests ways in which biology and/or genetics have often been invoked as authoritative foundations for American social policy and continue to be even as they are now encoded in concerns about the urban underclass. Rigid characterizations of the relationship between crime and race became frequent in scientific and medical literature during the late nineteenth and early twentieth centuries, particularly after the rediscovery of Gregor Mendel's laws of heredity in 1900 suggested a new model for how biological mechanisms might play a role in human behavior (Allen, 1989;

Stephan and Gilman, 1993). The subsequent proliferation of medical and scientific explanations for crime and violence, as the editorial suggests, increasingly contributed to a popular attribution of crime and violence differentials among social groups to various alleged racial and ethnic factors. Increasing reliance on biological and genetic explanations for violence in contemporary American scientific, medical, and popular discourse suggests that historical discontinuities with respect to race and violence research frameworks in American science may not be as sharp as some historians and scholars have theorized.

Nothing reflects the continuity of racially deterministic tales about race, crime, and violence more than contemporary lay and professional scientific debates about the NIH "Violence" Portfolio, which was officially characterized as the study of "antisocial, aggressive, and violence-related behaviors and their consequences" (National Institutes of Health, 1994). Even with the recent emergence of a "public health" approach, which largely stresses the socioeconomic context for violence prevention and reduction, many of these more sympathetic researchers also remain invested in a search for "root causes" that stigmatize racialized urban communities. The release of the National Research Council's now multivolume *Understanding and Preventing Violence* starting in 1993, as well as the proceedings of the NIH-sponsored Genetics and Crime Conference held in September 1995, have helped to bring scrutiny to medical and lay discourse on race and violence (see Reiss and Roth, 1993; Reiss, Miczek and Roth, 1994; Marshall, 1993; Angier, 1995). This is not to mention the use by Frederick Goodwin (the former head of the federal Alcohol, Drug Abuse, and Mental Health Adminstration Agency, now head of the National Institute of Mental Health) of the legendary metaphor of the "jungle" in 1992 to describe patterns of urban youth violence.

Most important for this analysis, however, I want to underscore how conclusions advanced by policy leaders and advisers continue a reliance on race and culture as variables with high predictive value. The increasing authority of a genetics-based racial determinism in violence research is particularly glaring, as exemplified in the now authoritative source from the National Research Council, *Understanding and Preventing Violence* (Volume II: Biobehavioral Influences). Volume II of the NRC's report concludes that aspects of social, individual, and biological factors can account for violent behavior. Sadly, however, the brief commentary on racial factors offers far-reaching conclusions that reify, yet again, race as a valid biological category for scientific research in the study of human aggression. This inclination is made apparent in the chapter entitled "Genetics and Violence," which contains a section on "Genetics, Race, and Violence" after a heading "Prospects for Future Human Genetic Research" (National Research Council, 1994: 21–58).

Subsequent debate on the merits of the NRC's findings as well as public outcry about theories and research on race and genetics related to the NIH-sponsored conference on crime and genetics in September 1995 at the University of Maryland, no doubt, influenced NIH's decision to convene an Advisory Panel on Antisocial, Aggressive, and Violence-related Behaviors and Their Consequences in June and September 1993. Conducted by twenty-nine experts in fields as diverse as criminal justice, sociology, public health, anthropology, ethics, and psychiatry, the 1993 NIH investigation referenced over three hundred violence-focused projects, with the majority of initiatives concentrated at the National Institute of Mental Health. The panel's work led the NIH to develop a more open process to evaluate the so-called Violence Portfolio. According to the final report released in April 1994, a central objective was "to review the NIH research portfolio in these areas and to evaluate it in terms of its relevance, adequacy, and responsiveness to social and ethical concerns." This statement existed alongside the firm declaration that:

> Violence, despite its horrible toll on the health of the public, has only recently come to be regarded in the United States as a public health problem. . . . Understanding violence and the many factors that affect it, assessing its toll on physical and mental health, learning to prevent it, and aiding the recovery of its victims are awesome challenges for our society. (National Institutes of Health, 1994: 38–40)

As a result of this process, we did see some challenges to the racial and cultural determinism in some of NIH's research. Many social scientists on the advisory panel, for instance, repeatedly pointed to the potential benefits of antiviolence initiatives in prisons and schools that gave greater priority to "issues of cultural competence," as well as conflict resolution and peer education programs. Nonetheless, deterministic racial metaphors and generalizations about communities would still abound in the final summary. As a result, the committee's stated general perception that "there are clear racial differences in the patterns and perceptions of violence in America" was never fully unpacked to explain how NIH's portfolio on aggressive behavior reproduces reductive definitions of race and culture in several of its major projects (National Institutes of Health, 1994: 68–69). Part of the reason for the continued ascendence of these more deterministic models is a competition for authority over this topic by various disciplines. The failure of the social sciences to trump the biological sciences on research in this area has hampered efforts to give visibility to violence as a complex socioeconomic phenomenon.

These science wars have important implications for public policy. For instance, the suggestion, as mentioned earlier, that "African American boys are naturally more active" and that there may be "predisposing" factors is a scientifically legitimated statement that has both historical resonance and dramatic contemporary policy implications. Though the NIH advisory panel left the question of a link between biology and violence open for debate, members in such organizations as the American Public Health Association continue to warn that biological, genetic, and medical models of violence steer "resources away from urgently needed social research and interventions," and doubly attack "minority youth, making them scapegoats while exacerbating their economic distress." We must therefore also continue to ask: How is race (re)defined in health policy and public policy in general? What about the question of mitigating influences on violent behavior? Would intervention through preventive initiatives stem these inherent factors? These are key questions that should inform the framing of race, crime, and violence as public issues, and whose answers will continue to have important policy implications.

Race, Violence, and the Politics of Prevention

The prominence of racially and culturally deterministic models of violence at NIH and among other researchers, we have seen, reinforces perceptions that there may be genetic bases to violence and aggression. The previous sections have suggested some of the ways in which these ideas have influenced the naming and definition of causality in professional and lay discourse even as those discourses construct an "urban underclass." This final section will analyze more directly how social policy discussions remain anchored in these evolving tales of inherent racial and cultural predisposition to crime and violence. In other words, what do deterministic explanations simultaneously justify and exclude in the social policy and criminal justice arena?

Despite the news that some school- and community-based initiatives have been moderately successful in the promotion of violence prevention and reduction strategies, more conservative critics (including both congressional Democrats and Republicans) continue to decry investment in such programs. Such investments would not work because, as one set of critics charges about urban "super-predators," "for as long as their youthful energies hold out, they will do what comes 'naturally': murder, rape, rob, assault, burglarize, deal deadly drugs, and get high" (Bennett, DiIullio, and Walters, 1996). This dire predictive model is also dramatized by a belief that because the youth population is expected to increase by between 15 and 20 percent during the next decade the rate of violent crime will almost unavoidably increase ("especially among young urban minority males") without stricter law enforcement.

In addition to being supported by such reductionist and racist cultural narratives, retrenchment in the violence prevention arena has also been supported by findings in the biological research community. A series of recent findings that serotonin, an organic chemical found in the brain and believed to be a regulator of emotions and aggression, helped to fuel the following caution about beliefs that violence can be prevented among youth:

> Violent families breed violent children. Violent children become violent adults. . . . Until recently, however, it was assumed that an inclination to violence was largely a matter of learned behavior. . . . But science is discovering another cause of destructive behavior which is at once frightening and fraught with hope. It is the biological component. . . . This is frightening because it implies that violent behavior cannot simply be "unlearned" by improving a child's circumstances or by teaching the benefits of gentle cooperation. Those things must be done, but they are unlikely to totally undo that which has become biologically embedded. (Chicago *Tribune*, 1993: Section 3, 2)

The Chicago *Tribune*'s editorial raises a central issue concerning social policy: the subject of whether intervention to stem violence has the potential to work in urban communities. It fundamentally illustrates the dangerous use of biological and cultural reductionism to question whether there is a limitation to the capacity of environmental factors to account for the majority of a child's actions. The metaphoric use of the term "breed" and the suggestion of a concomitant inherited predisposition might also lead one to conclude that the editors believe there are limitations or inherent, biologically embedded obstacles to preventive approaches in the inner city or elsewhere.

Some observers might find it puzzling as well that the *Tribune* also argued for the expansion of social welfare programs and that "early intervention such as the Head Start preschool program must be improved and made available to children at-risk." But the earlier analysis of the debate on NIH's violence-related research activities should have made it apparent that biological and cultural deterministic characterizations of race and culture can also be found in seemingly progressive public policy platforms that advocate the expansion of social welfare programs to mitigate poverty and violence.

Yet, at this historical moment, when a majority in the U.S. Congress apparently believe that the federal government has virtually no role in the provision of social welfare or the mitigation of poverty, deterministic arguments present ample justifications for incarceration as the significant, if not only, public policy for the management of crime and violence. Science critic and cultural theorist Dorothy Nelkin recently stated after a scientific meeting on genetics and crime that "genetic explanations are extremely convenient when you're trying to dismantle the welfare state" (see Angier, 1995: C1). "The idea of a criminal gene," she later noted, "also implies a hope of controlling crime, not through the uncertain route of social reform but through biological manipulation" (Nelkin, 1995: A27). The tales of race and violence that support the identification of violence as immutable among urban minority youth, in particular, reproduce a lexicon of race and culture that blames and stigmatizes various spatially located groups for crime and other social problems. As long as conservative media and theorists continue to fuel racialized and spatialized tales of "super-predators" that suggest that the urban environment is inherently dangerous, we will not tend to how problems of joblessness, residential segregation and isolation, and racism contribute to violence, crime, and substance abuse.

Conclusion

Mary Douglas (1992) has written that popular perceptions of "danger" and "risk" frequently support narratives that blame spatially concentrated ethnic and racial groups for public problems such as disease and crime. Indeed, we have seen this process at work in a new racial determinism that reinforces locating the causes of increased violence, crime, and substance abuse in the urban underclass neighborhood. This process is currently reinforcing a set of policy options to support incarceration and swelling federal and state budgets for prison construction, at the same time that opportunities for prevention are undermined (Gavora, 1996; National Criminal Justice Commission, 1996). Without a more visible social and political movement to redefine and critique powerful cultural axioms that place limitations on governmental responsibility, discussions of interpersonal violence will remain anchored by vulgar stereotypes and not the need for a redistributive social policy agenda.

Part IV
Tales of Domestic Policy

11

Welfare Migration as a Policy Rumor: A Statistical Accounting

Sanford F. Schram, Lawrence Nitz, and Gary Krueger

In 1996, the U.S. Congress succeeded in getting President Bill Clinton to eat his own words and "end welfare as we know it" by terminating the 61-year-old federal entitlement to public assistance and replacing it with block grants to the states. This historic retrenchment of public assistance was successful because of a variety of factors, including economic slowdown, wage stagnation, growing expectations that mothers take paid employment, increased concerns about welfare dependency, and heightened concern over the federal budget deficit (Danziger and Gottschalk, 1995). These contemporary factors took on an added intensity given that welfare has also historically been a source of resentment in a market-centered society where individuals and families are expected to provide for themselves (Piven and Cloward, 1993). Welfare has served as a convenient site for a symbolic politics that reinforces dominant norms about work and family via the ritualization of punitive treatment of recipients (Handler and Hasenfeld, 1991). As a result, welfare politics has often been easily driven by unsubstantiated stories regarding who gets welfare, how much, and how frequently. Often centered on a controlling metaphor, like "welfare queen" or "welfare migrant," welfare stories can be potent ways of reinforcing prejudicial stereotypes that in turn undermine support for providing public assistance (Gordon, 1994). Although such narrative practices are probably influential across a number of policy areas, they arguably are even more influential in shaping welfare policy.

As stories, policy-tales take a narrative form. As policy-tales, these stories often are narrated in the statistical register of quantitative research that is so preferred by policy makers (Stone, 1997). Such stories also often invoke an economistic idiom that evaluates things like welfare-taking in terms of what is economically rational. Related social scientific research has also often been couched in terms of models of economic rationality for explaining such behavior and the corresponding responses by governments (S. Schram, 1995). In what follows, we examine data concerning the especially pertinent policy-tale about "welfare migration"—i.e., that people move from one state to another in order to get higher benefits (Peterson and Rom, 1990). We suggest in our conclusions that like many of the tales that circulate about welfare today, the one about welfare migration implies that welfare recipients are economically rational but in illegitimate ways. We also conclude that this is a story whose popularity is associated more with deep-seated anxieties in society today than with empirical evidence.

Welfare Migration and WelfareTales

Much political capital has been made from stories about welfare recipients as coldly calculating nomads of self-interest who try to maximize their personal utility by trying to get the best welfare package (Tanner, Moore, and Hartman, 1995). Characterizations of economically rational behavior among welfare recipients unfortunately often translate into signs of illegitimate, self-serving behavior. Although welfare recipients are often depicted as ill-informed, undereducated, and irresponsible, they are also often characterized as benefit-maximizers exhibiting high levels of "bureaucratic-competence" and a crafty capacity for economic calculation (Murray, 1984).

Perhaps the most literal version of this sort of story is the welfare migration narrative. In recent years, it has gained substantial popularity, especially among state policy makers who have sought to revise welfare so as to discourage people from moving to their states to receive welfare (Peterson and Rom, 1990). Welfare migration as a policy-tale has taken anecdotal as well as statistical form. In Wisconsin, a state legislator spied on incoming buses from out of state in order to report tales of people going directly from the bus station to the welfare office (Hanauer, 1994). Others political officials commissioned statistical research (Peterson and Rom, 1990).

States all around the country have responded to these stories with much policy investigation and even some action, for instance trying as they did in California and Minnesota to set lower benefits for the newly arrived (Schram and Krueger, 1994). There is evidence that states with relatively high benefits have been lowering their benefits more rapidly over the past two decades because of a number of factors, including the fear of becoming welfare magnets (Peterson and Rom, 1990). States in general may be tempted to enter into a "competition to the bottom" and let their benefits decline in real value, most often by simply not raising them to keep pace with inflation (Schram and Krueger, 1994). By 1996, a number of states had established lower benefits levels for recent arrivals so as to discourage welfare migration into their state (Hughes, 1996).

Also, in this increasingly global, postindustrial world of accelerated electronic transfers of resources, the welfare migration tale often can easily tap prevailing anxieties about border crossings of a variety of kinds (Shapiro and Alker, 1996). In 1994, California referendum voters passed the now legally contested Proposition 187 prohibiting illegal immigrants from gaining access to education, medical care, and social services as well as welfare benefits. Others states have witnessed growing interest toward adopting proposals similar to California's (Schuck, 1995). The 1996 welfare reform included a controversial ban on welfare to legal immigrants (S. Schram, 1996). International welfare migration has been added to the narratives reflecting growing anxieties about welfare expenditures in late-twentieth-century America (Fix and Passel, 1993).

This upsurge in interest regarding welfare migration ironically took place within a legal context where the U.S. Supreme Court had ruled in *Shapiro v. Thompson* (394 U.S. 618, 1969) that the Ninth Amendment implied a right to travel, meaning that states could not impose durational residency requirements on citizens as a condition for the receipt of public assistance. In 1995, the Supreme Court returned a case to a lower court deferring a decision that could have overturned *Shapiro* (*Anderson v. Green*, 1995 WL 68473 U.S., February 22, 1995). In other words, welfare migration was denigrated even as it remained a constitutional right for U.S. citizens. Just as tales of selfish and sexually irresponsible young single women circulate to the effect of undermining the constitutionally guaranteed right to abortion (Faludi, 1991), tales of welfare migration undercut the political ground from the Court's prohibition on state durational residency requirements for the receipt of welfare (S. Schram, 1995). While the 1996 welfare reform abolished the prohibition on residency requirements, its increased workfare requirements are seen by some as precipitating a massive interstate migration of welfare recipients, this time in search of jobs (Hughes, 1996). Therefore, if for no other reason than its salience and frequency in welfare policy discourse, the welfare migration story deserves serious empirical examination, now more than ever.

Measuring Welfare Migration

As Russell Hanson and John Hartman (1994) have noted, most state studies on welfare migration are suspect because they usually simply estimate the percentage of recipients coming from out of state (most often defined as not having resided in the state five years prior to the study), but without adjusting those estimates for the percentage of the general population that is similarly from out of state. Therefore, finding that one-fifth of current welfare recipients are from out of state really does not tell us much about welfare migration, especially if one-fifth of the general population of the state is also from out of state.

Thomas Dye has summarized academic studies noting a shift between the first and second wave of these studies: "Early studies suggested that the poor migrate for job opportunities and family reasons with little knowledge of welfare rules and payments in various jurisdictions. More recent studies suggest that the poor migrate opposite net flows and toward high benefit states" (1990: 69). Other surveys of the literature provide a more skeptical account that questions whether second-wave studies actually offer strong evidence for welfare migration (Moffitt, 1992).

Welfare Benefit Variation as an Evanescent Cause

Our own analysis involves data that impinge on two issues concerning welfare migration. These issues are, appropriately enough, welfare and migration.

First, is there enough variation of state welfare benefits to induce migration? Paul Peterson and Mark Rom (1990) provide evidence that substantial variation across the states, as measured according the coefficient of variation (i.e., the standard deviation divided by the mean), has not declined over the past forty years. Dye, also using the coefficient of variation, finds as much variation as Peterson and Rom, but disagrees about what it means. Peterson and Rom see benefit variation as implying both a magnet that attracts people to move from low-benefit states to high-benefit states and a magnet that retains people by discouraging the reverse. While not dismissing welfare migration as an issue, Dye (1990) emphasizes how high benefits encourage the growth of dependency within a state. Also using the coefficient of variation, Robert Albritton (1989) suggests that there is actually less real variation across states once benefit levels are adjusted for the differences in the cost of living, as indicated by variations in per capita income.

Albritton includes Hawai'i and Alaska, but not Washington, D.C., in his calculations. As others have noted, given their remoteness from the other forty-eight states, Hawai'i and Alaska are not likely targets for welfare migration; whereas Washington, D.C., is (Hanson and Hartman, 1994). For our own calculations, we look at AFDC benefits, both in nominal terms and adjusted for the cost of living, but for the continental forty-eight states and Washington, D.C., and for the most recently available years of 1985 to 1993. We use the coefficient of variation to compare variation of adjusted to unadjusted benefits. (The standard deviation would be sufficient for examining change in benefits in constant dollars over time. The coefficient of variation is necessary for comparing adjusted to unadjusted benefits for these data are "entirely different in magnitude or units of measure." See Gaynor and Kilpatrick, 1994.) Consistent with Albritton's hypothesis, we find that from 1985 to 1993 the coefficient of variation for adjusted benefits is consistently below that for unadjusted benefits (see table 11.1). Taking

Table 11.1

	1985	1989	1993
Unadjusted benefits	.3470	.3433	.3488
Adjusted benefits	.3059	.2816	.2978

variations in the cost of living into account suggests that while there is still variation there is less than what the nominal value of benefits indicates.

Yet Albritton also finds that adjusted benefits, if not as much as unadjusted benefits, still vary with the per capita income levels of states. Richer states, according to Albritton, have a slight tendency to provide higher benefits even when benefits are adjusted for the higher cost of living in those states. This then would make them more attractive locations for recipients and therefore potentially "welfare magnets." Yet we do not find this to be the case in our own calculations, once we correlate the per capita income levels (*Statistical Abstract of the United States*, 1994) and welfare benefits (U.S. House of Representatives, Committee on Ways and Means, 1994) as a ratio of per capita income for each of the continental forty-eight states and Washington, D.C. Our data indicate that income levels are correlated with unadjusted benefits but not, as Albritton found, with adjusted benefits (see table 11.2). While richer states tend to provide nominally higher benefits, they are not more likely to provide higher benefits once we account for the higher cost of living in those states. Therefore, when we assess welfare benefits in real terms and for the relevant states, we do not find the variation that is suggested by looking only at nominal benefits, nor do we find that richer states are likely to provide higher adjusted benefits.

The real value of benefit variation is even less if we were to include food stamps, which since the mid-1970s all AFDC recipients receive, and which are reduced approximately thirty cents for each additional dollar in income, including AFDC, so that recipients in low-benefit states get more food stamps than recipients in high-benefit states (U.S. House of Representatives, Committee on Ways and Means, 1993). Using the coeffi-

Table 11.2

	1985	1989	1993
Unadjusted benefits	.30	.38	.33
Adjusted benefits	.02	.03	.03

(Correlations are presented as r^2 for purpose of comparison with Albritton's analysis.)

Table 11.3

	1985	1989	1993
Unadjusted combined benefits	.2258	.1771	.1663
Adjusted combined benefits	.2064	.1431	.1435

cient of variation for unadjusted and adjusted benefits, we find that variation is not only much smaller than for AFDC benefits alone but that it has declined in recent years as well (see table 11.3).

In fact the coefficient of variation for unadjusted combined benefits is only slightly above that for per capita income (see table 11.4). From this revised perspective, while there is still variation beyond the cost of living, it is debatable that there is still enough variation to prompt welfare migration.

Nonetheless, in what amounts to a story of incomplete economic rationality, or economic rationality based on incomplete information, migrants may be motivated by their subjective assessments of nominal benefit levels without taking adjustments for the cost of living and other benefits into account. However, we really cannot decide this issue until we track welfare migrants themselves.

The Magnitude of Welfare Migration

In order to track welfare migrants, we examined the Public Use Microdata Set (PUMS) (5 percent sample) of the 1990 U.S. Census for the contiguous forty-eight states and Washington, D.C. This sample provides a distinctively large number of out-of-state movers who can be tracked over a five-year period. The PUMS provides information as to the state of residence in 1985 for the people interviewed in 1990. We then can determine who has moved from state to state for that period, providing a larger representative sample of movers for a longer period of time than that analyzed in any of the previous major studies of welfare migration. The PUMS also supplies information on personal, family, and household characteristics including receipt of public assistance.

We focused on the approximately 435,000 single mothers with children under the age of eighteen in the PUMS. We examine poor single mothers

Table 11.4

	1985	1989	1993
Per capita income	.1511	.1699	.1564

with children under eighteen as our target welfare-relevant population who might be attracted to the prospect of receiving higher welfare benefits. We hasten to add that movement by this group does not automatically imply welfare migration. The target population may in fact be moving for similar non-welfare-related reasons that attract other populations.

We found that most single mothers (91.4 percent) were still living in 1990 in the same state that they were in 1985. We found a similar percentage (90.5) when we restricted the analysis to the 141,402 single mothers living in families in 1990 that reported annual incomes for 1989 that put them below the poverty line. In other words, poverty did not increase one's chances of moving out of state over the five-year period. Even accepting the questionable assumption that all poor migrants were welfare migrants, we find that they are a small proportion of their base population moving no more frequently than the corresponding non-welfare-related group.

Focusing on the target population of poor single mothers with children under eighteen, we find interesting contrasts between migrants and nonmigrants. Migrants are on average slightly younger, better educated, and white, with a slightly higher chance of having children under the age of six. They also have slightly higher average earnings and a slightly lower likelihood to be receiving public assistance in 1989. Their average income is basically indistinguishable from the average for nonmigrants as is the average benefit level of their state of origin, indicating that migrants are not more likely to come from low-benefit states. Migrants therefore do not conform to any particular stereotypes, racial or otherwise, that are often latent and sometimes explicit, in tales of welfare migration.

Given that we have a 5 percent sample of the relevant U.S. population, the 13,434 weighted cases of migrants in the PUMS translates into about 268,000 single mothers with annual incomes below the poverty line migrating out of state over the five-year period. In any given year, this works out to an average of no more than about 53,000 welfare migrants or no more than 2 percent of all the single mothers with annual incomes below the poverty line.

The real annual cost of welfare migration during the period under study is most likely to have been quite small. Migrants over the five-year period comprise no more than about 5 percent of the target welfare-relevant population, only about 47.5 percent of that small percentage are estimated to be receiving welfare in any one year, not all of these people move to higher-benefit states, and those who do are not necessarily getting benefits that are considerably higher than they got previously. Even if we assume that all of the migrants move to higher-benefit states and receive $150 more a month in welfare (approximately the standard deviation of monthly maximum welfare benefits offered by the different states in 1990), then the total bill to taxpayers for welfare migration would be approximately $90 million a year. It is about $45 million a year if we still assume they all move to higher-benefit states but account for the fact that only about half the migrants are receiving welfare in any one year. It is less still if we account for those who move to lower-benefit states. It is even less than that if welfare migrants receive an average increase below $150 a month. In 1990, government at all levels spent approximately $20 billion in AFDC benefits (U.S. House of Representatives, Committee on Ways and Means, 1993). Therefore, there is the distinct possibility that the real costs to taxpayers for welfare migration might be as little as 0.45 to 0.225 percent, in other words less than 1 percent, of the total cost of benefits paid out by the program each year during the 1985–90 period.

The total cost of all welfare migration may in any one year in fact be quite small. It is true that the overwhelming majority of public assistance expenditures are associated with mother-only families. Yet while other single mothers who are not poor for a whole year might move from one state to another and receive public assistance, many poor single mothers have incomes above eligibility levels and cannot receive public assistance. In any case, our cost estimates are only meant to be suggestive. What they suggest is that welfare migration is not a major cost for taxpayers.

Not only do we find that migration of poor single mothers is a marginal phenomenon for the 1985–90 period, our descriptive data suggest that it does not seem to be tied to welfare benefit levels. We found that poor women living in low-benefit states in 1985 were no more likely than those living in high-benefit states to have moved out of state by 1990. The percentage is about the same (7 to 15 percent) for most states, with no noticeable trend in either direction. There seems to be no correlation between the 1985 benefit levels and whether someone moved by 1990. For instance, indicative of the lack of correlation, we find that 7 percent of the women in the PUMS sample who lived in the lowest-benefit state in 1985 (Mississippi) moved out by 1990, while 9 percent of the sample from the highest-benefit state in 1985 (California) moved out by 1990. Whereas only nine of the samples of women from the twenty-six lowest-benefit states in 1985 had more than 10 percent migrating out by 1990, fourteen of the samples of the women from the twenty-five highest-benefit states did so, indicating no real difference and undermining the idea that women from low-benefit states are more likely to move to other states in quest of higher benefits.

We also found that poor single mothers living in high-benefit states in 1990 were no more likely to have moved in since 1985 than persons living in low-benefit states. Again we found no systematic variation across states by benefit levels, this time between 1990 benefit levels and whether someone moved in after 1985. For instance, seventeen of the samples of women from the twenty-six lowest-benefit states in 1990 had more than 10 percent migrating in since 1985, whereas only fourteen of the samples of the twenty-five highest states did so, indicating once again no real difference and undermining still further the idea that women in high-benefit states were more likely to have moved in from out of state. Our descriptive data therefore provide no evidence for either attraction or retention.

We did find, as do Hanson and Hartman (1994), that among the small minority of poor single mothers who were living in a different state in 1990 than they were in 1985, those that went to high-benefit states were slightly more likely to have been receiving welfare benefits in 1989 (the year for which the Census requests information). Yet we hasten to add that this is not different from the trend among the welfare-relevant population generally with nonmigrants receiving public assistance in each state in similar proportions as migrants and both being slightly more likely to be receiving public assistance in higher-benefit states. In addition, one important reason for this trend is that higher-benefit states have higher eligibility levels, enabling a greater proportion of single mothers with children living below the poverty line to qualify for and receive public assistance. Therefore, even this piece of evidence can be explained in a rather straightforward fashion to suggest that it too does not provide evidence of welfare migration.

If welfare migration were serious, we might expect to find that migrants not only were more likely to move to high-benefit states but that once there they would have a higher rate of receipt of public assistance than nonmigrants. In comparison to nonmigrants, migrants are, according to this logic, hypothesized to be disproportionately made up of persons seeking assistance. We would therefore expect that the difference in rates of receiving public assistance between migrants and nonmigrants would increase in the higher-benefit states where migrants were supposedly more likely to be moving in order to receive higher benefits. Yet we do not find that to be the case. If we compare the rate of receiving public assistance for migrants with that for nonmigrants in the form of a ratio of the former to the latter, we find that the ratio changes very little with benefit level and what change we find implies that migrants are not more likely to take public assistance relative to nonmigrants as benefits increase. The regression coefficient is negative ($b = -0.000104$) with a standard error of some size (s.e. = 0.000077), making for a statistically insignificant and even negative relationship ($t = -1.34$) between benefit level and the rate at which migrants relative to nonmigrants take public assistance. Regardless of benefit level, migrants and nonmigrants tend to receive assistance at about the same rate, and those rates increase slightly for both groups in higher-benefit states.

Hanson and Hartman (1994) suggest that because migrants have less informal social support from family and friends they are in greater need of public assistance. Yet despite their hypothesized greater need, we find that their rates of receipt of public assistance tend to approximate those of nonmigrants. The positive correlation of rates of receipt and benefit levels is also similar for both migrants and nonmigrants. Therefore, these data do not provide much evidence at all for welfare migration.

Conclusion

Welfare policy is driven by stories about welfare and its recipients. Stories about welfare migration are among the more influential policy-tales actively shaping welfare reform in recent years. Welfare migration has frequently operated as a powerful symbol often narrated in the policy arena in statistical form with the effect of undermining support for public assistance. The welfare migration story reinforces the symbolic power of depicting welfare recipients as illegitimate self-seeking people who are abusing the system. These stories tap deep-seated anxieties about the viability of social standards regarding self-sufficiency and personal responsibility in late-twentieth-century America. As such, stories of welfare migration are not easily repudiated by evidence to the contrary even as they are often tied to questionable data as they circulate in policy arenas.

Our own data analysis provides a basis for questioning whether there are significant causes or effects concerning welfare migration. We found that the causal agent, i.e., benefit variation, is less significant than often assumed, and the effect, i.e., movement by the target welfare-relevant population from low-benefit to high-benefit states, is equally insignificant for the five-year period 1985–90. Our estimates suggest that the annual level of welfare migration is quite small for the 1985–90 period, and probably for other periods of recent years. The annual cost of welfare migration is today probably minuscule in terms of the total welfare budget.

Yet stories of welfare migration are likely to persist despite the lack of data to support them, especially as welfare reform now allows states to use their discretion to enter into a "competition to the bottom" and try to outdo each other in cutting back on public assistance. Rumors of welfare migration are likely to become rampant. Reports on the extent of welfare migration are not likely to be very helpful even if they provide evidence suggesting it is a marginal phenomenon. These studies are often written in an economistic idiom that reinforces the idea that welfare migration is a questionable form of economic rationality that needs to be anticipated and countered by policy change. This insidious logic is often in service of allowing states to decide how to structure their own welfare programs so that they can fend off allegedly illegitimate interlopers who move in to take advantage of better benefits. The narrative idiom of these stories has therefore helped deemphasize the idea that welfare migration was before the 1996 reforms a constitutional right of U.S. citizens, while reinforcing the idea that it is now illegitimate behavior. The prevailing political climate with its emphasis on limiting the growth of the federal government and its welfare state is predisposed to accept stories in this idiom even when evidence to the contrary is available.

This logic persists however even in arguments on behalf of nationalizing public assistance. Peterson and Rom (1990), for instance, argue for a national welfare guarantee on the grounds that it is needed to counter the welfare migration that state variation in benefits encourages. When applied to governments, their economistic idiom helps us understand how welfare as a redistributive program will operate most rationally at the national level. Yet, national welfare reform narrated in this way still runs the risk of reinscribing welfare recipients as illegitimate benefit-maximizers while deemphasizing their now contested rights to migration. And it does all of this on the basis of a weak empirical foundation.

A better approach would be to question both the facts and the narrative associated with welfare migration. For instance, Carol Stack (1996) uses ethnographic data to provide a more contextually rich description of African Americans' reverse migration, back to the South, in recent years. She concludes that for the low-income African Americans she studied, "the resolve to return home is not primarily an economic decision but rather a powerful blend of motives" (xv) including especially the desire to build a better future for themselves and their children. She details how such moves even involve migrating to rural areas with fewer economic opportunities but where family ties and a sense of community are stronger. Stack's work therefore suggests how we can develop better explanations once we provide a more detailed description of the variety of motivations associated with migration by the poor. For instance, the fact that most poor single mothers living in poverty do not move out of state could be explained by the fact that the real value of welfare benefits do not vary as much as is often assumed. Yet women's failure to move to another state may also be explained by the fact that they are more interested in things other than welfare for improving their families' prospects. Safety, economic opportunities, better housing, and better schools are more important than welfare. These things may be gained while relocating within the state to be closer to family and friends. Once we see poor single mothers as working toward having access to the same things that most other people want, an alternative logic that better explains the data of welfare migration becomes available.

The welfare migration story has proven powerful in policy deliberations. Part of the explanation is that there are studies available that suggest it is a real phenomenon. Part of the explanation is that welfare migration is convenient politically, justifying retrenchment as a necessary move to make welfare less attractive to outsiders who are seen as not deserving the support of state taxpayers. Therefore, challenging the power of the welfare migration story is more than an empirical exercise; it also involves contesting politically convenient assumptions about what is rational for the poor and everyone else. The power of the welfare migration story will only start to fade when the rationality of people living in poverty is treated as similar to everyone else's and everyone is treated in terms broader than those narrowly focused on economic gain.

12

Tales of the City: The Secret Life of Devolution

Joseph Kling

It should not come as a surprise to those familiar with the study of methodology in the social sciences that policy analyses, and the proposals to which they lead, may be understood as forms of ideological narrative. For hypotheses in the realm of policy study are inherently political, and policy researchers, whatever their political leanings, all have points to make, stories to tell. Of course, as long as researchers acknowledge and control for the value biases inherent in their work, the presence of bias does not necessarily invalidate or corrupt what researchers do. But the storytelling that lies at the base of all social research is about more than bias. It is about the ways in which the practical intellect, unable to function without investing experience and action with meaning, constructs reality in counterpoint/conformity to and with received notions of an ordered world.

Informed readings of public policy decipher the way policy-tales construct and reinterpret everyday experience, uncover the political implications of these tales, and if so disposed, offer alternative narratives with alternative meanings. But I want to argue that, alone, the textual deconstruction of a policy discourse is insufficient to reveal the policy's social meaning. To allow us to understand the force of prevailing policy stories, to let us grasp how they came to take hold in public consciousness, to provide us with a basis for engaging them, critical discourse needs to confront the specific historical and social conditions that sustained their original acceptance.

In this chapter I will look at the historical roots of the current drive toward devolution. Devolution, the philosophy of governance at the heart of the Contract with America (Gillespie and Schellhas, 1994), is a call for both privatization of public services and a "return of power to the states." It is a *story* about how ordinary Americans have lost control over the conditions of their lives, and how the dismantling of federal regulations of the marketplace, including the reduction of social services, will restore that control. We should note that once its consequences began to be felt, this tale of the happy effects of the retreat from federal support for social services encountered various degrees of resistance from the public. By the 1996 election, in fact, the Contract with America had almost disappeared from public discourse. Nevertheless, "devolution" is a doctrine that arguably will set the stage for public policy debates for the next several years. It has already had devastating effects; the passage of the historic welfare reforms of 1996 that end the federal entitlement to public assistance for families with children is only one example.

It is my contention that any effort to situate the narratives currently buttressing the policies of federal devolution needs to keep 1968, and Richard Nixon's election, sharply in focus. In that year, reacting against what they perceived as assaults on their hard-won yet always tenuous economic and social gains, and feeling abandoned by the political party that once had protected their interests, constituencies once assumed by the conventional wisdom of American political science to be unquestioningly loyal to the Democratic Party began to give their support to the Republicans (Matusow, 1984: 395–439).

For those concerned with the processes by which public policy stories come to shape and reorder social decision, what is most telling about the 1968 shift in political orientation is the way it reversed what had become, since the New Deal, the received readings of American politics. The Great Society and the War on Poverty, a set of state-initiated programs designed to broaden the reach of New Deal democracy to include the black urban poor, were portrayed by those opposed to such measures as utopian, overly centralizing, disruptive of the social order, and incompatible with the basic value of American individualism. At the same time, programs and initiatives clearly designed to restrict the widening of opportunity structures were trumpeted as strategies for popular empowerment. Washington bureaucrats and intellectual elites, the story ran, had usurped the agency of the people; the Nixon administration was going to return it to them. As the election results demonstrated, the argument, convoluted as it was, won its point with its intended audience.

The issue, I contend, is not that these stories were told. That elite sectors will resist economic and social democratization is one of the few constants on which political science can depend. What is not obvious is why, after thirty-five years of support for welfare state politics, large numbers of people in the working and lower-middle classes began to question efforts designed both to equalize American society and to involve the poor in the process of reshaping their circumstances. We need to look at the story behind the fortunes of these contested stories. Race, it should be obvious, will play a pivotal role.

In attempting to explain the ideological reversal that began with the Nixon presidency, the following essay looks at the interplay of a number of factors. First, it examines the notion of devolution itself, a double-edged political construct that emphasizes the *process* of decentralization, rather than the substance of what is being decentralized. Second, the analysis looks at the first New Federalism, a set of proposals introduced by Nixon in the early 1970s. While its block grant proposals met with only limited legislative success, and never directly opposed the assumptions of the New Deal, the New Federalism nevertheless represents the opening wedge in the Republican Party's bid to capture the flag of populism.

Third, the essay discusses two different sets of stories that were used to justify the New Federalism. One set was fairly respectable, and dealt with questions of administrative efficiency. The other, less savory, was seldom explicitly acknowledged by those who relied upon it in their efforts to dismantle the Great Society. These tales were grounded in the sentiment that federal antipoverty policy discriminated against hardworking, savings-oriented, middle-income white people, and favored undisciplined, present-oriented, lower-class black people in inner-city ghettos. It is important to recognize that these two sets of stories worked independently of each other: concerns about the fragmentation and lack of coherent planning in Great Society programs, and arguments that policies developed from the center could be insensitive to overall local needs, were often legitimate, and not necessarily racist in intent. But they were—and remain—marvelous camouflage for those who wished to use them in that way.

A Shift in Stories

Viewed *abstractly*, "devolution" is a policy stance that begins with the presumption that all governmental action belongs at local levels. Federal intervention is legitimate only for reasons of national security, protection of economic exchange, or maintenance of the most minimal of social standards. Unless these concerns are at issue, government should expect that all domestic federal mandates will be turned over to the states to define and administer, "or, where possible and appropriate, removed altogether from governmental hands and made the responsibility of private citizens, families, churches, or other civic institutions" (DiIulio Jr. and Kettl, 1995: 2).

The problem is that in a nationally organized economy, federal retrenchment from the arena of social policy results in a retreat from what Julian Wolpert (1993) refers to as "social generosity." Viewed *concretely*, that is, in terms of its substantive policy consequences, devolution turns out to be about much more than a revisioning of American federalism—if, indeed, it was ever about that at all. It is, rather, part of the contest over what the nature of the social contract will be under conditions of postindustrial capitalism. John Donahue, in his study of privatization, put the matter well:

> it is not simply the emergence and entrenchment of special interests that has bedeviled postwar American politics, but also the erosion of traditional public values and the failure to restore them or to replace them with a new consensus on the claims citizens can make on their fellows. . . . [For] the assessment of spending proposals requires attention not only to the material goods citizens seek, but also to the moral purposes they endorse. . . . (1989: 30)

What we are witnessing, in other words, is the decline of the mythic power of the public sphere. The next section looks at the beginnings of this decline in the Nixon administration's conscious attempt to destroy the Great Society, an attempt that brought devolutionary politics onto the public agenda for the first time since the New Deal.

"Devolution" as Complex Policy Construct

Generically, "devolution" is the black hole of public policy analysis. It sucks in discrete policy functions and conceptually crushes them into an indistinguishable mass. For, as undifferentiated narrative construct, "devolution" confuses the commitment to *decentralize administrative functions* with the desire to *constrict public purposes.* The point of contemporary conservative rhetoric is precisely to eradicate the distinction between these two activities. "Isn't it time we got Washington off our backs?" the Contract with America asked. "Too many people in Washington believe that government is the only solution to our problems. When it comes to creating jobs, government is more often the problem rather than the solution" (Gillespie and Schellhas, 1994: 125). These are slogans that oversimplify what is an inherently complex set of policy processes.

John J. DiIulio and Donald F. Kettl point out that the concept of "devolution" can be applied to three separate activities: *setting* policy, *financing* policy, and *administering* policy. "The content and character of federal-state relations thus depends not only on whether the national government is expanding or contracting its activities in given areas, but on which mix of responsibilities Washington is assuming or shedding, centralizing or devolving" (1995: 9). Unless the three aspects of "decentralization"—which I refer to as regulative devolution, fiscal devolution, and functional, or administrative, devolution—are kept present to discussion, debates over federalist strategies become carried out within the now incontestable assumption—incontestable in the sense that there is no longer any language available with which to contest it—that "that government governs best which governs least." The most powerful tool for controlling the direction of public policy is finally conjured up: alternatives to prevailing governance philosophies are eradicated from public discourse.

While regulative, fiscal, and functional devolution overlap and condition one another, they speak to independent practices. It is one thing for the federal government to seek, for example, generalized day care while providing states with sufficient funds to set up, coordinate, and oversee such programs. It is quite another for the federal government to not assume responsibility for the provision of day care, leaving it to the states to determine whether they want publicly sponsored day care and then, if they do, to find the money to fund it.

Recognition that the notion of devolution is not adequately encompassed by the phrase "getting the government off our backs" is absolutely critical to any informed policy discourse. But DiIulio and Kettl, having acknowledged the complexity of the concept, go on to argue that the policies put forth in the Contract with America do not, in fact, represent any basic shift from New Deal assumptions.

> The Contract preserves the national government's role in making, administering, and funding the vast array of post-New Deal and post-Great Society domestic policies and programs. That the Contract is considered so "revolutionary" by so many testifies only to the rhetorical resurgence of pre-Hoover era ideas about politics and governance in America. . . . Viewed historically, the Contract represents the final consolidation of the bedrock domestic policies and programs of the New Deal, the Great Society, the post-Second World War defense establishment, and, most importantly, the deeply rooted national political culture that has grown up around them. (1995: 60)

This is a remarkable reading of recent American politics. For the stories of the New Deal and its programmatic offspring are quite different from the ones told by the writers of the Contract.

The presumption of New Deal stories was that the modern capitalist state had some level of responsibility to correct for the dysfunctions inherent in the operation of capital markets. These dysfunctions include the markets' inability to compensate individuals adequately in the face of structural and frictional unemployment, and their inherent inefficiency in the provision of social goods, such as public education, generally accessible health care, and adequate housing for low-income workers and the poor. The Contract seems to assume that markets have no dysfunctions or weaknesses: that the unequal access to a minimal standard of living, which is the necessary by-product of a market system, is simply the way things are supposed to be, and therefore not an appropriate arena for collective action.

The new stories of public policy revive the myth that the virtuous individual will succeed and prosper, and that the irresponsible will fail and fall to the bottom of the social ladder. We are thus justified, as a polity, in ending the principle of entitlement. Society is out of the picture; no individual need worry about any other individuals save those in his immediate family or community. Going along with what they interpret as a new social consensus, the party responsible for the New Deal officially retreats from whatever limited progress the nation had made toward legitimizing the concept of social rights. President Bill Clinton, a Democrat, with the support of the majority of his congressional party, signs the welfare reform bill—also known as the "Personal Responsibility and Work Opportunity Reconciliation Act of 1996"—and carries to fruition a political enterprise that began with the election of Richard Nixon.

The New Federalism

The attack on the principle of social responsibility made its formal appearance at the Republican National Convention in Miami Beach in 1968. From five years of government programs for the unemployed, for the cities, for the poor, Nixon told the millions watching his televised acceptance speech, the country had reaped only

> an ugly harvest of frustrations, violence, and failure. . . . Instead of Government jobs and Government housing and Government welfare, let Government use its tax and credit policies to enlist in this battle the greatest engine of progress ever developed in the history of man—American private enterprise. (1968: 676)

The point, Nixon insisted, was not to abandon the inner-city poor, but to find ways of letting the market improve their condition.

Admittedly, one must be careful when tracing the roots of current devolutionary policy back to Nixon, who for example, has been linked with those presidents who expanded the welfare state and were committed to a politics of redistribution. "The welfare state was legitimated by Roosevelt's New Deal, Harry Truman placed civil rights on the national agenda, Lyndon Johnson founded the Great Society, and Richard Nixon called for welfare reform and signed into law food stamps, aid to the disabled, and the indexation of the social security program" (Peterson, 1995: 36). Further evidence for the position that the New Federalism did not represent a radical break with welfare state principles lies in the fact that it could look for antecedents to its block grant proposals in the 1940s and early 1950s, in the years of the Truman administration. For Truman had supported block grants in the fields of public health and welfare, although both proposals were defeated by the Congress (Conlan, 1988: 23). And revenue sharing was first proposed by Walter Heller, chairman of the Council of Economic Advisers in the Kennedy and Johnson administrations (Judd and Swanstrom, 1994: 273). Even the political administrators of the War on Poverty, dismayed by the maze of categorical grants that made any sort of rational coordination or oversight impossible, looked to block grants and revenue sharing as ways out (Conlan, 1988: 24–26).

It is probably true that Nixon had no ideological interest in challenging the New Deal. "The Federal Government will still have a large and vital role to play in achieving our national purposes," he told the country in his 1971 State of the Union address (1971: 228). And while one could never quite trust Nixon's rhetoric, this is not a language designed to undermine public commitment to New Deal principles. "[I]f the goal of improved performance required nationalizing certain shared or local functions—such as welfare or environmental regulation . . . ," Timothy Conlan writes, "Nixon accepted that conclusion" (1988: 12).

Under Nixon's tenure, expenditures for federal programs providing food, housing assistance, and medical care for the needy increased by more than 250 percent (Peterson, 1995: 81). During Johnson's administration the food stamp program made available to the poor only surplus agricultural commodities; Nixon's advisers revised the program so that food stamps could be exchanged for virtually any product sold in a grocery store (Peterson, 1995: 115). In 1970, a rent subsidy program was introduced, which paid the difference between the monthly cost of an approved housing unit and 25 percent of the recipient's income (Peterson, 1995: 59). The Family Assistance Program, though ultimately defeated by the Congress, sought to abolish Aid to Families with Dependent Children and replace it with a federally established minimum income floor, substantial increases in government support for families in poorer states, and a larger welfare budget (Conlan, 1988: 29). According to Conlan, the Nixon administration never intended to reverse the course of governmental activism or to restrict the growth of government spending (20).

On the other hand, it is simplistic to read Nixon's agenda of dismantling direct federal responsibility for community action projects as no more than an antibureaucratic twist on principles consistent with the New Deal consensus. Indeed, it is surprising the ease with which political scientists extract Nixon's proposals from their historical context. The political intent of the plans to turn control of social programs over to the states and cities was hardly a secret. They were designed to take advantage of the rising backlash, on the part of constituencies once loyal to the Democratic Party, against both the Great Society's general focus on social change and its particular focus on the black urban poor. The people who voted for Nixon

> were people who might have voted for Johnson in 1964 and might even have supported civil rights but who had been profoundly shocked by recent events—by students sneering at old values, by blacks rioting in the ghettos, by rising crime rates which made the streets a place of fear. (Matusow, 1984: 400)

Thus, to understand the beginnings of devolution, one must understand this white backlash, the ways in which the Republican Party appealed to it, and the failure of the Democratic Party to counter it.

The Two Rationales

The stories designed to put an end to the Great Society can be grouped into two grand narratives that came from two directions simultaneously. The first narrative focused on the issue of the relation of the federal government to the cities and localities it was trying to transform. The narrative was, on one level, about both administrative and political processes, and drew on traditional concerns in administrative theory about coherence, efficiency, and accountability in the implementation of federal programs at local levels. The second narrative was crudely expressed in the idea that "blacks were getting too much," and grounded in white resentment against the undeniably race-specific intent of allegedly universal antipoverty legislation.

Concerns about the administrative efficiency of the programs of the Great Society had emerged as early as 1966, when the Bureau of the Budget initiated a series of field studies in five states to assess the grant administration process. The findings were critical, particularly of the complexity and fragmentation of the federally supported programs, which, the staffers argued, "inhibits the development of a unified approach to the solution of community problems" (cited in Advisory Commission on Intergovernmental Relations, 1977: 11–12).

A 1968 study of federal aid programs in Oakland, California, was critical not only of their lack of coordination, but of the way they undermined local processes for setting and overseeing policy.

> Despite Federal expenditures in recent years totaling many millions of dollars, the visible results of Federal involvement in Oakland are few. . . . Public officials and residents (particularly those in the ghetto) tend to feel that Federal programs often fail to meet their needs. City officials in particular indicate that categorical aid programs sometimes skew city priorities: they are not developed to meet specific needs expressed by the city, they frustrate central administrative control over local functions, and they impede comprehensive planning and budgeting. (Cited in Advisory Commission on Intergovernmental Relations, 1977: 12)

These became familiar complaints about Great Society programs, particularly those administered by the Office of Economic Opportunity. The Oakland report itself was issued by a task force of executives representing eight federal agencies in the San Francisco area. It cannot simply be discounted, therefore, as the grumbling of a group of local officials upset with their loss of control over local programs and federal monies.

Attacks on the bureaucratic structure of War on Poverty programs continued in such works as Daniel Patrick Moynihan's *Maximum Feasible Misunderstanding*. Moynihan was especially dismayed by the seeming commitment of the Office of Economic Opportunity to undermine the representative institutions of local government. His book brought together, in systematic fashion, the arguments emerging in the policy community that, laudable as the goal to end urban poverty was, it could not be achieved without the participation and support of the formally elected local political leadership and their representatives.

One need not agree with Moynihan's criticisms of either the community action movement or the policies that mandated the direct participation of the poor on the boards of community action agencies to recognize the problems that emerge when official structures of accountability are bypassed. If nothing else, one should recognize that those holding the power of office are going to use all the resources at their command to hold onto their prerogatives. The men and women in the Office of Economic Opportunity were approving, from Washington, thousands of independent Community Action Projects in urban neighborhoods all over the country. They should not have been surprised when state and local Democratic leaderships began to demand control over the funding and supervision of these programs invading their turf.

The push for decentralization from the policy community critics focused on *administrative* disengagement. They defined the problems in terms of the absence of coherent planning, obstacles to effective coordination, and a loss of political and fiscal accountability. This set of stories never brought into question the right of the federal state to define national purposes and to engage in redistributive policies to realize those purposes—not the stories told by the federal administrators, who longed for coherence in planning, not those recounted by Moynihan, who had a Madisonian fear of direct democracy, and certainly not those put forth by the Democratic mayors and their cohorts, who were not so much disturbed by the principle of categorical grants as by the question of who controlled them.

It is here that the set of narratives specifically designed to undermine the programs of the Great Society comes into play. For the administrative critiques of the War on Poverty were easily co-opted by those who wanted to resist its equalizing goals and to maintain existing levels of economic and racial stratification. The argument for *administrative* devolution allowed them to have it both ways: to be opposed to nationally based programs for greater racial equality, but to talk only about the enhancement of individual freedom through less government regulation of daily life. In that sense, stories about devolution have not changed much at all.

The stories that brought Nixon to power always had race and class as their core, with the language of local control as their cover. Nixon's tales of turning government back to the people were designed to speak directly to those strata in the republic who felt most threatened by the liberal effort to use redistributive policies as a means of ending racial inequality. These groups had little enough as it was, and good reason to fear that it was *their* resources that were going to be redistributed. What they did have, they knew, was constantly vulnerable to job loss or economic downturn. They were not about to risk their tenuous economic and social status at the behest, as they saw it, of affluent intellectuals and policy makers who did not mind slightly higher taxes in pursuit of lofty social goals, whose schools had the best students and most qualified staff, and whose property values were not at risk from residential integration.

Lillian Rubin tapped into the character of these resentments in her case study of a school desegregation conflict that took place outside of San Francisco, in a suburb she called Richmond. To the community's working-class and lower-middle-class opponents of desegregation, Rubin observed,

> race was never an abstract problem far from home . . . for it is to their jobs, their neighborhoods, their schools that the first challenge is made. . . .
>
> Feeling powerless and deeply threatened, and therefore passionately angry, the working-class and lower-middle class anti-integrationists moved into the political arena in large numbers. Fearful that they would bear the lion's share of the costs of the impending social change . . . they reached for the stereotypes that reinforced their prejudices and that legitimated the scapegoating of blacks. . . . (1972: 203–4)

The political call to turn the determination and control of social policy over to local arenas appealed to these groups, as no one believed that they intended to use that power to support federal efforts to make the public sphere more inclusive.

The language in which Nixon called for "localizing power" masked a national drive to end federally developed programs of economic and racial equalization. The New Federalism, in its invocation of the magical formula "smaller government equals increased local power equals more individual freedom," blurred the distinction between goal-setting and implementation, between regulative and functional devolution. It never directly attacked the principles of the New Deal, as Ronald Reagan's programs did a decade later. But it fostered a social atmosphere in which white middle-income workers could easily transform their resentments against the War on Poverty, and their resistance to the integration of neighborhood schools, into the angry conviction that the federal government was intruding illegitimately into matters of strictly local concern.

Those who argued that government should withdraw from its commitment to broad-based programs for social equity began to put themselves forward as the deputies of the common people. Liberals—who assumed that, since Franklin Roosevelt, *they* were the ones who had stood for a public philosophy against the privatist vision of the wealthy—suddenly found themselves attacked as defenders of special interests and as uninterested in the plight of ordinary people. The terms of mid-century American political discourse were being turned upside down.

As I pointed out earlier, Nixon (1971) reaffirmed the principle that the federal government had a central role to play in achieving national purposes. But he then went on, in the same speech, to announce details of the revenue sharing plan, and to promise to "return power to the people." Unashamedly, he used a rhetoric that recalled both John F. Kennedy's inaugural address and New Left appeals for participatory democracy. Nixon, it turned out, shared the populist idealism of America's youth. He said: "Millions of frustrated young Americans today are crying out—asking not what will government do for me, but what can I do, what can I contribute, how can I matter?"

> And so, let us answer them. . . . Let us say to all Americans: "We hear you. . . . We are going to give you a new chance to have more to say about the decisions that affect your future—a chance to participate in government—because we are going to provide more centers of power where what you do can make a difference that you can see and feel in your own lives and the life of your whole community." (1971: 228)

This from a president whose domestic campaign had been grounded in reaction against the state's promotion of desegregation, who was committed to eviscerating the participatory components of the antipoverty programs, who was unalterably opposed to social activism, and who, under the guise of a call for law and order, had campaigned with the promise to end marches and demonstrations.

What did Nixon believe those frustrated young Americans, to and for whom he claimed to be speaking, want to participate *in*, one wonders. Mobs stoning buses that were carrying children to integrate neighborhood schools, perhaps; or the National Guard, where, in an increasingly repressive political environment, ill-prepared young men might shoot and kill unarmed student protesters their own age; or, most empowering of all, the military, where America's youth could participate in the remaking of their society by fighting in Vietnam. Unfair charges, perhaps, but at the same time, understandable reactions to Nixon's cynical use of American political rhetoric.

While it is true that none of Nixon's speeches directly attacked the principles of the welfare state, and that the president was content to work within the confines of the New Deal consensus still firmly in place when he took office, his 1971 State of the Union message was a seminal moment in setting the tone for what has, by now, become the common coin of political discourse. Nixon's tales opened a path for those in the society who were seeking ways to end the public policy commitment made by the Kennedy and Johnson administrations to the black urban poor. This is the point in recent American history when the conditions necessary to shred the notion of Social Contract behind the Great Society began falling into place.

The Democratic Party also bears some responsibility for the rise of the New Federalism. For local Democrats were under pressure from their middle-class constituents to curb expensive, racially oriented programs, control unruly behavior in the ghettos, and stop rising crime rates. These officials, facing fiscal crises, were frustrated by their lack of direct access to antipoverty funds, and wanted federal resources in their own hands. Congressional Democrats, rather than insist that centralized policy setting was necessary to extend democratization, and that uniform standards of social equity could only be developed and maintained at the federal level, yielded to their local colleagues' demands. They supported revenue sharing in the form of the State and Local Fiscal Assistance Act of 1972, reinforcing the message that the liberal politics of the Great Society had indeed undercut the power of ordinary citizens.

By failing to search for and offer a set of coherent alternatives to Nixon's New Federalism, liberal policy makers weakened the political ideal that had given the modern Democratic Party its identity. For, from the time of Roosevelt's election in 1932, the Democrats had stood, in principle at least, for the idea that under democratic capitalism, there was a federal responsibility to guarantee to all citizens access to those life necessities that the workings of the market failed to provide. By retreating from the New Deal commitment to nationalized standards of social equity, however, the Democrats did their part in easing the way for the return of the unthinkable. Generally accepted by academics and the policy community as a permanently resolved political question, the legitimacy of the minimalist New Deal welfare state began to reemerge as a contested issue. With Reagan's election in 1980, the conservative movement, held in check for a few years by Nixons fall from grace, unleashed a full assault on the welfare state.

Conclusion: The Force of Political Narrative

Stories situate people, provide them with context, and construct the realities in and through which they live. Clifford Geertz called these stories "ideological maps"—

> projections of unacknowledged fears, disguises for ulterior motives, phatic expressions of group solidarity—they are, most distinctively, *maps of problematic social reality and matrices for the creation of collective conscience.* Whether, in any par-

> ticular case, the map is accurate or the conscience creditable is a separate question. . . . (1973: 219, italics added)

Policy-tales are often efforts to redraw and thereby offer new maps to people. Yet we do not fully understand the dynamics by which social groups come to follow one set of these maps as opposed to another. In the end, I suggest, people choose the maps they wish to follow, and listen to the stories they want to hear.

Emerging political awareness is shaped by preexisting frameworks of belief, the particular character of people's everyday experiences and ways of life, and the extent to which groups believe the derived ideologies flowing into the stream of public discourse are consonant with their interests. Within that matrix, however, there is an autonomy to political consciousness. We are all somewhat manipulable, no doubt, but not as manipulable as current convention seems to suggest, with its reliance on spin doctors, marketing specialists, and talk show stars. Those who would shift a society's narrative direction must pay close attention to the ways its members construct social belief out of the everyday terrain they experience themselves to be living in and moving through. Media representation is part of that experience, but not its totality. For agents of change to reach down to the levels of independence on which ordinary people make immediate political decisions, they must respect the latter's capacity for thoughtful deliberation and choice.

It is unclear what combination of stories, strategies, and immediate experience might help move people away from support for privatization and regulative devolution, and back toward narratives of public responsibility and social generosity. Unhappily, it may require the impact of the social and economic devastations that will course through the body politic over the next few years. Even now, governors and mayors complain that under the new Personal Responsibility and Work Opportunity Reconciliation Act of 1996, they will not be receiving sufficient federal funds to train people for jobs, provide necessary day care, and make sure that adequate health services are available. They worry that more children will go hungry, and homelessness will increase. It is after the fact, but they worry.

As these reverses become more difficult to hide, as the tragedies of individual lives make their way more frequently onto the evening news, as the decline of social services affects more and more people, the stories of public policy may help redirect a change in course once again. The American working and middle classes may yet come to construct a discourse that links, in common dilemma, all those in some way dependent on the social wage.

13

The Entrepreneurial Gloss: The Myth of Small Business Job Growth

Phillip H. Sandro

This chapter examines a powerful tale about the promising role of small business in the economy of the United States. The small business tale reverberates among legions of politicians, bureaucrats, business lobbyists, economic development practitioners, workers, and even left-leaning activists in communities and unions from the United States to Italy to England. The tale has become part of "the common sense," as Antonio Gramsci put it (see the introduction to his 1971 work), and goes something like this.

First, small business firms since the early 1970s have been generating the vast majority of new jobs and will constitute the majority of the job base in the future. Second, small business firms are the engine of economic growth and are at the cutting edge of the economy, driving technological dynamism, change, and innovation. In short, the story goes, we have traversed into a new economic epoch whereby secular growth will be led by the dynamic synergy of clusters of small firms.

The policy implications of this tale are many. The chief implication is that development planners should do everything possible to promote the start-up and retention of as many new small businesses as they can. Specific policy measures suggested to achieve these ends fall mostly under the rubric of classic eighteenth- and nineteenth-century economic liberalism: get government out of the way, deregulate and cut taxes, and eliminate other barriers to the free flow of capital, trade, information, investment, and people. Tough medicine but well worth the payoff in job creation.

The ability of the small business tale to take hold so deeply reveals the power of an underlying or prior "metastory" that says free markets create a rising tide of economic growth that lifts the boats of even the least of us. According to the small business tale, big government, unions, welfare rights advocates, environmentalists, and numerous other groups rigidify markets and choke job creation in the small business sector. The small business tale is thus couched in populist terms.

The small business tale is now being challenged by recent and very convincing research that shows most of its claims to be either misguided or just plain wrong. Yet for now, the tale tenaciously retains its grip. In this chapter I will examine how the small business tale was socially produced, how the tale obscures our view of the economy, how the tale functions in our political economy, and whose interests the tale serves and hurts.

I will argue that the tale functions to rationalize a set of economic and social policy changes sought by major transnational corporations (TNCs) for purposes of their enhanced accumulation (profit). Ironically, these TNCs are not primarily responsible for propagating the small business tale. Furthermore, I will argue that the economic and policy changes sought by TNCs are indeed in their short-term interests but not in their long-term interests. Thus, the small business tale is ultimately dysfunctional for large units of capital, for small businesses, and certainly for the various strata of non-owning classes in the United States. Yet few see this dysfunctionality at present. Thus is the power of tales.

The Approach

This is a neo-Marxist account of the dynamic process of late capitalism that examines the role of tales in giving rise to mystifications that rationalize economic change. On the structuralist-poststructuralist analytical spectrum, then, this analysis lies toward the structuralist end of the continuum. The research that I will review suggests strongly that the small business story is what is called a "tall tale" in the introduction to this volume. Because the tale is so tall I contend that it can be refuted factually. Jean-Francois Lyotard (1984), a postmodernist, contends that it is difficult to distinguish between "factual knowledge" and "narrative knowledge" because "the facts" are delivered through the vehicle of narrative discourse. The narrative through which facts are communicated inevitably compromises and muddies "factual knowledge" so as to render it indistinguishable from what could be just another myth or story. I contend that the tallness of the small business tale overcomes the difficulties of distinguishing between factual and narrative knowledge.

Without throwing out the Marxian framework or being closed to its omissions, I do entertain an insight espoused by some postmodernists. The insight is that structures need ideological rationalization and that ideology can often operate through tales or discursive practices. These tales or discursive practices can become deeply, uncritically, and unconsciously embedded in day-to-day life so as to be vital to the reproduction of structures. I contend that the consideration of tales and other discursive practices potentially deepens the analysis of what Marxists call the "superstructure" (laws, religion, culture, belief systems . . .).

The Tale: Origin and Development

Celebration of small entrepreneurs is a centuries-old tradition in the United States. However, in the early 1980s MIT researcher David Birch (1987) propelled the celebration of small business to unparalleled heights when he concluded that 88 percent of all net job creation between 1981 and 1985 was in firms of twenty employees or less. Birch argued that a region's economy will be successful to the extent that it is able to start up and retain new businesses. After the publication of Birch's findings numerous other researchers and popularizers elevated Birch's research and its implications to the status of a full-blown "tale." These included the Organization for European Cooperation and Development (1985), George Gilder (1984), and special reports in *Business Week* and the *Wall Street Journal* extolling the virtues of small business job creation. Within a few years anyone worth their salt in policy circles knew that small firms were creating most of the jobs. A tale was born.

Eager to be associated with job creation, legislators, bureaucrats, and policy wonks rewrote numerous laws, regulations, and programs in both Europe and the United States to favor the small business sector.

In addition to claiming that most of the net new jobs are created from the small business sector, proponents of the small business tale argue that small firms are the key to productivity-led growth because they are leading technological change and new product innovation. During the 1980s Birch, Gilder, and scholars such as Giovanni Dosi (1988), Michael Piore and Charles Sabel (1984), and Zoltan Acs and David Audretsch (1987) made assorted arguments that small firms are the fountain of technological innovation and creativity, are systematically privileged by new technologies such as computer-controlled factory automation, or are leaders in new product innovation.

There is another, yet connected, variation of the small business tale that extols the possibilities for prosperity with local control made possible by "small firm-led industrial districts" in Italy, eastern Asia, and North America. A number of scholars (Piore and Sabel, 1984; Bagnasco, 1977) characterize these districts as spatially concentrated clusters of small and medium-sized firms using flexible computer-controlled technology. Firms in these clusters compete, yet, on a collaborative basis, share information and technology. They form intricate yet fluid buyer/supplier linkages while resisting hierarchy of control among themselves. Furthermore, some characterizations of industrial districts raise the possibility for increased local control by emphasizing the strategic importance to these districts of a "social infrastructure" that includes activist local and regional governments and civic associations. These industrial districts are thought to be led by small and medium-sized firms.

It is this "industrial district model" with its politically inclusive, locally controlled growth model that resonates with some of the left wing in the United States and Europe, and for understandable reasons. Industrial districts are seen as a countertendency to the loss of economic sovereignty and local control wrought by the decentralized globalization of production since the early 1970s.

We have then two variations of the small business tale: the competitive-individualistic entrepreneurial tale that finds support among a broad range of conservative constituencies, and the industrial district tale that offers hope to many liberals and other local control advocates. The problem is that both of these tales are misguided and dysfunctional.

What's Wrong with This Picture?

Bennett Harrison in *Lean and Mean: The Changing Landscape of Corporate Power in the Age of Flexibility* (1994) has mounted the most influential challenge to the small business tale. He has compiled a solid body of evidence that demonstrates that the employment share of the small business sector as a percentage of the total has barely changed since the late 1950s.

First, Harrison finds flaws in Birch's methodology. After much criticism of his research, even Birch admitted in an interview in the *Wall Street Journal* that his early numbers were "silly" (Wiesel and Brown, 1989). Harrison then critiques and updates a number of subsequent studies that look at small business job-generation patterns. Indeed, average firm size in the United States declined from a very large 1,100 people in 1967 to 665 in 1985, still a large figure by Birch's standards. Harrison outlines five plausible explanations for this decline, only one of which is a growth of small firms (1994:40):

- Vertical disintegration of the big firms, to escape unions, high wages, and "bad business climate"
- Closures concentrated among the largest companies and units
- A secular shift from manufacturing (with its generally larger facilities) to services (with its generally smaller facilities)
- The strategic downsizing of large conglomerates as part of a retreat into core competencies
- A genuine disproportionate growth in the activity of small firms

Harrison and his colleague Barry Bluestone have found extensive support for the first four explanations (1988), but little that backs up the fifth, the core of the small business tale.

To examine this fifth explanation, Harrison updates an International Labor Organization (ILO) study that covered the performance of small firms in France, Italy, the United Kingdom, West Germany, Japan, Norway, Hungary, Switzerland, and the United States (Sengenberger, Loveman, and Piore, 1990). The ILO researchers defined a small business as one hundred employees or less, five times Birch's definition. With "small" defined as five times larger than Birch's definition, Harrison still finds that the long-run share of small firms has barely changed since at least the late 1950s (Harrison, 1994).

Another questionable assumption made by Gilder, Birch, and other proponents of the tale is that small businesses are leaders in "process innovation" and "new product innovation." The evidence, however, suggests that small businesses are technological laggards on both accounts.

The process innovation argument focuses on the role of new technologies such as computer-controlled factory automation that facilitates a system of "flexible specialization." Flexible specialization is a production strategy that allows firms to flexibly target niche markets by reaching economies of scale and therefore breakeven points at lower levels of output than under a mass production system. Smaller firms are said to be "favored" by these technologies and are therefore more viable and competitive than before (Acs and Audretsch, 1987).

However, empirical tests of penetration rates of these technologies by firm size undermine these claims. Kelley and Brooks (1991) and the U.S. Bureau of the Census (1989) in separate studies have concluded that computer programmable machinery is positively related to firm size, just the opposite of the small firm story. Similar conclusions have been reached for the United Kingdom, Japan, and Italy (Harrison, 1994: 62–63).

With respect to new product innovation, small and medium-sized firms again appear to lag behind larger establishments. Studies of Germany, the United Kingdom, and even the high-technology sector in the United States suggest strongly that the tale popularized by Birch and Gilder et al. just does not hold up. It is larger firms with deep pockets that disproportionately foster new product innovation.

A third weak point regards the assumption that decentralized, nonhierarchical industrial districts led by small firms already exist in sufficient numbers. The upshot of recent research is that they may have existed in the 1970s but that their very success created the conditions for their demise in the 1980s. Again, the most rigorous research has been done by Harrison. He studied three of the most celebrated industrial districts and concludes that all three were characterized by cooperative, fluid networks of small firms in their early years through the 1970s. However, in Italy's Emilia-Romagna disrict, the Sasib company, a strong firm in the cluster, was bought out by the conglomerate Olivetti, which then bought and pressured other supplier companies in the district to serve the interests of the parent firm. The Venito district was also characterized in the 1950s as a web of cooperatively competitive firms, one of which was Benneton. Yet by the 1980s the little Benneton Company evolved into an immense multinational conglomerate forging a "core" of closely owned large firms that controlled successive "rings" of highly dependent subcontractors who in turn put out low-wage work to small shops and homes in an adaptable "periphery." Power and control became highly asymmetrical between core and periphery. Again, this is the opposite of the popular image of nonhierarchy and cooperation. Prato, perhaps the most celebrated, idealized, and archetypical industrial district, boomed until the early 1980s, when it began to fall under the weight of its own unproductive fragmentation, losing market share to larger, more rationalized, productive, and "modern" global competitors. None of these examples fit the picture of industrial districts that have captivated those on the liberal-left end of the political spectrum.

What Is Obscured by This Tale and Who Benefits?

The small business tale in its various forms obscures, rationalizes, and legitimates the contradictions of an evolving industrial order quite different from that envisioned by the tale. What is emerging as a dominant organizing principle in the world economy is a complex of globally networked production systems led by increasingly "lean," downsized, yet large "core" firms. These core firms are linked to other large and small firms operating in different industries, regions, and countries through joint ventures, supply chains, strategic alliances, and other intercorporate "webs" (Harrison, 1994; Reich, 1992).

While European, Japanese, and U.S. production networks interact, they differ in their production, locational, and governance structures. Yet there is a common underlying developmental tendency: an increased shift toward hierarchical core-ring production systems, led increasingly by large, powerful transnational firms (increased concentration). Small firms are increasingly important in production networks as larger firms are outsourcing more of their functions to smaller firms. But smaller firms are not leading this process. They are dependent upon it.

That the small business tale is misguided does not explain what it legitimates or the contradictions it rationalizes. Flexible networked production systems are achieving remarkable gains in productivity and appear benign at first blush. Yet this method of production carries with it contradictory aspects. It has served as the resolution to a prior crisis of profitability in the 1970s. Flexible networks help resolve this crisis because their aim is to lower production costs (thereby increasing profit rates) by achieving maximum "flexibility." Flexibility means many things, but above all it means capital mobility in myriad forms. But capital mobility is contradictory. On the one hand it is necessary to restore corporate profits. On the other hand it undermines workers' bargaining power over wages and working conditions and undermines the influence of the state in economic affairs. Capital mobility decreases job security, has devastated communities through deindustrialization, continues to destabilize community institutions and life, and is increasing the level of inequality in the United States and elsewhere (Ranney, 1994). Thus, production networks are not economically neutral. The small business tale, to the extent that it rationalizes the need for capital mobility, obscures the contradictory nature of this whole process.

Nor are production networks politically neutral. In the 1970s and 1980s corporations aggressively pursued a set of government policies that would facilitate various forms of capital mobility. The economic crisis of the 1970s played a role in delegitimizing liberalism, creating an opening for a federal government whose conservative policies were quite responsive to this corporate agenda. Government responses included myriad forms of deregulation: the New Federalism that allowed firms to more easily whipsaw state and local governments for "better business climates," and cuts in the social safety net, putting downward pressure on wages and helping to drive people into an ever-increasing number of low-wage jobs. The National Labor Relations Board was reconstituted into an entity unsympathetic to labor, and striker replacement bills were passed. Corporate tax rates and income tax rates for upper income brackets were decreased. The North American Free Trade Agreement and a revised General Agreement on Tariffs and Trade were sanctioned by Congress, which, by reducing nontariff barriers to trade, may further undermine local, state, and federal sovereignty over health, safety, and environmental regulations (Ranney, 1994). I argue below that the small business tale has played a significant role, perhaps ironically, in rationalizing these policy changes and obscuring their contradictions.

How Does the Small Business Tale Rationalize the Transnational Agenda?

The small business tale was promulgated and popularized in the 1980s by free market conservatives and energetically operationalized by the small business lobby. Large transnational corporations (TNCs) are not chiefly responsible for the telling of these tales. Yet I argue that they are beneficiaries. How does this happen? More specifically, since both large and small firms seek to influence policy, why aren't those internationalist class fractions of the ruling class, known in some circles as "trilateralists," who are instrumental in the forging of international production networks, countering the small business tale? Marxists have long noted the intraruling class fracture between international capital and domestic (national) capital.

Why aren't large conglomerates threatened by all the talk of supporting small firms? I contend that part of the answer lies in the changing relationship between TNCs and small businesses. I argue that in the emerging system of flexible networked production the relationship between the internationalist corporate sector and the small business sector is changing as large TNCs increasingly outsource to small firms the production of inputs that were formerly produced internally. This differs from the "Fordist" mass production model with high proportions of internally produced inputs. Thus, any policy that reduces the cost structure of small businesses increasingly reduces the cost structure of larger core firms by lowering input costs.

I also contend that the agendas of TNCs and small businesses are more congruent than in the past because now, more than in the past, both large and small firms put a huge premium on flexibility and therefore capital mobility. Thus, in many respects, government policies sought by the small business lobby coincide or compliment one another. Almost nothing in the way of policy recommendations trumpeted by the small-is-beautiful ideologues is inconsistent with the agenda of the transnational "core" firms in command of production networks. It used to be said that what's good for General Motors is good for the country. Perhaps the rub here is that what's good for small business is increasingly good for GM. Let's examine this further with but a few, out of many, examples.

As mentioned in the early sections of this chapter, advocates of the small business vision advise a return to classic economic liberalism and see large government as a major problem. Their solution: shrink government and use the money saved to cut corporate tax rates further. Large conglomerates have no material reason to object to tax cuts for small businesses because these cuts lower their own cost structures to the extent that they use small firms as suppliers. Additionally, to the extent that campaigns to cut taxes for small business pave the way for general corporate tax cuts, the objective interests of small and large capital are increasingly coincident.

States and localities are advised, according to the tale, to provide tax "holidays" and scores of other variances and incentives in order to encourage small business retention and start-ups. Many of these small businesses are suppliers in the production networks of larger firms. There is no reason why large firms would object to any policy that would decrease the cost profiles of their suppliers.

According to the tale, government is too big in another sense. Small entrepreneurs are hamstrung by costly and burdensome regulations. Some give up or are put out of business, choking off the best source of jobs in the economy. So: deregulate. Unleash the entrepreneurial spirit, in Gilder's words, and let those that create the most jobs do what they do best. Again, there is nothing here that large conglomerates aren't already energetically lobbying for, albeit in a less public and more sophisticated way. All of this deregulation may hurt consumers where they live or workers where they work. But the small business tale promises a greater counterbalancing tendency: jobs. The key to successful production networks is flexibility and mobility. Regulations create inflexibility and less mobility. If they can be swept away by a tide of free-market small business advocacy, there is no reason for the leaders of production networks to object.

Some variations of the small business tale complain that large conglomerates control industrial policy, and yet they aren't creating the jobs. Despite this anti-big business rhetoric, the small business tale still stands to benefit large U.S. conglomerates, for according to the small-is-beautiful free market advocates, government is once again the problem. The solution is to get government out of the business of business and let the market give the signals; the government must not try to control big business by picking winners and losers in an "industrial policy." If government is delegitimated generally, and there is a climate that is hostile to coherent, coordinated, overarching government planning and regulation, then it is easier for *individual* transnational and other large firms to wrest concessions, favors, and assistance from the state that may be good for that *particular* firm but bad for the economy as a *whole*. In other words, the coherency that would come with planning may undermine "corporate welfare" as we know it.

Furthermore, if the state were seen as a legitimate instrument of economic and industrial policy planning, then there would be an increased possibility that a national discussion or political debate would occur that might ask, "toward what ends do we have an economy?" But this would present the state with a legitimation problem. In order to reproduce the tale that we are a democracy, unions, other workers, the unemployed, communities, welfare recipients, immigrants, women, the disabled, communities of color, environmentalists, consumer protection advocates, and others might insist on being included in this discussion. But these groups have tales of their own, some of which are anticorporate. Assuming that these groups were legitimated by their inclusion into a national debate, they would invariably gain political leverage. But, as I've outlined earlier, the corporate sector (in concert with the state) has spent the past twenty years systematically undermining the influence of these groups because they are elements of inflexibility. Thus, the small business tale plays an important role in manufacturing consent. It undermines the legitimacy of the state in economic affairs. By doing so the tale increasingly privatizes political discourse on economic policy. It therefore severs potentially dissident groups from at least one arena (the state) where political discourse on economic affairs occurs. The small business tale attempts to win over these groups with the promise of new jobs. They may not be great jobs, but since small businesses create most of them it's the only game in town.

There is a tradition of tales that characterize big business as greedy, too powerful, and in control of Washington. Survey after survey tells of an American people that associates its economic insecurity with the actions of large firms. Given this negative image, most large firms wisely lobby for much the same agenda that small businesses lobby behind the scenes while the small business tale takes the case to the public. The small business tale makes the coinciding policy agendas of large and small businesses more palatable. People may be more inclined to support policy changes for the little struggling entrepreneur trying to create jobs. They are less likely to support the same policy changes for transnationals that have deindustrialized and taken jobs abroad or downsized and increased unemployment.

This Is a Dysfunctional Tale

There is evidence to suggest that the small business tale is dysfunctional because it reinforces U.S. business practices that achieve short-term profits at the cost of long-term competitive advantage, market share, and growth.

There is a significant corpus of best-practice management literature in U.S. business school texts and leading business media that strongly advises firms to follow what Harrison has dubbed the high-road strategy (1994: 211–15). Informed by Japanese and European experiences, the high-road strategy includes a cluster of practices that enhance long-run productivity and growth through mechatronic and organizational techniques in collaboration with government and labor, all in the context of "patient money" and industrial planning that allows for a long-term planning horizon. This literature suggests that if adopted, these practices would help firms in U.S. production networks realize greater increases in the levels of downstream profits, market share, and growth. Some of the leading and most dynamic U.S. firms are adopting elements of the high-road approach. By contrast, most are unable to do so until a critical mass of firms do.

Explication of the specific elements of current best-practice management literature is beyond the scope of this chapter. It suffices, however, to say that its prescriptions taken as a whole are distinctly non-laissez-faire. They legitimize government involvement in industrial policy. They require large and small firms alike to sacrifice some flexibility and some autonomy for longer-term gains. They call for labor-management cooperation in the European or Japanese sense. The small business tale takes direct aim not only at these best-practice management prescriptions but at their ideological foundations. The small business tale characterizes them as too social democratic, too regulatory, too inflexible. The result is that the bulk of U.S. firms continue to trade off long-term market share for short-term profits.

The use of the metaphor "high road" does not imply that production networks organized along these principles are without contradictions or are benevolent toward workers and communities. Harrison characterizes both Japanese and German industrial policies as "high road," but clearly states that their production networks rely on very exploitive relations of production outside of the "core firms" and their primary "ring" of suppliers. While the relative merits of social democratic economic policy are debated incessantly on the left, the main point here is that elements of that approach could boost long-term productivity, market share, and growth of firms in U.S. production networks but that the small business tale is so powerful that it plays a role in dysfunctionally blinding most U.S. firms to that possibility.

Conclusion

The small business tale undermines democracy in the name of democracy. It does this by severing voices that might resist corporate agendas from public economic discourse by severing the state from a legitimate role in economic policy formation. On the other hand, to critique the tale is to reinstate the state as a "contested terrain" in economic policy discourse, to open up the state as one arena where questions concerning the purpose of an economy may be raised. Reconnecting the state to economic policy formation or "deprivatizing" economic policy debate allows heretofore unthinkable questions to be posed. For example, should we have democratic control over the economy? In what areas and to what extent? This is not to say that the state will yield to demands that arise out of these questions. But the state can be used as a strategic vehicle to legitimate and strengthen groups heretofore defined by the small business tale as enemies of job creation.

To critique the tale is also to understand that a system of increasingly networked economic concentration is emerging—*not* a system increasingly led by small firms. A less obscured view of the economy creates the possibility of a more efficacious economic development policy. The combined effects of reinstating the state as a contested terrain on matters economic, a more activated citizenry, and a less obscured analysis of the economy may pose a threat to the state's ability to mediate the contradictions between capital and the many groups that may demand fundamental reinclusion into policy-making process after years of exclusion. These contradictions may not be easily reconcilable, which may pose a threat to the "democracy tale" itself. Thus, embedded in the small business tale are some of the most fundamental tenets of free market conservative ideology. Interrogating the small business tale questions these tenets and so challenges the prerogatives and flexibility of capital itself.

14

The Vanishing White Man: *Workforce 2000* and Tales of Demographic Transformation

Joel Best

We live in anxious times. As we approach the end of this millennium, we no longer take the idea of progress for granted, and our doubts shape our recollections of the past and our expectations for the future. Increasingly, history is told in terms of devastation, exploitation, and oppression. Contrast the generally upbeat bicentennial celebration of 1976 with the focus on genocide, environmental despoliation, and other crimes of the Old World against the New that characterized 1992's muted commemoration of the 500th anniversary of Columbus's voyage.

Similarly, our anxieties shape our vision of the future. Earlier predictions of technological utopia now seem naive (Corn and Horrigan, 1984). Instead, apocalyptic scenarios for the near future abound: global war ending in firestorms or nuclear winter; ecological catastrophe brought on by overpopulation, exhausted resources, or a polluted environment; spreading AIDS or other incurable viral epidemics; economic collapse; terrorism and political anarchy; and on and on (Karplus, 1992). Throughout the twentieth century, Americans have spoken of rapid social change; today, they routinely assume such change will be for the worse.

These doubts shape our understanding of even the most mundane social issues. Sociologists describe the processes whereby issues come to public attention as social problems construction (Spector and Kitsuse, 1977; Holstein and Miller, 1993). That is, social problems are produced or constructed through claims by those who hope to attract the attention of the press, the public, and policy makers. This focus on social problems construction is fundamentally different from traditional, objectivist sociology's equating social problems with harmful social conditions. Constructionists argue that conditions are not problematic in and of themselves; they must be defined as social problems through claimsmaking. While so-called strict constructionists attempt to limit their analysis to the content of claims, most researchers are contextual constructionists, who locate claims within their structural and cultural context (Best, 1995).

Claimsmaking is a competitive process; claims compete for attention in a social problems marketplace (Hilgartner and Bosk, 1988). And, because doubts about the future are widespread, claims that depict especially threatening social problems tend to find their way to the top of the media and policy agendas. This means, of course, that claimsmakers find it easier to promote their causes when they adopt apocalyptic rhetoric. This chapter examines one recent instance of doomsaying: projections of a dramatic transformation in the U.S. workforce. It offers a contextualist interpretation, contrasting claims about dramatic, troubling change with other, contradictory evidence. The story begins with a modestly dramatic fanfare: the federal government released a report projecting trends in the composition of the U.S. workforce. But the drama promptly turned into comedy: the official summary of the report's findings contained an important error that exaggerated the nature of the projected changes. That error quickly took on a life of its own, and the mistake was repeated and amplified in the repetitions. Attempts to correct the record have gone unnoticed; the error lives on because it makes claims by both liberals and conservatives seem more dramatic.

Statistics in Contemporary Claims

Statistics are a standard element in modern social problems rhetoric. Objectivist analysts often treat statistics as straightforward measures of problematic social conditions. Numbers imply facticity; they seem solid, incontrovertible. Of course, this is an illusion. Constructionist sociologists warn that official statistics must be understood as products of organizational practices (Kitsuse and Cicourel, 1963; Bogdan and Ksander, 1980); even the most authoritative data reflect their political context and the limitations of data collection (Alonso and Starr, 1987; Choldin, 1994). While this does not mean that statistics are worthless, it does suggest the importance of interpreting numbers carefully.

There are at least three reasons why such care is often absent when social problems claims incorporate statistics. First, efforts to draw attention to social problems typically focus on neglected social conditions, and one symptom of neglect is the paucity of good data: accurate, authoritative statistics are often not available. As a consequence, claimants find themselves encouraged to produce their own statistical estimates, even if these are nothing more than best guesses or ballpark figures. However, once these numbers enter public discourse, their limitations are soon forgotten, and in the absence of more authoritative statistics, the claimsmakers' figures may become widely accepted.

Second, claimsmakers' estimates almost inevitably exaggerate a problem's size. This exaggeration need not be cynical; convinced that a problem is serious and neglected, and invited to estimate its scope, claimants may produce large numbers that they believe to be more or less accurate. Because dramatic claims are more competitive in the social problems marketplace, it is no surprise that the statistics offered by claimsmakers tend to err on the side of overestimating the problem's magnitude. Thus, critics have documented exaggerated statistics in claims about a wide variety of social problems, including missing children (Best, 1990), homelessness (Jencks, 1994: 1–3), elder abuse (Crystal, 1987), date rape (Gilbert, 1994), and workplace violence (Larson, 1994).

Third, many statistical claims fail to receive critical examination because neither the claimsmakers nor their audience have the skills to properly interpret them. Mathematician John Allen Paulos uses the term "innumeracy" to refer to the mathematical equivalent of illiteracy—"an inability to deal comfortably with the fundamental notions of number and chance" (1988: 3). The widespread willingness to uncritically accept and repeat statistical claims should be recognized as a form of innumeracy. Too often, claimsmakers present figures of dubious validity, the mass media repeat those numbers, and policy makers and the public respond to the imagery in those claims. In this way, questionable statistical claims can shape both perceptions of social problems and proposals for policy solutions. Many of these elements—including statistical exaggeration, innumerate manipulation, and uncritical repetition—can be found in the contemporary discussions of the changing American workforce as depicted in *Workforce 2000.*

Workforce 2000

In 1987, the U.S. Department of Labor commissioned *Workforce 2000* (Johnston and Packer, 1987), a report from the Hudson Institute, a well-known neoconservative think tank. *Workforce 2000* analyzed anticipated changes in the U.S. economy and workforce through the end of the century; it projected relatively healthy economic growth, increased productivity, an aging workforce, growing demand for educated workers, and so on. While this might not seem to be the stuff of dramatic claims, one finding would become the focus of considerable attention:

> The small net growth of workers will be dominated by women, blacks, and immigrants. White males, thought of only a generation ago as the mainstays of the economy, will comprise only 15 percent of the net additions to the labor force between 1985 and 2000. (Johnston and Packer, 1987: 95)

It is important to understand exactly what this passage meant. For the most part, the authors of *Workforce 2000* drew upon existing data, especially data collected by the federal Bureau of Labor Statistics. By examining BLS data, we can reconstruct the evidence for *Workforce 2000*'s claims about the changing composition of the labor force. This reconstruction is necessary, not because *Workforce 2000* made false claims, but because it presented its findings in a manner that confused virtually everyone who encountered them.

Population growth produces a larger workforce: the U.S. civilian labor force was 122 million in 1988, and is projected to be 141 million in 2000 (see table 14.1). Currently constituting a bit under half the workforce, white males are the largest single category of workers. To be sure, their share of the workforce is shrinking and will continue to decline, from 47.9 percent in 1988, to a projected 44.8 percent in 2000.

This relative decline is not due to falling numbers of white male workers; their ranks will grow from 58 million to 63 million during the same period. However, other categories of workers—women, blacks, Asians, and Hispanics—are increasing at faster rates. These changes reflect several

Table 14.1

Civilian Labor by Sex, Race, and Hispanic Origin, 1976–2000 (numbers in thousands)

	1976		1988		2000	
	Workers	Percent	Workers	Percent	Workers	Percent
Total	96,158	100.0	121,669	100.0	141,134	100.0
White	84,767	88.2	104,756	86.1	118,981	84.3
Males	51,033	53.1	58,317	47.9	63,288	44.8
Females	33,735	35.1	46,439	38.2	55,693	39.5
Black	9,565	9.9	13,205	10.9	16,465	11.7
Males	5,105	5.3	6,596	5.4	8,007	5.7
Females	4,460	3.6	6,609	5.4	8,458	6.0
Asian/other	1,826	1.9	3,709	3.0	5,688	4.0
Males	1,036	1.1	2,015	1.7	3,029	2.1
Females	790	0.8	1,694	1.4	2,659	1.9
Hispanic*	4,279	4.4	8,982	7.4	14,321	10.1
Males	2,625	2.7	5,409	4.4	8,284	5.9
Females	1,654	1.7	3,573	2.9	6,037	4.3

Source: Fullerton, 1989: Table 4.

**Note:* This is a separate tabulation. The data above include persons of Hispanic origin under other racial categories (i.e., the percentages for whites, blacks, and Asians/others total 100 percent).

familiar processes. The proportion of women who are in the workforce continues to grow; 57 percent of women over 16 were in the labor force in 1988 (up from 47 percent in 1976), a figure projected to rise to 63 percent in 2000. Asians and Hispanics make up the majority of recent (and anticipated) immigrants. Immigrants tend to be young adults, and the birthrate for native-born whites lags behind those of other groups. As a consequence, the average age for white workers is somewhat higher than for blacks, Hispanics, and Asians. Taken together, these trends ensure a steady, gradual decline in white males' proportion in the workforce. In fact, non-Hispanic white males are expected to account for only 31.6 percent of the people entering the workforce between 1988 and 2000 (see table 14.2).

Thanks to their growing labor-force participation rate, white women entering the workforce will actually outnumber white male entrants. More important, the population entering the workforce is quite different from those workers projected to leave (because of death, retirement, and so on). Nearly half (48 percent) of those leaving will be non-Hispanic white males.

This discrepancy between the populations entering and leaving the workforce accounts for the *Workforce 2000* finding quoted above. From 1988 to 2000, roughly 13.5 million non-Hispanic white males will enter the workforce, but some 11.3 million will leave, resulting in a net increase of about

Table 14.2

Projected Workforce Entrants, Leavers, and Net Change, Moderate Growth Scenario, 1988–2000 (numbers in thousands)

	Entrants		Leavers		Net Change	
	Number	Percent	Number	Percent	Number	Percent
White, non-Hispanic	28,597	66.8	19,393	83.0	9,204	47.3
Males	13,522	31.6	11,257	48.2	2,265	11.6
Females	15,075	35.2	8,136	34.8	6,939	35.7
Hispanic	6,486	15.1	1,145	4.9	5,341	27.4
Males	3,558	8.3	681	2.9	2,877	14.8
Females	2,928	6.8	464	2.0	2,464	12.7
Black	5,385	12.6	2,329	10.0	3,056	15.7
Males	2,423	5.7	1,121	4.8	1,302	6.7
Females	2,962	6.9	1,208	5.2	1,754	9.0
Asian and other	2,364	5.5	504	2.2	1,860	9.6
Males	1,232	2.9	282	1.2	950	4.9
Females	1,132	2.6	222	0.9	910	4.7
Total	42,832	100.0	23,371	100.0	19,461	100.0

Source: Fullerton, 1989: Table 7.

2.3 million. These 2.3 million white males will account for only about 12 percent of the total net increase in the workforce. Or, as the *Executive Summary to Workforce 2000* stated: "Non-whites, women, and immigrants will make up more than five-sixths *of the net additions* to the workforce between now and the year 2000, though they make up only half of it today" (U.S. Department of Labor, 1987: xx; emphasis added).

Why did *Workforce 2000*'s authors choose to report their results in this relatively obscure, technical language? Was there a hidden agenda, or was it simply an effort to make the report's findings seem more striking? Presumably claims that white males would form "only 15 percent of the net additions to the labor force" seemed more dramatic than, say, noting that white males' share of the workforce would drop from 48 percent to 45 percent. Phrased that way, the likely response to the report would have been indifference—among those who bothered to pay attention.

In any case, the meaning of "net additions to the labor force" was not self-evident, even to those responsible for publicizing the report. In releasing the *Executive Summary* for those too busy to read the full report, the Department of Labor made a classic, innumerate blunder. According to the executive summary: "Only 15 percent *of the new entrants to the labor force* over the next 13 years will be native white males, compared to 47 percent in that category today" (1987: xiii; emphasis added). This equated the original, confusing notion of "net additions to the labor force" (estimated at 12 to 15 percent white males) with the more easily understood—albeit far different—concept of "new entrants to the labor force" (estimated at 32 percent white males). (A parallel mistake appeared in the original *Workforce 2000* report: a chart showing the demographics of the net increase in new workers was mislabeled "new entrants to the labor force" [Johnston and Packer, 1987: 95].)

Commentators seized the simpler, mistaken statistic and began repeating—and improving—it:

- White men would make up just 12 to 15 percent of the people joining the workforce between 1988 and 2000. (Dobrzynski, 1995: D1)
- While white non-Hispanic males made up 47 percent of the labor force in 1985, they would make up only 15 percent of new workforce entrants between 1985 and 2000. (Litvan, 1994: 49)
- Of the 26 million new workers [1990–2005], 85 percent would be members of minority groups, women and immigrants. (Williams, 1992: D20)
- Almost two-thirds of the new entrants to the labor force between 1985 and 2000 will be female. . . . (Jamieson and O'Mara, 1991: 19)
- Eighty-five percent of new entrants would be members of a minority. . . . In contrast, . . . the Economic Policy Institute suggests . . . that most 1990s labor market entrants—in fact two-thirds of the total number—

> will be non-Hispanic whites, not minorities. . . . But no matter which projections are more accurate. . . . (Diamante, Reid, and Giglio, 1995: 60)

These statements appeared in authoritative mainstream sources (including the *New York Times*, twice, and *Nation's Business*). They reveal that few commentators appreciated the distinction between "new workers" and "net entrants" to the workforce; each statement erroneously speaks of the former, instead of correctly referring to the latter. Other commentators adopted fresh—but even more confusing—imagery to make the *Workforce 2000* findings clear. For example, *Working Woman* magazine quoted economist Audrey Freedman: "Now for every ten jobs there may be eight applicants. Four are women, and three are immigrants. Of the four young men applying, only two are white, and one may take drugs" (Sandroff, 1990: 59). The *New York Times* cited Mae C. Jemison, an African American astronaut, for this claim: "By the year 2000, less than 25 percent of the nation's high school seniors will be white males . . ." (1993: B13). Another newspaper story cited projections by David Hayes-Bautista, a professor in UCLA's School of Medicine and director of the Chicano Studies Research Center: "By the year 2030, the U.S. work force is projected to be 50 percent Hispanic, 20 percent Asian and African-American and 30 percent Anglo" (Hoagland, 1991: A8).

The error was further compounded by those who confused "new entrants" with the entire workforce, leading to assertions that white males would soon be a tiny fraction of all workers. Other commentators apparently failed to distinguish between labor-force participation rates and workforce composition. Presumably, one—or both—of these errors explains the extraordinary claim by Warran Furutani, a member of the Los Angeles Board of Education, who told a congressional hearing that "By the year 2000, nearly 65% of the total workforce will be women" (U.S. House of Representatives, 1989b: 69). When the commentators finished, the findings of *Workforce 2000* had been mangled beyond recognition.

What is perhaps most striking about the confused commentaries on *Workforce 2000* is the degree to which they fly in the face of common sense. Who, after a moment's thought, could believe that, in little more than a decade, two-thirds of all workers would be women, or that white males would form only a tiny share of those entering the workforce? Why didn't people question these claims?

It's not that they weren't warned about the distinction between new workers and net entrants to the workforce. At a 1989 congressional hearing on *Workforce 2000*, Janet Norwood, commissioner of the U.S. Bureau of Labor Statistics, noted the confusion: "The distinction between the total number of entrants and the net addition to the labor force is important because the demographic distribution of the *total* number of entrants by race, sex, and Hispanic origin is much different from the demographic composition of the *net* change of 21 million. The two concepts are different and must not be mistaken for one another" (U.S. House of Representatives, 1989a: 49; emphasis in original). Apparently few paid attention; virtually every other witness at the same hearing offered, without challenge, at least one garbled statistic. Similarly, although the press has run stories (including one in the *Washington Post* in 1990 that was picked up by other papers) explaining that the *Executive Summary* had misinterpreted the *Workforce 2000* findings (Crittenden, 1994; Swoboda, 1990), confused descriptions of the future workforce remain common. Despite the numbers being obviously ridiculous, despite efforts to correct the errors, claims about the vanishing white male worker endure. Why?

Exploiting Demographic Change

Obviously demographic change is a feature of contemporary U.S. society. The population is aging, thanks to longer life expectancy and the post-baby boom decline in fertility. There is considerable immigration and, for the first time in U.S. history, immigrants from both Asia and Latin America greatly outnumber those from Europe. Immigration patterns and differences in birthrates are causing the majority white population to grow more slowly than the minorities of African, Hispanic, and Asian descent.

Of course, most societies, at most moments in their history, experience some sort of demographic change and, not infrequently, their members define such change as troubling. Certainly U.S. history has been marked by nativist and anti-immigrant movements, eugenics campaigns, and calls for population control. The responses to *Workforce 2000* can be understood within this context: the garbled assertion that white males were vanishing from the workplace became the centerpiece for a variety of warnings about demographic change. Contemporary pessimism about the future turned relatively technical, mundane labor statistics into a sign of impending disaster.

Perhaps the most striking feature of the shocked reactions to *Workforce 2000* was the range of claims that could be linked to workforce projections. Commentators on both the right and the left found meaning in the imminent disappearance of white male workers. *Workforce 2000* was released by the Department of Labor during the second Reagan administration. Although it was the finding regarding the proportion of white males among net workforce entrants that captured the attention of most commentators, the main thrust of the full report was very different. The report worried that the national supply of sufficiently skilled workers might prove to be inadequate to fill the jobs of the future—jobs that would require more education and greater skills. (For a critique of *Workforce 2000*'s "supply push" approach to labor policy, see Mishel and Teixeira, 1991.) The shrinking pool of white male workers "thought of only a generation ago as the mainstays of the economy" was simply one aspect of a potentially inadequate labor supply. Thus, *Workforce 2000* was a Labor Department contribution to Reagan-era claims that drugs in the workplace, schools' failure to prepare students for the workforce, and other aspects of contemporary culture threatened the nation's ability to compete in international trade.

But claims about threatened white male workers also contributed to a darker conservative interpretation. By supposedly documenting the vanishing white man, *Workforce 2000* seemed to offer hard evidence of immigration and affirmative action gone out of control. Thus, Richard Bernstein's (1995) critique of the multiculturalism movement uses *Workforce 2000*-based claims that only 15 percent of new workers will be white males to argue that multiculturalism could have catastrophic, divisive consequences as the workforce changes.

The same *Workforce 2000* claims appealed to liberals, who also found ways to couple the changing workforce to pessimistic scenarios for the future. Most often, they argued that women and minorities (who supposedly would constitute the vast majority of new workers) were ill-prepared to fill the jobs of the future. As Representative Augustus Hawkins, Chairman of the House Committee on Education and Labor, put it: "the population which will be the most critical to our nation's future employment and productivity needs—women and minorities—is the least prepared to take its place in the workforce of the 21st century because of historical discrimination in education and employment, and because of poverty and poor academic preparation" (U.S. House of Representatives, 1989a: 3). Some even worried that the Social Security system might collapse in the early twenty-first century, because the minimally skilled workforce of low-paid minority workers would be unable to support a growing population of retired white male workers. Naturally, these scenarios could be used to endorse a range of educational, job training, and affirmative action programs, such as Hawkins's proposed Workforce 2000 Employment Readiness Act of 1989.

These government programs had private-sector counterparts:

> Ten years ago, nobody called himself a "diversity trainer." Today, there are some five thousand nationwide, with more hanging out their shingles daily. The trainers—or "facilitators"—trace the origins of their profession to 1987, when the Hudson Institute released its report, *Workforce 2000*, predicting that by the end of the century only 15 percent of those entering the workforce would be American-born white males. *Workforce 2000* was taken as a firebell in the night by many American-born white male businessmen: It happened to General Custer, it can happen to us. (Ferguson, 1994).

By the mid-1990s, references to *Workforce 2000* had diminished in general-circulation newspapers and magazines, but they remained common in the business press, particularly in specialized periodicals on personnel and human resources issues. Like diversity trainers, executives responsible for personnel could enhance their value to their corporations by repeating claims about dramatic changes in the workforce.

Conclusion

There is nothing terribly surprising about the story of the reactions to *Workforce 2000.* Hoping to command attention in the social problems marketplace, claimsmakers crafted the report to emphasize the changing nature of the workforce. Innumeracy allowed both the claimsmakers and their audience to garble the report's findings, highlighting the dramatic—albeit mistaken—claim about the virtual disappearance of white males from the future workforce. This error took on a life of its own; it continues to be cited—by conservatives and liberals, journalists, government officials, and people in the private sector—as evidence of a dramatic, troubling demographic transformation in the immediate future. *Workforce 2000,* then, is yet another example of doomsday rhetoric in social problems construction.

It is, however, important to consider some implications of these claims, implications that rarely get articulated or examined. The subtext in virtually all *Workforce 2000* claimsmaking is that female, immigrant, and minority workers are different from—and probably less qualified, less competent, and less desirable than—white males: "the labor market will be increasingly comprised of disadvantaged minorities over the next 13 years" (Johnston and Packer, 1987: 90). There is no discussion of the possibility of assimilation, no acknowledgment that those desirable white male workers are descendants of the Irish and the southern and eastern Europeans whose arrival produced nativist outrage in earlier eras. There is no recognition that the gaps in educational attainment and standardized test scores between whites and minorities have been closing, no mention that females, on average, complete more schooling than males. Instead of depicting demographic change as gradual, something that is likely to continue to be accommodated through ongoing shifts in culture and social structure, claims inspired by *Workforce 2000* envision a sudden lurch into a threatening future.

Once again, we are reminded of the unfashionability of the idea of progress. It would not be impossible to view twentieth-century U.S. history in terms of improved health, a rising standard of living, greater equality, increased education, and other indicators of social progress. But references to improvements in the past and calls for further progress are uncommon. Instead, contemporary social problems claims seem to depend upon imagery of impending societal collapse, rather than any promise of a good—let alone great—society. Claimsmaking rhetoric emphasizes threats, loss, decline, and the prospect of things getting much worse. Poised at the beginning of the third millennium, we prefer the rhetoric of fear to the rhetoric of hope. Our glass is not just half-empty; it is leaking—probably through a big crack.

15

Schooling Stories: Three Paths, Two Tragedies, One Vision

Ruthanne Kurth-Schai and Charles R. Green

The narratives and recurrent imagery of educational policy discourse—those exemplary stories that describe and advise and dominant symbols that signal and shape—have an ambivalent status in educational policy. On the one hand, the concept *tale* in policy analysis is usually employed invidiously with the assumption that the "rational analyst" is beyond needing such a construct, but is aware that particular tales are "at work" to perpetuate certain values, perspectives, and practices. On the other hand, all participants in policy communities tell stories (Skoldberg, 1994; Kahne, 1996). From Plato's advice in the *Republic* (625)—e.g., ". . . we should do our utmost that the first stories that they hear should be so composed as to bring the fairest lessons of virtue to their ears"—to William Bennett's current preferred examples in *The Book of Virtues* (1993), educational stories, we are told, are important. All of us, moreover, can tell schooling stories that are at once personal and shared in our culture and politics. Finally, the participants in formal schooling are actively involved in storytelling—stories are the essence of educational philosophies, curriculum, pedagogy, and public policy discourse.

Our educational tales are predominantly cast in journey terms with metaphoric paths with distinctive features leading to desired destinations. This idea resonates across many cultures. For us in the West, our formal educational journeys are rooted in the word "curriculum," which means running a course, often one complete with hurdles. A pathway for learning (a route already mapped for us but one we must take ourselves) seems especially apt as we metaphorically travel through internal (personal) and external (social/historical) landscapes. "In traveling a Pathway we make stops, encounter and overcome obstacles, recognize and interpret signs, seek answers, and follow the tracks of those that have something to teach us" (Cajete, 1994: 55).

Three Paths, Two Tradegies, One Vision

In this chapter we identify three clusters of educational explanations, descriptions, and prescriptions that present distinctive but interrelated paths and their associated tales of direction and destination. We map and interpret these three educational policy paths on a "philosophical grid," point to each path's pedagogical emphases, and suggest some distinctive features of their associated politics. Philosophy itself comes from reflection on and refinement of the tales, metatales, and archetypes that form stories. Educational stories evolve and are consciously constructed to answer perennial philosophical questions about reality, social order, knowing, and meaning. In U.S. public policy, education is mythologized as the great equalizer of persons and as a main route to a democratic society. Our stories promise opportunities for both individual fulfillment and social participation. *Essentialism, progressivism,* and *holism* become alternative but connected educational pathways with exemplary tales employed to realize these ambitions.

Essentialism (Plato, 1961; Russell, 1926; Adler, 1982; Hirsch, 1987) and progressivism (Rousseau, 1911; Dewey, 1916; Brameld, 1956; Freire, 1973; Weiler, 1988) dominate current educational policy and associated political conversation. The essentialist and progressive educational forms are described in tales of individual struggle for personal fulfillment and social democracy. These tales become tragic as educational paths are blocked or fail to lead either to personal fulfillment or to a vibrant democracy. Despite sincere intentions and efforts, inevitable flaws result in, at best, partial successes. The tales may include some declarative elements that are "romantic exceptions" in which the good should and, on rare and heroically effortful occasions, does triumph over significant challenges. There are even a few (dark) comic moments of parody and satire in the exemplary tales, but the dominant resolution remains personally and socially tragic. Our educational ambitions are not met; we are neither personally nor democratically fulfilled.

The third educational path with its distinctive stories, here called holism (Krishnamutri, 1953; Bopp, et al, 1989; Miller, 1992; Bowers, 1993), is much less coherent than the essentialist and progressive forms. We explore it to clarify its defining visionary characteristics in hopes of moving beyond the propensity for tragic resolutions of educational policy. We do not believe educational policy tragedy is inevitable. It is possible to develop tales strategically and encourage recurring images that provide a new political vision and policy imagination for education. Holism offers a third path, connected to the other two, but branching out with inspirational/adventure tales that provide a vision of escape from tragic resolution by transforming conceptions of personal fulfillment and democracy (while working toward their realization) within a global/planetary context of sustainability (a challenge not foreseen by those who plotted the essentialist and progressive tales).

Essentialism

"Eddie Thompson is now a judge."

She said that aloud even though she was completely alone in her office. Her computer had been on screen saver for a long time, but she was staring intently at it as if it were a cloudy window.

"Judge Thompson has become one of our star graduates," she mused. When he was in school and she was a Master Teacher, the District had been known statewide for its academic excellence. But it had declined in recent years as it struggled with a changing population, a city in transition, new program initiatives, and all sorts of state mandates. A lukewarm state assessment last year had in fact become a core issue in the recent school board election and the victories of two new members who had promised "reform."

She was troubled as she continued to stare at the screen. While she was mindful of her rather precarious position as the district's first female superintendent, she found herself feeling the most concern for the prospects of her own children. Rachel was just starting middle school and Nathan was a junior at one of the high schools. It had been a long time since the voters had approved a school bond issue and the state was barely staying even with inflation in its share of the budget. The buildings were sliding toward disrepair. There wasn't enough money for all the requests. Staff morale was on the edge.

She was troubled but not confused. Eddie Thompson, an African American from a poor inner-city family, had made it. Now he was a judge. He had gotten into a good college and had gone on to a law career in large part because these schools had equipped him to compete. The school board election was over and so was her ambivalence. There had been enough problem-bashing, hand-wringing, and passion about everyone's favorite code words, from "multiculturalism" to "creationism." She knew what programs and what directions were needed. Eddie Thompson signaled the need for basic, focused, well-disciplined instruction. Advanced literacy, cultural knowledge, critical thinking, and competence in science and mathematics were what prepared students for this competitive world.

In the silence of her office she could hear voices of opposition. One she could almost see in her darkened computer screen, the Master Teacher from Nathan's high school. He, who was also on the union negotiating team, would talk eloquently of elitism, of freezing the teachers out of participating in policy making, and of dividing students by narrowing recognized achievement to a short list of criteria. The drop-out rate would increase, he would predict, because many students would not be supported by either their situation or their families. They would not be motivated by stiffer academic demands, and they would just leave school, become lost to society, or perhaps worse, fall into drugs and crime. The Master Teacher was very persuasive at these meetings and he was really good in the classroom. But his educational progressivism was demonstrably flawed in principle and practice.

Years ago, this district had not been hesitant about academic excellence, in advocating the highest forms of integrity, or in recognizing the best knowledge and the best learning. Seasoned teachers should be listened to, but it was the elected school board members and the superintendent they selected who were responsible for setting school policies, shaping the organization, and prescribing the curriculum. Meeting tough standards for learning things that really mattered was what got Eddie Thompson to the bench, not having teachers and students participating in well-meaning diversions. Trying to get the current Eddie Thompsons to feel included by lowering academic standards, by caving in to popular culture, by offering electives that encouraged avoidance of basic learning that was essential, and by not insisting on the highest levels of learning and character, all had contributed to this familiar crisis.

The state assessment was painful for her, but it had been mostly accurate. She could see the faces of the school board in her computer screen. She could hear their voices in her quiet office. They would quickly agree with the direction she would propose to them tomorrow. They would join her in challenging the drift away from what was essential and in moving toward teaching what all of them knew to be right. They knew Eddie Thompson, too. They knew what had gotten him onto his achievement track and now he is a judge.

Essentialism: Rooted in tales told about the American Revolution, the Declaration of Independence, and the U.S. Constitution, and elaborated in response to late-nineteenth-century growth and diversification, public education's philosophy and policy became centered by the efforts to provide universal access to a common literacy, a common core of knowledge, and common values applicable across time and cultures (Spring, 1994).

The essentialists depict the educational journey as largely an individual quest for distinctive excellence through which one accumulates the knowledge base and cognitive abilities necessary to live a productive life. The individual learner's progress is acknowledged and rewarded by achieving and maintaining position in competitive intellectual, social, and economic hierarchies. It was the hope of the common schools movement that by mandating mass, public education, the path toward personal and material fulfillment would be open to all individuals, regardless of their social position. Public schooling, through teachers as primary agents, would assume the role of guiding individuals along a narrow but clearly defined path by holding learners accountable to universally held standards of excellence. The teacher, as trusted authority, would skillfully lead learners to humanity's highest thoughts (e.g., Socratic method) and to the most useful tools for shaping the world around them (e.g., scientific reasoning). As all would be offered the same invitation to excel, manifest differences in needs, abilities, and interests would be understood and accepted as differences in personal motivation, effort, and merit. As all would follow a singular, upward path toward shared goals, learners would experience a sense of solidarity and purpose through schooling. By assembling individuals to assume earned roles in established hierarchies, much the way industrial assembly lines produced standardized products for mass consumer markets, public schools would also play an important role in preserving social unity, stability, and continuity.

Tragedy begins to take shape as tales of exemplary success teach that to win means others must lose, and there is always "more" that must be won and possessed. Distinctions among civilization, citizenship, and commerce are blurred as knowledge becomes explicitly treated as a commodity. Among the implications for democracy is the shift in locus of power (responsibility for advocacy) to rest squarely on the shoulders of each individual—the student, parent, teacher, administrator, school board member, legislator, tax payer. Theoretically one gains power and influence in these roles through individual achievement. In reality public schooling promotes selective and largely static hierarchies of knowledge, economic security, status, and power. While essentialist stories promise otherwise, individual merit and effort seldom overcome the barriers imposed at birth. Universal access to a standardized, meritocratic, commercialized educational system does not result in universal access to self-fulfillment or in democratic participation. Tragically, political passivity, a risk-aversive stance toward social/political change, proliferation of adversarial and defensive social/political relationships, and a predominant focus on organized efforts to control from above an increasingly diverse population comprise the unintended legacy of essentialist educational policy.

Progressivism

"I can't believe this is happening again!" he had almost shouted as he stormed out of the room. He knew he had slammed the door as he left. Now, seated in his darkened classroom, he also knew he had again failed to make the school board understand. "They just don't get it!" he muttered.

It wasn't that way in his classroom. Even in the dark he could make out the "organized chaos" of the physical features—the clusters of desks, the oddly angled tables, the computers with several chairs at each. He could feel the presence of his students, what they were going through, their unique yet paradoxically common configurations of energy, confusion, and insight. He could identify with their struggle, their evolving dreams, their confrontation with greed, violence, and various forms of oppression right here in this school. He was proud of their achievements on group projects, especially their work in developing a student governing system that satisfied them.

Down the hall, in the auditorium, the school board members were quibbling over parliamentary procedures so that they could pass quickly this year's litany of elitist educational reforms to be imposed on already overburdened teachers and troubled students. The superintendent was pushing strategies to improve standardized test scores, narrow and specialize the curriculum, increase school discipline, and enhance student and teacher performance through even more strenuous competition and top-down control.

"Twenty years of struggle for another meeting like that?" He had worked hard and smart, mobilizing scarce resources, creating alliances, and attacking the "system" in many places. His first teaching position was at Central—the largest, toughest, most traditional school in the district. That was where he wanted to be, where his idealism and energy were most needed. He had risen quickly through the ranks of the union, had become influential on the endless curriculum development committees, and had been a vigorous worker on several school board campaigns. He had become visible in the whole district as a student advocate, an active colleague for his fellow teachers, and a major thorn in the side for the administration. His friends often referred to him as tireless and heroic. His opponents saw him as preachy and disrespectful. He reflected again on what he saw as his few successes outside his own classrooms, beyond the walls of his own school. Most of his efforts had been blocked, not by principled argument, public debate, or systematic analysis, but instead dissipated by a thoughtless school bureaucracy and ignored by an out-of-touch school board.

He was tired, deeply tired, of trying to extend progressive programs beyond his classroom and small circle of like-minded colleagues. Now it was taking most of his attention just to focus on his own students in this school, in this difficult neighborhood, and on the daunting challenges these students faced. The evening's anger was ebbing as he promised himself again to withdraw from his union activities, quit going to school board meetings, and commit his efforts fully to his students in his classroom. He knew he made a difference there. The union was negotiating around the edges of conditions of work—important maybe, but not central to these kids' needs. The school board wasn't listening—the administration couldn't listen! The classroom was the best he could do.

Progressivism: Progressive educators also pursue universal access to personal fulfillment, but turn their path toward overt equity goals. Knowledge is still acquired largely through personal effort and merit, but now with the goal of acquisition redirected from mainly personal gain toward granting *voice* and *influence* to the disadvantaged. Knowledge is explicitly acknowledged as power. Learners are encouraged to accumulate knowledge so they can increase their power to advocate for themselves and for others who share their concerns and interests (Dewey, 1916; Shor, 1992). The teacher, as broker, gathers and guides the learner through multiple resources and varied experiences so that students might join together in the social construction of knowledge that is valued based upon its relevance and utility for specific persons in specific communities (e.g., the project method, Kilpatrick, 1921). The definition of valued knowledge is thus expanded beyond the narrower cognitive conceptions that became standardized along the essentialist path to assert value for the emotional aspects of identity and the reality of education as an explicitly political project.

Education remains largely an individual journey but one that leads to broadened self-identities and community responsibilities. Broadened identities are achieved through greater cultural integration and community participation, in flatter educational hierarchies, with interchange of teacher and learner roles. Classrooms are to extend into community life. Communities are called upon to restructure patterns of social and economic privilege to guarantee movement from goals of equal access toward goals of equal power, participation, and performance for all learners in public educational systems. Equal opportunity to pursue personal fulfillment and economic security is to be supported by equitable school financing. Democracy is to be advanced by teaching advocacy skills and by developing strong school-community partnerships.

Struggling to move from present inequities toward a more egalitarian future, pervasive and abstract systems of social exploitation are identified and demystified so that individuals need no longer attribute their positions of disadvantage primarily to personal inadequacies. Personal identity is defined in relation to oppositional oppressor/oppressed categories as a means of first clarifying the causes and dynamics of social injustice and then motivating principled social action to alleviate it (Freire, 1973).

It is here that a second tragedy begins to unfold as hopes for progress are raised but not fulfilled despite intense efforts expended. Although progressivism provides significant insight into the nature of the gap between the haves and have-nots, the feasibility of its proposed strategies to bridge the gap and to improve the quality of social relationships is deeply problematic. In an increasingly complex and troubled world, is it possible to sustain dialogue and to work together constructively across difference merely when the oppressor and the oppressed are made fully aware of the implications of their positions for their own lives and the lives of those they love (Narayan, 1988)? Is it possible to redistribute valued resources (wealth, status, power, opportunity) on a large scale, or to expand the resource base to bring all up to the quality of life experienced by those who are now socially and economically stable and secure? Though deep in the heart of every progressive lives the hope that with sufficient commitment and skill such questions can be answered "yes!" years of valiant but failed attempts have proved otherwise.

Progressivism remains ambivalent on individual achievement while defining democratic participation as pursuit of an agenda of personal gain or commitment to advancing the cause of an organized interest/identity group. Social concerns constructed out of personal and interest group agendas are then addressed at the risk of a failure to build common values and community. Building advantageous coalitions grows more difficult, policy imagination is diminished, and political tragedy interweaves with classroom discouragement. Universal access to an educational system driven by individual and special interest group advocacy does not result in universal access to self-fulfillment and deepened democratic participation (Lowi, 1969; Barber, 1992, 1996; Sandell, 1996).

Progressives cannot easily adopt common essentialist responses to an increasingly obvious educational tragedy by giving up (passively accepting privilege) or by adopting a cynical nostalgia (attempts to return to a golden age). Some progressives retreat to niches of control (e.g., a grant-funded program, a charter school, an innovative classroom) and try harder. There is passion that grows out of continued failure and an admirable willingness to persist in the face of unbeatable odds. Such educators and policy advocates become portrayed by themselves and others as perpetual burnout victims. They risk drifting toward lower expectations for themselves, their students, and their society. They increasingly settle for exceptional "romantic" moments of success and learn to thrive on failure-driven passions without a broader, inspiring, and sustaining tale.

The intertwined paths of essentialism and progressivism that are our current educational policy lead to nonsustainable material and cultural expectations in an increasingly fractured social order (Bowers, 1987). By continuing to follow these paths we set ourselves up for either apathy and cynicism or repetitive and debilitating experiences of failure. Deep tragedy is the inescapable resolution of these dominant educational tales.

Holism

Suddenly things snap into focus.
I've been pursuing unity all my life,
But could only glimpse the monstrous vision in fragments;
It has haunted me for years.

Each time I sighted it, I struggled to make it concrete.
At first, it seemed I only had a sculptor's yard of unfinished figures
Then it slowly began to make sense,
Gathered from glimpses and inferences.

More and more, this mysterious life comes together.
It may take years more to reveal the whole.
That's all right.
I'm prepared to go the distance.

Holism: In this short poetic meditation, Deng Ming-Dao (1992: 346) offers a fleeting glimpse of the unique form of storytelling embraced by educational holists across time and cultures, that of the *inspirational adventure tale.* Such tales are told to focus our attention on the most intense and significant learning experiences of our lives—those times when we deeply *know* and, in response, are deeply *changed.*

While not new, holism remains an unclear, promissory path aspiring to reconstruct the American educational metamyth to enrich the objectives of personal fulfillment and social democracy while adding considerations for sustainability. Part of the holists' political difficulty is a strategic attempt to avoid sharp debate and direct conflict with travelers and maintainers on the other paths. Thus, a major challenge for holism is to define itself positively and integratively—to attempt to incorporate the best of what other perspectives have to offer rather than defining itself in opposition to their inadequacies. Perhaps an even tougher problem for holists is the tendency for opponents to dismiss them as fuzzy-minded, romantic, and fundamentally naive in their refusal to engage in "intellectual criticism wars" or the common forms of "educational politics as usual." To avoid becoming a third failed educational path, holists must evolve a deliberately integrated approach to philosophy, pedagogy, and policy—an effort of imagination that transcends conventional categories and "politics as usual." They must write a plausible adventure tale.

This will be a tale of knowing. What does it mean to deeply know? For holists, deep knowing is essentially *relational;* it occurs within a context of connections that are close, personal, intensive, gracious, compassionate, just, enduring, mutually beneficial; relationships that are, in a word, *intimate.* Holists struggle to support the development of intimate relationships across multiple dimensions of learning: *intrapersonal learning* (relational experiences promoting full development and integration of mind/heart/body/spirit); *interpersonal learning* (experiencing intimacy on a person-to-person basis, building connections that build community); and *transpersonal learning* (connecting in life-affirming ways with nonhuman entities and broader social and physical systems and forces).

As each individual is fundamentally connected to the whole of humanity and nonhuman nature, deep knowing is at once intensely personal and fundamentally communal (Bowers, 1993). Personal transformation occurs in *communion* (i.e., connection, communication, resonance, and harmony) with broader social and biophysical worlds and is then radiated through intricate webs of relationship. Its effects are strengthened and enhanced when communion is created across dimensions of difference. Life is sustained, not when interaction across difference is merely tolerated or actively restricted, but when those possessing unique and distinctive attributes interact and evolve together. Individual, societal, and biophysical diversity is cherished and protected because it provides opportunities for creative synthesis and renewal. Thus it is through efforts to initiate and sustain intimate, diverse, and multidimensional relationships that deep knowing and deep change occur.

Holists reach beyond the essentialist and progressivist paths as they struggle to develop and integrate a *spiritual* dimension along with the intellectual, emotional, moral, and political dimensions of learning and life. Within a holistic context, spirituality is described and experienced as the inspirational "kaleidoscopic" moment at which understandings that have beckoned yet eluded one suddenly "snap into focus." Though extremely difficult to capture in words, such moments are characterized by an intense and elegant integration of insight, sensation, and emotion. Valued knowledge, in a spiritual context, is received as a *gift* (Kurth-Schai, 1992). It is not earned and acquired through individual effort or merit, but instead is bestowed as a blessing, and thus received with feelings of elation, surprise, wholeness, and humility. The inspirational quality of such moments is further enhanced by the simultaneous experience of deep *mystery*—the complex interplay of doubt, fear, and wonder that challenges our deeply held illusions of control and certainty and compels us to abandon these. Herein lies the centrality of the spiritual element of holist tales, for only if we are "haunted" by "monstrous" and beautiful visions; only if we are driven by intense joy, curiosity, and uncertainty can great risk taking and adventure, can deep learning, take place.

Holists' key themes—intimacy, inspiration, spirituality, resonance, communion, risk, mystery, and adventure—are strange ones to introduce into educational policy conversations. But their political implications include a nonoppositional style with emphasis less on rhetorical claims and more on successful holistic performances. A holistic educational policy turn implies stories that will emerge through attempts to imagine and act upon three interrelated transformations: one intellectual, one technological, and one political.

(1) *A transformed conception of teaching/learning:* If sustainable self, societal, and environmental identities and interactions are the objectives, the conceptual transition from treating knowledge as commodity to understanding knowledge as gift must be accomplished. Knowledge is a gift to be received, developed, and shared by all. Its gift quality is a function of its ability to develop and sustain intimate relationships through its exchange. In this view, learning involves deriving personal meaning from intense, complex, and multidimensional experience; determining how the gifts of knowledge received or constructed might be made accessible and beneficial to others; and remaining continually open to new insight gained through participation in varied and diverse relationships. It is through full engagement in these processes that each individual's identity as a uniquely *gifted self* can emerge. Holism introduces into educational policy discourse a conception of excellence that is inclusionary, diversified, and defined within the context of significant social relationships; one that values self-development and self-expression balanced with sensitivity and creativity in response to the needs and contributions of others.

Specific challenges include helping all participants (students, teachers, administrators, policy actors) whose educational experiences have emphasized competition to regain the levels of confidence, trust, and respect necessary for constructing knowledge in collaboration with others; to develop imaginative approaches to advocacy and conflict resolution that are not defined, motivated, and ultimately defeated by oppositional category traps; and to develop new ways to organize resources and assess the quality of educational interactions and outcomes. Overall, processes of teaching and learning centered on gifts defy passivity and uniformity, and challenge current conceptions of predictability and control.

(2) *A transformed conception of the nature and role of technology:* The industrial assembly line (long-serial technologies) model for essentialist public education rolled-off standardized "products" for what was understood as its labor and consumer markets. Progressivism became shaped largely as a *mediating technology* in which schools and teachers tried to broker among groups (of knowledge makers and users) and build communities—not just assemble status-ready individuals. *Holistic technologies,* in closer harmony with human and nonhuman natures, are possible and necessary in order to transform education. This type of technology is based on expanding conceptions of information (not just instrumental data), is informed by a more diverse understanding of human learning (not only narrow cost/benefit problem-solving), and must be responsible to its human and nonhuman constituents (not just to existing dominant hierarchies). Such "open reflective systems" will require transformed philosophies, pedagogies, and policies. Technologies of the material are one of the distinguishing achievements of our present culture and metaphors in our policy stories. Technologies of the spirit are a new requirement for the holists' educational vision and a challenge to our collective imaginations.

(3) *A transformed politics:* Educational systems that include both conventional competitions and gift exchanges are imaginable, inspiring, and imperative. Public policies for what is needed (sustainable self-fulfillment and social democracy), but not yet well understood or supported, require a politics that reduces the contingent either/or oppositions, and is broadly accessible and accountable. To the politics of essentialism, holism can add more diverse, inclusive, and loftier goals than the quest for private virtue and the privileges of personal economic success. For progressives, holists can add inspiration to familiar interests and communion to fragile coalitions. The politics for this requires openness, creativity, and courage with a political imagination broadly defined, expressed, and experienced; with participation broadly understood and practiced in all parts of life; with coalitions becoming broader, deeper, and understood as intrinsically dynamic; with operating conceptions of power becoming multipolar and multiparadigmatic; and with an expanded sense of political time (beyond short-term budget and election cycles).

In their politics of schooling, holists do not reject the visions and achievements of essentialism and progressivism, but try to understand these intertwined tragedies in order to move in ways that incorporate the best of their aspirations. Holists give us "glimpses and inferences" of an inspiring destination, a fragmentary sketch of an adventurous and risky path, and a vision that is at once educational and political. By valuing a broader range of knowledge (cognitive, emotional, spiritual, and political) and by inventing deeper learning situations (diverse pedagogies and flexible technologies situated in many places) public education can be shaped by successful holistic performances. Policy analysts and evaluators can take such holistic opportunities to broaden and deepen their criteria and methodologies. All of us could take these challenges to become adept in less oppositional, more inclusive, and situationally imaginative political conversations.

Conclusion

The politics of schooling require new tales and reinterpreted myths to inspire and renew travelers for their adventuresome journey along the familiar paths of essentialism and progressivism and especially as they join the new path of educational holism. Perhaps constructing an intelligible holistic educational inspirational/adventure tale and reshaping our social myths will not be such an extensive challenge. Gregory Cajete reminds us that "Our lives are expressions of the myths we live by and that live through us," and challenges us to begin "the process of living a mythically literate life." That is: "to live life with conscious reference to more than day-to-day concerns . . . and to live a life of cultivated relationships with significant people, practices, institutions, and the world, based on guidance from inner and creative sources" (1994: 118). From such collaborative and creative efforts, new narratives will emerge, new paths will be explored, and new schooling stories will be told to reflect and guide public educational policy.

Part V
Tales of Global Policy

16

Rumors of Apartheid: Myth and Stereotype in U.S. Foreign Policy Toward South Africa

Donald R. Culverson

Research on U.S.-Africa relations traditionally focused on Cold War-driven assumptions that limited policy options and the range of domestic participants in policy making (Young, 1984). However, political turmoil in southern Africa in the mid-1970s compelled scholarly reevaluation of U.S. linkages to the problems in that region, as well as the scope of domestic involvement in the policy-making process. Scholars recognized how civil and human rights interests began to intrude upon the policy domain of state agencies and transnational corporations (Clough, 1991).

However, these approaches remain incomplete, as they overlook critical linkages between foreign policy formulation and domestic political culture. Foreign policy ideas and imagination emerge from national political values and the material arrangements that sustain them, along with elite efforts to orchestrate agendas. American experiences from slavery, colonialism, and segregation, as well as civil rights activism, shaped attitudes toward Africa and joined with strategic decisions and commitments embodied in the Cold War to supply the foundations of policies. In a similar vein historian Michael N. Hunt's analysis of U.S.-China relations emphasizes "how powerfully a sense of national mission, stereotypes about 'Orientals,' and a dedication to a particular path of political and economic development combined to shape the American approach to China" (1987: 163).

Although productive during the early Cold War years, confidence in such beliefs eroded with U.S. disengagement from Southeast Asia and with congressional and other domestic challenges to presidential dominance of foreign affairs. Claims and complaints by groups traditionally excluded from policy debates gained legitimacy, and revealed not only the encroachment of new interests, but also perspectives and norms different from those held by more established members of the polity (Tolley, 1990). First world/third world, short-term/long-term, human rights/militarization, corporate/local autonomy, and other tensions acquired political salience as proponents expressed concerns about policy problems as well as visions of more equitable foreign relations. The quests for new ways in which to interact with the global community can be usefully viewed as stories that present commonsense ways to talk and think about creating meaning and order in foreign policy. Such foreign policy stories provide explanations of the origins of conflicts and their likely trajectory. They offer a cause for adherents, a sense of flow and direction for passive bystanders, and warnings to challengers.

This chapter explores presidential responses to decolonization movements in Africa, and focuses on the Carter and Reagan administrations' storied constructions of apartheid and the problems it posed for policy makers. These constructions relied upon political ideals and myths nourished in American exceptionalism, and invoked notions of domestic race relations and political reform as appropriate models to guide reforms in South Africa. In contrast to earlier presidents, who faced few obstacles in sustaining friendly relations with Pretoria, Jimmy Carter and Ronald Reagan confronted steady domestic and international opposition to efforts to shape the pace of change in one of the last colonial outposts in Africa (Metz, 1986).

Initiatives by Carter and Reagan toward political turmoil in South Africa represent stories designed to distance new administrations from the presumed failed policies of their predecessors, and to define an appropriate American role in southern Africa's transformation. Some of the stories relied upon deep historical roots, while others simply invoked triumphant moments as guiding ideologies (Staniland, 1983). This chapter examines how these stories revolved around three central elements that shaped U.S. responses to the challenges posed by apartheid: (1) the global political climate, its opportunities, and limitations, (2) race relations, and (3) identification of the appropriate mechanisms for guiding political change. Understanding these stories offers insights into how each administration constructed South Africa and the problem of apartheid in ways that reinforced the outlines of its policy preferences.

Stories as Instruments of Engagement and Evasion in U.S.-South African Relations

Public debate about U.S. policy toward South Africa intensified after the 1960 Sharpeville massacre of black protesters and the 1976 Soweto uprisings. Although American relations with that region originated in the late eighteenth century, the domestic constituency for Africa consisted of small groups of businessmen, diplomats, and missionaries with direct ties to

South Africa. Consequently, concern about racial domination, and its centrality to the production and distribution of wealth in southern Africa, rarely penetrated U.S. political discourse.

American images of Africa derived from the myths and stereotypes furnished by European colonialism, but acquired a momentum of their own. Literature, film, and journalism periodically revived and enlarged upon the "Dark Continent" as the appropriate theme for situating Africa in the landscape of American global experiences (McKinley, 1974; McCarthy, 1983), and for reinforcing the relationship between the United States and South Africa. Scholarly concentration on economic and strategic relations seldom explored how cultural dimensions of crossnational ties strengthen mutual dependencies. For example, American business played a major role in establishing South Africa's mining infrastructure and in developing its agriculture, radio, film and tourist industries (Hull, 1990). South Africans viewed the U.S. as a source of ideas on management and social control, rather than just technological innovation and markets. Additionally, as linkages expanded between intelligence and law enforcement agencies, foundations, universities, and churches, these ties enlarged the repository of American images that fortified dominant myths about Africa.

Political developments throughout the international community converged at the end of World War II to gradually erode the foundations of America's special relationship with South Africa. African decolonization movements grew rapidly, as did the U.S. social justice community. Civil rights and human rights groups capitalized on the material and symbolic opportunities provided by wartime mobilization to strengthen linkages between their demands and those emanating from anticolonial forces. Furthermore, the defeat of fascism generated consensus around the world on the abhorrence of political systems based on the denial of basic human rights (Shepherd, 1977). Yet South Africa, frightened by demands for black political rights, elaborated and codified its system of racial separation (Lodge, 1983). The resulting conflicts, symbolized by state violence against blacks, increased charges of Washington's indifference to Pretoria's gross violations of human rights (Clough, 1991).

The social construction of reality that provided coherence to U.S. policy toward South Africa and other states in southern Africa maintained an immunity to changes in the domestic interest articulation system for decades (Minter, 1986). These stories arose from colonial and Cold War notions of power, economics, racial hierarchy, obligation, and morality, and explained a world composed of separations—causes from effects, present from future, and "we" from "they." Policy makers expressed broad principles and goals, but their views of African societies as requiring order, strong nation-states, and regional security reinforced stereotypes circulating among less informed audiences (Staniland, 1991).

The private and public comments of American policy makers from the 1940s through the 1960s hinted that old stereotypes maintained a significant place in the fabric of institutional thinking about Africa. For example, Sumner Welles, Franklin Roosevelt's expert on colonial matters, concluded that independence for Africans was inconceivable as they represented "the lowest rank of human beings" (Hunt, 1987: 162). This pattern of thinking continued with the Truman administration. As late as 1946 the president's private references to blacks as "nigs" and "niggers" suggest that he had not abandoned a mind-set about race derived form his formative years in Missouri (Hunt, 1987).

Prominent State Department officials such as George Kennan and Dean Acheson aggressively endorsed Eurocentric worldviews that relegated Africa to the margins of U.S. global concerns (Brinkley, 1992). Despite the potential problems posed by failure to address racial questions in both the United States and South Africa, Truman administration officials remained captive to orientations that encouraged identification with white supremacist states in southern Africa. Indicative of this spirit, Waldermar Gallman, U.S. ambassador to South Africa, stressed the "common heritage and experience that have left an identical imprint on the character and outlook of both peoples," especially the effort to "force the frontier back" (quoted in Borstelmann, 1993: 199).

The Eisenhower administration drew its understanding of South Africa almost exclusively from the apartheid government. Pretoria's staunch anticommunism accelerated the expansion of U.S. diplomatic, intelligence, and military agency ties to South Africa, and reflected administrative hesitance in addressing racial conflict at home. With pressures mounting to amplify federal desegregation efforts, Dwight Eisenhower assured his southern supporters that while he shared their anxieties about integration, white racism reflected badly on America's image abroad (Cook, 1981: 173). As decolonization evolved from an idea to a postwar reality, U.S. officials adopted a "middle road" strategy that acknowledged the right of self-determination for colonized peoples, but warned against "premature independence" that could undermine European interests (Byroade, 1953).

The killing of unarmed black protesters at Sharpeville in 1960 revealed the Eisenhower administration's sensitivity to the South African government. The State Department disciplined public affairs officers for publicly declaring that the United States "condemns violence in all forms" and that it upheld the right "of all African people in South Africa . . . to obtain redress for legitimate grievances by peaceful means" (*New York Times*, 3/23/60: 1). The president distanced himself from the remarks by explaining apartheid as a "touchy thing" and insisting that critics remain sensitive to the needs of a U.S. ally (*New York Times*, 3/26/60: 2). Eisenhower's reactions reflected less concern with the injustices of the apartheid system than with the violent images it furnished its critics.

The election of John F. Kennedy in 1960 and Lyndon Johnson in 1964 seemingly produced mandates for reforming race relations abroad as well as at home, but the deference of both presidents to Cold War concerns reduced inclinations to challenge the colonial regimes in southern Africa. These doubts resulted in the dominance of policy discourse by elements most conciliatory toward South Africa within the administration, Congress, the Democratic Party, and the business community, and hindered civil rights momentum from spilling over into foreign affairs.

Although Kennedy assembled an impressive array of policy makers with experience in Africa, their interest in accelerating the pace of decolonization could not overcome the entrenched Europeanist perspectives of veteran cold warriors such as Dean Rusk, Paul Nitze, and George Ball, a protégé of Dean Acheson. Ball strongly opposed demands from administration liberals that Kennedy pressure South Africa to moderate its apartheid institutions (1968: 226–59). While Ball's realist approach emphasized Pretoria's contributions to the anticommunist struggle, less refined arguments emerged from business leaders and members of Congress. Clarence Randall, former president of Inland Steel, urged Kennedy to remain patient with Pretoria as "the white people of South Africa are charged with a great responsibility toward the black people, and they know it. At heart they are our kind of folk. In the end they will do right. Let us give them a little more time" (quoted in Randall, 1963: 80). Missouri Representative Clarence Cannon echoed these sentiments in criticizing Kennedy for acting in favor of "the jungle Bantu and against the white man, who was there before the native African" (*New York Times*, 3/4/63: 5).

As administration efforts to alter policy discussion on South Africa faltered, they increasingly limited African initiatives to diplomatic communities at the United Nations and Washington, and the emerging black American constituency for Africa. Rising U.S.-Soviet tensions in the early 1960s reinforced the dominance of the CIA and the Defense Department in shaping Johnson administration responses to South Africa. Adhering to the idea of Pretoria playing a vital role in resisting Soviet influence in southern Africa, this outlook rationalized American reluctance to challenge that government.

Africanist and other attempts to inject humanitarian concerns into American policy experienced further isolation as the Treasury and Commerce departments accepted the inflexibility of the South African government, but encouraged corporate engagement as a way of addressing U.S. military and economic concerns. For example, when disagreements emerged within the administration in 1964 over whether to permit the Lockheed Corporation to honor its contract to sell antisubmarine aircraft to the South African air force, Secretary of Treasury Douglas Dillon urged immediate approval as the "South African payments alone of about $85–100 million in 1965–66 would be a major step toward achieving the sales target for the military component of our balance of payments program" (quoted in Noer, 1985:162–63). Secretary of Commerce Luther Hodges offered a simpler rationale. "If we do not allow sale of the Lockheed aircraft the French and British will pick up the business" (quoted in Noer, 1985: 163). By the end of Johnson's term, the Cold War orientation remained unshaken as government and corporate officials constructed Pretoria as an ally (Ball, 1968: 259) and the bustling city of Johannesburg as "the Detroit of South Africa" (Myers, 1968: 96–97).

As Eisenhower's vice-president in the late-1950s, Richard Nixon strongly urged reevaluation of U.S. ties with Africa independent of the needs of the European colonial powers. However, the "new" Nixon who entered the White House in 1969 refined the global realist outlook that assigned southern Africa and racial discrimination to the periphery of East-West relations. After Nixon took office, National Security Council (NSC) adviser Henry Kissinger and his staff conducted a comprehensive review of all regions of the world and produced a series of National Security Study Memoranda. NSSM 39 concentrated on U.S. relations with the white states of southern Africa, and outlined five options:

1. Developing a stronger relationship with the white regimes, while ignoring their domestic policies as factors in deciding U.S. relations
2. Encouraging communication with the white regimes, rather than ostracism, as a way of producing moderate change in their domestic policies
3. Symbolic dissociation from the white regimes, but maintaining substantial relationships with them
4. A substantial reduction in ties with the white states
5. Adoption of a lower profile and reduction of the U.S. presence in the region. (El-Khawas and Cohen, 1976: 103–5)

The administration chose option two, which resulted in the upgrading of relations with South Africa and the other settler-dominated states in southern Africa. However, each of the five options rested on the assumption that the white-controlled states would remain in power and that they had removed any threats of black insurgency. While NSSM 39 expressed dominant administrative perspectives on southern Africa's linkage to broader security concerns, it may have concealed more traditional racial attitudes and stereotypes. According to *New York Times* reporter Seymour Hersh White House staffers who monitored presidential telephone calls found that Nixon repeatedly referred to blacks as "niggers," "jigs," and "jigaboos," and that Kissinger frequently expressed contempt for black people (1983: 110). NSC aides overheard another conversation with Kissinger in which Nixon commented on Secretary of State William Rogers's successful trip to Africa: "Henry, let's leave the niggers to Bill and we'll take care of the rest of the world" (Hersh, 1983: 111). Roger Morris, a member of Kissinger's NSC staff, assessed the impact of these attitudes:

> There is no documentary evidence—save perhaps the inaccessible White House tapes on national security subjects—that this racism was the decisive influence in Kissinger-Nixon policies in Africa, Vietnam or elsewhere, policies for which there were other arguments and reasons, however questionable. But it is impossible to pretend that the cast of mind that harbors such casual bigotry did not have some effect on American foreign policy toward the overwhelming majority of the world which is nonwhite. (1977: 131–32)

Recognizing the institutional and individual attitudes that shaped U.S. policy toward South Africa is not simply to label them racist. Nor is it to say that reliance on familiar analogies and constructions of Africa indicated pathology. The point emphasized is that this generation of policy makers developed in a segregated world in which blacks occupied subordinate roles and where Europeanist concerns circumscribed their worldviews. African crises presented challenges that encouraged drawing from familiar but limited personal and national experiences with African Americans and Africans.

The Cold War reinforced the tendency to impose customary frameworks on Africa. Ironically, it inspired three developments that undermined the foundations of the early postwar order. First, the international spotlight exposed America's own racial problems and accelerated the pace of civil rights legislation. Second, civil rights advocates attempted to extend their agendas into foreign policy arenas. Third, expanding U.S. economic, military, and political commitments required enhancement of the public and private sector institutional infrastructure for interaction with the external world. Each development blurred established distinctions between domestic and international politics, and provided insights into how foreign policy acts as a mirror on one society, much as a lens through which it projects national aspirations and values on other societies.

The Search for a New South African Story: Carter and the Revival of the Civil Rights Dream

In the spring and summer of 1976 presidential candidate Jimmy Carter campaigned heavily on the theme of morality in foreign and domestic policy making. Carter attempted not only to implicate the Nixon-Ford administration in the corruption surrounding Watergate and the policy failures in Vietnam, but also to suggest that the emerging global community presented a more hospitable climate for promotion of American interests. After his election, Carter outlined a commitment to develop a more restrained, populist foreign policy. The centerpiece of this policy, the use of human rights as a criterion in assessing the effectiveness of American external relations, represented a significant departure from other Cold War presidencies. Carter officials' initial rhetoric implied an eagerness to work with the international community to enforce respect for human rights (Carter, 1977: 957–62). This optimism produced a global story that stressed how participation in multilateral arrangements promoted restoration of American influence and power.

Carter administration stories about race extended the human rights focus by acknowledging America's racial past and repackaging the 1960s civil rights achievements as lessons to export to the world. Furthermore, Carter saw the civil rights experience as a tool for sharpening America's focus on the fragile states of southern Africa.

> It would be a great help to this nation if people in public life were to be made aware of the problems of Africa through a significant Black interest in Africa. Americans might not have made the mistakes we made in Vietnam had there been an articulate Vietnamese minority in our midst. (quoted in *Africa Report*, 1976: 20)

To reformulate strategies toward Africa Carter assembled a team of policy makers that included Ruth Schacter Morgenthau, Anthony Lake, Goler Butcher, Donald McHenry, Richard Moose, and Andrew Young, who not only had experiences dealing with African issues, but also represented important links to two underrepresented constituencies in the foreign policy-making process, professional Africanists and black Americans. Young, the former civil rights activist who was appointed ambassador to the United Nations, played the administration's most visible role on southern Africa. He expressed this faith during the 1976 campaign by proclaiming that America's triumph over segregation represented a model for Africa.

> I think our country has established through our own experience in race relationships, and particularly in the South, an understanding of this very sensitive issue of black and white people within the same community . . . with the special knowledge in our country, I think we might be a help in Africa. (quoted in Danaher, 1985: 161)

The new ambassador's confidence in civil rights narratives continued well into his first South African visit when he urged blacks to appropriate the 1960s boycott strategies employed in the United States. Moreover, he warned Afrikaaner politicians and businessmen that they had met their match in Carter, who shared their rural, fundamentalist Christian origins and outlook (*New York Times*, 5/23/77: 1). Carter officials' use of civil rights analogies led to charges by former diplomat George Ball (1977) that they promoted "happy multiracialism" as the remedy for apartheid.

While administration appraisal of the international climate and its prescriptions for race relations reform departed from convention, its outline of appropriate mechanisms of political change in South Africa varied only slightly from earlier U.S. postures. This story, perhaps the one most widely shared within the administration, allotted a major role for enlightened corporate capital (Coker, 1986). Carter described his expectations:

> I think our American businessmen can be a constructive force in achieving racial justice within South Africa. I think the weight of our investments there, the value the South Africans place on access to American capital and technology can be used as a positive force in settling regional problems. (*Financial Mail*, 1976: 1)

Young echoed this theme in asserting the priority of the economic arena as a catalyst for political integration. Relying on civil rights imagery, he argued that contrary to popular belief, the "private sector began to move toward desegregation in the South as early as 1960–61, while Congress didn't get around to the Civil Rights Act until 1964" (U.S. Congress Committee on Foreign Affairs, 1977: 6–7). Earlier, Young expressed reservations about the divestment movement's call for more punitive measures: "I don't see sanctions. I would see an arms embargo of course, but sanctions have seldom worked" (*New York Times*, 1/3/77: 3).

This reconstruction of America's struggle with racial segregation granted policy makers a framework for envisioning South Africa's transformation. More often than not, it identified the problem, proposed a remedy, provided a rationale for American action (or inaction), and pronounced rhetoric that enjoyed substantial credibility among policy makers, the corporate community, and selective publics. However, just as their domestic stories about "we shall overcome" ignored the roles of leftists, nationalists, and labor activists, administration attempts to encourage dialogue between contending forces in South Africa prefigured conversations among the Nationalist government, the business community, and "legitimate black leaders" (*New York Times*, 10/18/77: 1). The civil rights stories selectively borrowed from stages of the southern movement such as the freedom rides, and fast-forwarded to Atlanta's rise as a black business mecca, while ignoring obstructions that confronted the movement's northern shift and expanded social justice agenda. The civil rights narratives supplied an entree into racial crises in southern Africa, but they obscured matrices of power relationships that invalidated assumptions about the symmetry between America and South Africa. The resulting constructions of apartheid increased policy-maker reliance upon rhetoric rather than political will, and generated a kind of policy discourse unable to respond to entrenched obstacles to change in the United States and in South Africa (Nixon, 1994).

Reagan and Constructive Engagement

The Reagan administration demonstrated complete rejection of Carter's approach to the global community and its interpretation of how to confront the problems of racial inequality in southern Africa. From Reagan's perspective responsibility for the turmoil in the region rested with the Soviet Union. During Carter's first year in office, Reagan insisted that U.S. concern with human rights in southern Africa "clouds our ability to see this international danger [e.g., Soviet interests] to the Western world" (*New York Times*, 6/10/77: 1). As president four years later Reagan embarked upon a costly military buildup designed to reassert U.S. dominance and contain Soviet influence. Reagan stories reinforced the notion that any Soviet gain represented a U.S. loss, and that maintaining a strong South Africa, even at the expense of overlooking its internal policies and military aggression in the region, served American security interests (Fatton, 1984).

Reagan assembled a team of Africa policy advisers for the 1980 campaign, but avoided comment on that region. The group included Richard Allen, Nixon's liaison to the Portuguese dictatorship, diplomat Ernest Lefever, and academics such as Hoover Institute historian Peter Duignan, who favored détente with Pretoria, and Georgetown University political scientists Jeane Kirkpatrick and Chester Crocker (Deutsch, 1980: 4–7).

Unlike Young and his successor McHenry, who devoted considerable effort to delegitimizing South Africa, Kirkpatrick, Reagan's ambassador to the United Nations, allotted new space for a relationship with Pretoria. She believed that the United States could not work with Marxist states, which she labeled totalitarian. Yet South Africa, an authoritarian regime, presented no such problem as she felt that "racist dictatorship is not as bad as Marxist dictatorship" (*The Economist*, 3/29/81: 34) Crocker, who had contributed to Nixon's NSSM 39, became assistant secretary of state for Africa and developed its constructive engagement policy. He urged Americans to consider the needs and insecurities of whites before endorsing demands for majority rule (Crocker, 1992). In addition to accepting South Africa as an "authoritarian" state, the administration envisioned expansion of the republic's role in the Western defense system (Reagan, 1981: 196–97).

The administration relied upon a set of racial stories long discredited throughout Western democracies. From Reagan's perspective the existence of a system of racial discrimination provided insufficient evidence to call for dismantling apartheid. Like Nixon's relaxed stance toward the settler states a decade earlier, Reagan viewed white South Africans as a force of stability, with Western values and institutions. At press conferences Reagan announced the end of apartheid, the repeal of segregation laws, and the government's restoration of black citizenship rights.

> South Africa has eliminated the segregation that we once had in our own country, the type of thing where hotels and restaurants and places of entertainment and so forth were segregated—that has all been eliminated. (Quoted in Green and McColl, 1987: 144)

In response to criticism that constructive engagement served as U.S. endorsement of the South African state's killing of black demonstrators, Reagan declared: "But I think to put it that way—that they were simply killed and that the violence was coming totally from the law and order side ignores the fact that there was rioting going on in behalf of others there" and "it is significant that some of those enforcing the law and using guns were also black policemen" (*New York Times*, 3/21/85: 1). Reagan maintained that turmoil in South Africa resulted from "blacks fighting against blacks, because there's still a tribal situation involved there in that community" (*New York Times*, 6/14/86: 1). To him apartheid existed merely as an anachronism for blacks until they acquired the skills to enter the modern economy, rather than a politically refined, technologically advanced, internationally reinforced system of racial inequality that constrained black life from cradle to grave.

Reagan expressed confidence in American corporate capital, rather than government intervention, as the most effective means for promoting political modernization in South Africa. He maintained that U.S. companies utilized "what was called the Sullivan code," which merited credibility because "Sullivan is a black clergyman" (*New York Times*, 5/21/86: 1). From this perspective, change unfolded through peaceful and gradual means that would not disrupt market forces, which stimulated evolution toward Western democratic values and institutions. As what became the successful international sanctions drive intensified, Reagan drew from racial and corporate narratives to discredit demands for punitive actions against South Africa:

> The truth is that most black tribal leaders there have openly expressed their support of American business investment there, because our American businesses go there and observe practices with regard to employees that are not observed by South African companies. (*New York Times*, 12/7/84: 1)

Perhaps no other twentieth-century president relied upon stories as did Reagan (Combs, 1993; Rogin, 1987). Consistent with the major thrust of his presidency, Reagan's stories about South Africa relied on dichotomies: black unrest resulted from Soviet subversion, the United States should resist impulses to intervene in the internal affairs of Pretoria, and American corporations represented the most important forces of change in South Africa. The corollary to this interpretation—that blacks could not resist Soviet domination, that the white South African government should command America's respect as it maintained stability and upheld Western values, and that U.S. companies acted as agents of reform—arose from assumptions that guided Nixon initiatives toward southern Africa. Reagan stories also attempted to legitimate understanding of apartheid in ways that rationalized détente with the white supremacist government in Pretoria, as well as its campaigns of destruction against neighboring black states in southern Africa (Minter, 1994).

Conclusion

This chapter has suggested that stereotypes and myths reflect policy-maker perceptions of other societies, and that they encourage use of parallels from more familiar cultures and episodes. This approach challenges frameworks that focus on geopolitical strategy and elite interests as the primary foreign policy determinants, and it compels blending those ingredients with national experiences in race relations and social change to produce more comprehensive understandings of U.S. policy toward South Africa. Additionally, it emphasizes how policy-maker constructions evolve in accordance with changing national aspirations and locations within the global system.

Traditional crisis-driven studies of U.S. interaction with Africa derive from an assumption of limited American influence because of European colonial dominance. However, recent analyses suggest that America's role in Africa, especially in South Africa, is best explained not as an autonomous force, but as a global power that directly and indirectly exerts influence through multiple structures and agents (Nye, 1990). This perspective raises questions about how American stories about apartheid may have camouflaged the South African state's pathology and delayed the full impact of international sanctions.

Since the late nineteenth century the United States and South Africa have maintained a mutual attraction that led to enhancement of each country's integration into an expanding global system (Vieira, Martin, and Wallerstein, 1992). Policy-maker rationalizations of the relationship relied on stories about the benefits of access to natural resources and markets, and white South African contributions to the struggles against communism. Informed by American exceptionalist notions of the world as pliable, these dominance and control stories seldom, if ever, acknowledged the debilitating consequences for nonwhite South Africans. Furthermore, they ignored how these constructions retarded the development of the civil and human rights infrastructures that matured in the post-Vietnam era as critical instruments for enabling Americans to understand and interact with political transformation movements throughout the world. As South Africa looks to the United States for models to assist its transition to a nonracial society policy makers will undoubtedly again face the temptation to recirculate stories about the instructiveness of American race relations and social change experiences. Perhaps the break in the cycle will occur, not only with the enlistment of more representative stories and storytellers, but with a willingness to question how past stories have been told.

17

National Security Tales and the End of the Cold War

Joseph Peschek

In the winter of 1993–94, Americans learned that the U.S. government had sponsored radiation experiments on human subjects for over forty years, often with only questionable consent. According to details provided by Department of Energy Secretary Hazel O'Leary, the experiments included irradiating the testicles of prison inmates, placing radioactive milk in cereal and feeding it to mentally retarded children, and giving radioactive pills to pregnant women. U.S. soldiers were also deliberately exposed to radiation during the Desert Rock exercises in Nevada during the 1950s.

One of the most bizarre experiments took place in the northwest corner of Alaska in the late 1950s. The Atomic Energy Commission (AEC) hoped to study the impact of radioactive fallout on the Arctic environment by monitoring the effects of an aboveground Soviet nuclear test. When the wind blew in an unanticipated direction after the test, frustrating the monitors, radioactively contaminated material from an underground test site in Nevada was hauled in and dumped. Native Alaskan villagers in Point Hope, Kivalina, and Noatak were not told that their environment had been laced with radioactive isotopes that, in at least one site, exceeded by over one thousand times the amount permitted by federal regulations.

What explains these actions? An answer was suggested by an aide to Secretary O'Leary, Robert Alvarez, who stated, "The public record is very clear that the United States Government engaged in deliberate acts of deception against the American public in the 1940s and 1950s in order to prosecute the nuclear arms race" (quoted in Lewis, 1993: A17). Nuclear radiation was seen as an important weapon in the context of the Cold War. Following the bombings of Hiroshima and Nagasaki and the nuclear tests at the Bikini Atoll, a 1947 report of the Joint Chiefs of Staff concluded "of primary military concern will be the bomb's potentiality to break the will of nations and of peoples by the stimulation of man's primordial fears, those of the unknown, the invisible, the mysterious" (Quoted in Makhijani, 1994: 25). The irony of this study was pointed out in a report of the International Commission for the Prevention of Nuclear War and the Institute for Energy and Environmental Research: "Thus, in about the same period that the U.S. military was engaged in reassuring the U.S. public about the safety of tests and, implicitly, of radioactivity, it was considering the threat of radiation to 'break the will' of nations and of peoples" (quoted in Ridgeway, 1994: 15).

In 1950 Joseph Hamilton, a biologist working with the AEC, warned that the tests might have "a little of the Buchenwald touch" (quoted in Schneider, 1993: A8). But the Cold War legitimized a wide array of means to the end of containing the communist foe. Its amorality was underscored by the 1954 Doolittle Report to President Dwight Eisenhower on covert activities, which argued, "there are no rules in such a game. Hitherto acceptable norms of human conduct do not apply" (quoted in Brands, 1993: 61).

Our growing knowledge about the experiments on human subjects, details of which have been trickling out for many years, can serve as a point of departure for reflection on the Cold War and the national security state in the United States. In many ways the Cold War was the crucible in which the tests were conceived and conducted, and the exaggerated sense of threat that drove them was also used to justify arms buildups, military interventions, covert operations, and lying to and deception of the public.

In this chapter, I explore the politics of the Cold War by discussing the role of regnant national security tales, especially those involving Soviet "threat inflation," in two periods of Cold War mobilization: the onset of the Cold War under Truman in the 1940s and the return to Cold War tensions under President Jimmy Carter in 1979–80. These tales helped to shape U.S. foreign policy and American public opinion, and sidelined alternative approaches to national security. One of my aims is to show the contestable and constructed character of the assumptions on which policy was based by contrasting official, public explanations of policy with competing facts and assessments that were put forward within the U.S. state at the time, and disclosed by critical scholars later. I also suggest that the official Cold War paradigm, with its emphasis on Soviet perfidy, prevailed because it was functional to the global projects of U.S. policy planners. An alternative story about the objectives of national security policy, which went well beyond containment and reveal much about American politics and economics, can be sketched by rereading key statements and texts by state officials. In that sense I offer an "internal" reading of the Cold War and do not present a full-blown explanatory theory of its intersystemic and structural dimensions. In a brief conclusion, I indicate how the legacies of the Cold War limit thought and policy in the 1990s.

Making Cold War I

> The task of a public officer seeking to explain and gain support for a major policy is not that of the writer of a doctoral thesis. Qualification must give way to simplicity of statement, nicety and nuance to bluntness, almost brutality, in carrying home a point.
>
> —Dean Acheson (Quoted in Brands, 1993: 33)

In 1993 a Pulitzer Prize was awarded to David McCullough for his massive, sympathetic biography of Harry S. Truman. During the 1992 presidential campaign McCullough was invited to the White House to brief George Bush on the man from Missouri. Bill Clinton and Ross Perot also sought to associate themselves with the Truman legacy. Though his approval ratings were middling when he was in office, Truman is revered by many politicians and much of the public today. Yet as Gar Alperovitz and Kai Bird pointed out in a critical review of McCullough's book, there is a vast discrepancy between what historical records show and what is widely believed about Truman, the president who shaped the defining features of America's Cold War foreign policy (Alperovitz and Bird, 1993).

Consider the atomic bomb. Truman learned of the Manhattan project only after succeeding Franklin Roosevelt in April of 1945. In four months' time he would twice order use of the new weapon, ending the Pacific war in moves that were applauded for their sober realism. In recent years scholars have called into question the official rationale for the use of bomb, as J. Samuel Walker, chief historian of the Nuclear Regulatory Commission, explained: "The consensus among scholars is that the bomb was not needed to avoid an invasion of Japan and to end the war within a relatively short time. It is clear that alternatives to the bomb existed and that Truman and his advisers knew it. . . . It is certain that the hoary claim that the bomb prevented one-half million American combat deaths is unsupportable" (Walker, 1990: 110). The "hoary claim" was made by Truman himself, who said he never lost any sleep over his decision. But historian Barton Bernstein has concluded, "there is no evidence that any top military planner or major American policy maker ever believed that an invasion [of Japan] would cost that many lives" (1986: 38). Declassified files show, according to Bernstein, that military planners thought an invasion would result in 20,000 to, at worst, 46,000 American deaths. Beyond the issue of American casualties is the question of whether the U.S. practiced "atomic diplomacy" to strengthen its position against the Soviet Union. If this is true, then "the bomb was dropped not as the last act of World War II, but as the first act of the Cold War" (*In These Times*, 1995: 2).

These issues were central to the controversy over an exhibit on the dropping of the atomic bomb that opened in June 1995 at the Smithsonian Institution's National Air and Space Museum. The exhibit, which featured the fuselage of the Enola Gay, the B-29 that dropped the bomb on Hiroshima, had been greatly scaled back from an earlier plan that included photos of the bomb site and a narrative that challenged the necessity of dropping the bomb in order to end the war with Japan. This version was withdrawn after it was attacked as unpatriotic by the American Legion, the Air Force Association, and eighty-one members of Congress. Columnist Charles Krauthammer wrote that such exhibits "reflect the extent to which the forces of political correctness and historical revisionism, having captured the universities, have now moved out to dominate the museums and other institutions of national culture." He recommended that the museum "display the restored Enola Gay in reverent silence, with only a few lines explaining what it did and when" (quoted in *In These Times*, 1995: 2). In this way was the prevailing story of the atomic bomb protected from contamination.

By 1947 the Soviet Union was replacing the Axis powers on the American enemies list. In an "all-out" speech to Congress on March 12, Truman committed the United States to a global struggle with the Soviets, declaring that "It must be the policy of the United States to support free peoples who are resisting attempted subjugation by armed minorities or by outside pressure." Truman's address took place in the context of an internal conflict in Greece that was falsely depicted by American officials as an attempted Soviet takeover. Joseph Stalin was hostile to the left-wing guerrilla movement in Greece and provided no assistance to it. America was coming to the aid of an undemocratic right-wing Greek government, previously propped up by the British, that engaged in a "white terror" campaign against its critics. "Right across the country," Daniel Yergin has written, "people suspected of leftist sympathies were being fired from their jobs, refused new employment, harassed, beaten up, arrested, deported, and often killed" (1977: 291). A pattern was set. The Soviet hand was seen behind every revolutionary struggle, while U.S. officials, cast as agents of freedom in a historic drama, bolstered repressive regimes against the Red Threat.

Inflating the Soviet threat helped to "scare the hell" out of the American people, in Senator Arthur Vandenberg's words, and built public support for Truman's containment policy. As Emily Rosenberg points out, the concept of "national security" entered political discourse in the mid-1940s because it provided "common discursive terrain" that united various political actors around one basic goal: "the necessity of vigorous American global involvement in the postwar world. Usage of the new term snowballed after 1945, along with the attempt to marshal popular support for globalist and then strong anti-Communist policies" (Rosenberg, 1993: 280). The National Security Act of 1947, which created the National Security Council, the Central Intelligence Agency, and the Department of Defense, was the institutional embodiment of this new concept.

Inside the government, out of public view, analysts reached quite different assessments of Soviet capabilities and intentions, as several investigations of declassified documents show. For example, Frank Kofsky studied U.S. intelligence reports from 1946 to 1948 and found that "estimates of Soviet intentions were virtually unanimous in concluding that the Soviets currently had no wish to initiate hostilities with the West" (1993: 275). But intentions are one thing, capabilities another. Matthew Evangelista studied the capabilities of Soviet conventional forces in 1947–48 and found them extremely limited. As late as 1950, for example, half of the transport of the Soviet standing army was horse drawn. Many U.S. intelligence reports at that time underscored the decrepit state of Soviet forces. But partly in order to gain congressional and popular support for NATO, Soviet force capabilities were inflated by the U.S. military and State Department. Evangelista concludes, "the evidence now available shows that in the late 1940s the 'Red Juggernaut' was anything but" (1982–83: 138). These conclusions are consistent with the analysis of the State Department's Policy Planning Staff, in its first paper in 1947: "The Policy Planning Staff does not see communist activities as the root cause of the difficulties of western Europe. It believes the present crisis results in large part from the disruptive effect of the war on the economic, political, and social structure of Europe and from a profound exhaustion of physical plant and spiritual vigor" (quoted in Campbell, 1992: 26).

These studies indicate that American policy makers had an operative definition of security centering on economic interests and the control of resources in a reconstructed liberal-capitalist international system. Historian Melvyn P. Leffler has demonstrated that American officials developed a truly global conception of U.S. security prior to the onset of the Cold War, indeed even before the end of World War II. Moreover, defense analysts and intelligence officials of the time viewed the Soviet Union as a secondary challenge to an American-defined world order. As Leffler put it, "American assessments of the Soviet threat were less a consequence of expanding Soviet military capabilities and of Soviet diplomatic demands than a result of growing apprehension about the vulnerability of American strategic and economic interests in a world of unprecedented turmoil and upheaval" (1984: 349). In a later study Leffler quoted Truman: "If Communism is allowed to absorb the free nations then we would be isolated from our sources of supply and detached from our friends. Then we would have to take defense measures which might really bankrupt our economy, and change our way of life so that we couldn't recognize it as American any longer" (Leffler, 1992: 13). Reacting to the negative consequences of economic and political nationalism in the 1930s, American policy planners sought to shape a world system, based on free trade and capitalist production under American hegemony, that would promote economic growth, prevent a new slump, and forestall radical change at home, while undercutting war and revolution abroad.

These findings, based on archival research, do not resolve disputes over the origins of the cold war. Nor are they incompatible with recognizing Stalin's tyranny in those domains where he exercised control. But they undercut any view of the United States as a merely reactive party in the face of an implacable Soviet threat. They also tell a tale of national security at variance with the story presented to the American people during the Cold War.

Making Cold War II

The Carter years provide excellent material for a study in the politics of foreign policy and the role of national security tales in its making. A president less committed to Cold War policies than his predecessors ended his term embroiled in a "second Cold War" with the Soviets. Carter came into office as an advocate of military spending cutbacks, human rights, nuclear arms reductions, and a less confrontational approach to the Soviet Union. In a speech at Notre Dame University on May 22, 1977, Carter proclaimed, "We are now free of that inordinate fear of communism which once led us to embrace any dictator in our fear" (quoted in Smith, 1986: 66). By 1980 his rhetoric had changed. Carter spoke gravely of threats to peace represented by the hostage crisis in Iran and the Soviet invasion of Afghanistan, warned of the steady growth and increased projection of Soviet military power, and stated that "I am determined that the United States will remain the strongest of all nations" (quoted in Smith, 1986: 228).

One of the myths of the 1980s was that U.S. defenses were "neglected" during the Carter years, as the American government practiced "unilateral disarmament." But consider the following. After the Soviet invasion of Afghanistan in December 1979, Carter's policy package included reinstatement of draft registration, an embargo on grain exports to the Soviet Union, withdrawal of U.S. participation in the summer Olympics in Moscow, sales of military-related equipment to China, and new levels of support to client regimes in the third world. These steps came on the heels of the NATO decision to station 572 new medium-range nuclear missiles in Europe and shortly before the signing of Presidential Directive 59, a war-fighting nuclear strategy.

Carter's shift toward militarism predated the crises over Iran and Afghanistan, to which it was often seen as a response. Well before the hostage seizure in Tehran and the Soviet move on Kabul, the Carter administration supported modernized nuclear forces such as the MX missile; Trident submarines and missiles; and air-, sea-, and land-based cruise missiles, moved to upgrade third-world intervention capabilities through development of the Rapid Deployment Forces, and raised real defense expenditures every year in office, in sharp contrast to the decline in defense spending under Richard Nixon and Gerald Ford. Finally, despite President Carter's personal commitment to human rights, his administration did not seriously reduce material assistance to repressive pro-American regimes in the third world.

What explains Carter's move from the managerial politics of "global interdependence," associated with the Trilateral Commission and the Atlantic wing of the foreign policy establishment, to remilitarization and a new Cold War? Part of the answer is that public discourse about foreign policy, during the late 1970s, was increasingly dominated by the national security tales of a rapidly mobilizing Cold War policy current. Carter faced growing political pressure from a "Prussian" bloc of military officers, intelligence operatives, Cold War intellectuals, arms producers, and some domestic capitalists. Their flagship organization was the Committee on the Present Danger (CPD), whose founding statement in 1976 proclaimed, "The principal threat to our nation, to world peace and to the cause of human freedom is the Soviet drive for dominance based upon an unparalleled military buildup. . . . The Soviet Union has not altered its long-held goal of a world dominated from a single center—Moscow" (quoted in Sanders, 1983b: 183). America needed to get over its "Vietnam Syndrome"—the reluctance to militarily intervene in third world conflicts—and prepare to use force if necessary.

The CPD regarded Carter's early globalist approach as a new form of appeasement and a rationalization for a "loss of will" among the leadership class. The CPD had submitted fifty-three names to Carter for possible appointments and failed to receive a single one. "My views are unprintable," said Eugene Rostow, a prominent CPD member, in reference to the new Carter team, while another CPD leader, Paul Nitze, added, "Every soft-liner I can think of is in government" (quoted in Sanders, 1983a: 7). In 1977 the Senate Foreign Relations Committee held hearings on Carter's nomination of Paul Warnke to head the Arms Control and Disarmament Agency and serve as chief SALT negotiator. Warnke, a strong advocate of arms control and a defense adviser to George McGovern in 1972, was opposed by the CPD and other right-wing groups, who worked with Senator Henry Jackson, a major critic of détente. In his testimony Nitze characterized Warnke's views as "absolutely asinine, screwball, arbitrary, and fictitious" (quoted in Cox, 1982: 78). Warnke won Senate confirmation, but only by a vote of 58 to 40, a portent of political difficulties for Carter. In 1978 Carter expended much political capital on the Senate with his Panama Canal treaties, which were passed by 68–32 margins, only one vote over the necessary two-thirds majority. At about the same time all thirty-eight Republicans in the Senate broke with the "bipartisan spirit" of post-war American foreign policy and published a sharp attack on Carter. "In 15 short months of incoherence, inconsistency, and ineptitude," the Senate

Republicans argued, "our foreign policy and national security objectives are confused and we are being challenged around the globe by Soviet arrogance" (quoted in Reston, 1978).

A classic case of the shaping of national security discourse by the construction of a threatening enemy is the famous "Team B" report of 1976. In that year, under pressure from the CPD hawks, President Ford ordered CIA Director George Bush to establish an outside panel to evaluate the national intelligence estimates the CIA makes of Soviet capabilities. The panel, which came to be known as Team B, was comprised of hard-liners, several of whom were members of the CPD, including Richard Pipes (the chair) and Nitze. Though their report was not published, its contents were deliberately leaked to the press and widely disseminated just before Carter took office. Essentially the report argued that the Soviets were engaged in a massive military buildup, were outspending the United States on defense two to one, and were developing a civil defense program on the assumption that they could survive a nuclear war. Therefore, it was claimed, the United States must abandon the illusions of détente and counter these moves with its own military buildup. All of these claims were subjected to criticism, even within the foreign policy establishment, but by 1980 the arguments of the CPD and their allies in other hard-line policy groups were shaping public perceptions of the Soviet Union. Admiral Stansfield Turner, Director of Central Intelligence under Carter, described Team B as "outsiders with a right-wing ideological bent" who had an impact on official analysis: "The CIA team [Team A], knowing that the outsiders on Team B would take extreme views tended to do the same in self-defense" (Turner, 1985: 251).

The SALT II treaty became the object of intense opposition by conservative groups. The Committee on the Present Danger focused on elite opinion in Congress and the media. According to Dan Caldwell, the CPD from its founding in 1976 through December 1979 participated in 479 TV and radio programs, press conferences, and other public forums, distributed more than two hundred thousand copies of its pamphlets and reports, and had its leaders testify before Senate committees on seventeen different occasions during the hearings on SALT II. The mass public was reached through such organizations as the American Security Council, the American Conservative Union, and the Coalition for Peace through Strength, with combined memberships in the hundreds of thousands. These groups produced a series of short films sounding the alarm about alleged U.S. military weakness, one of which, "The SALT Syndrome," the Carter administration took seriously enough to circulate a sentence-by-sentence rebuttal (Caldwell, 1991: 104–5).

The national security tales that fueled this second Cold War were sustained by a high level of institutional, financial, and political organization that was part of the broader right-turn in American politics that began in the mid-1970s. To argue that Carter's rightward shift was in part a reaction to such forces is not necessarily to claim that it was based on an incorrect reading of international events. Indeed conservative policy currents in the United States argued that Carter was coming—too little, too late—to recognize reality. But were the tales of the right based on an accurate reading of international politics, or were the myopic perceptions of the 1940s being recycled? Examples in the areas of Soviet defense spending, nuclear strategy, and third world conduct exemplify the processes of threat inflation that occurred during the Carter presidency.

President Ronald Reagan and others claimed that in the 1970s the Soviet Union engaged in "the most massive military buildup in history," far outstripping the efforts of the laggard United States. Yet in the 1980s several reports of Reagan's own CIA in effect admitted this claim was overstated. First, total Soviet military spending was miscalculated, since the CIA's method was to estimate the costs of Soviet weapons and equipment in terms of what they would cost in the United States at prevailing dollar prices for materials and labor. Since wage and material costs were higher in the United States, Soviet spending was overstated. Second, the rate of growth of Soviet defense spending, previously thought to average 4 to 5 percent annually in the Carter period, leveled off after 1976 to a 2 percent annual rate, less than the growth rate of U.S. defense spending. Third, the largest category of Soviet defense spending, procurement of military hardware, was essentially flat in 1976–81, the CIA analysts later reported.

With regard to Soviet strategic capabilities, it was a central argument of the right that advances in Soviet nuclear forces had rendered U.S. ICBMs susceptible to a devastating first strike by only a portion of the Soviet long-range missiles. The cultural and psychological resonances of the "window of vulnerability" are obvious. Nitze used this scenario in his testimony against the SALT II treaty in 1979, and it was a central rationale for developing the MX missile and other modernized nuclear forces. Yet in 1985 General Bennie L. Davis, commander of the Strategic Air Command, told a Senate subcommittee on strategic and theater nuclear forces that existing missile silos were in much less danger of Soviet attack than previously thought and that the "whole question of a 'window of vulnerability' that was raised some years ago did not relate specifically to the vulnerability of missile silos." Reagan's Scowcroft Commission on strategic forces had already made a similar point (Ottaway and Pincus, 1985).

Finally, Soviet behavior in the third world in the 1970s was alleged to have violated the rules of détente and was taken as evidence of untamed aggression and expansionism. But the pattern of third world conflicts was not one of unbroken Soviet gains. While it is true that the Soviet presence in Angola, Ethiopia, Vietnam, and several other countries grew, the USSR lost influence in a number of countries in the 1970s, among them Egypt, and its acquisition of economic resources or strategic assets, such as the base at Cam Ranh Bay in Vietnam, was rather limited. It is also important not to confuse later Soviet involvement with Soviet instigation; political turmoil in third world states often has complex indigenous roots, as in Afghanistan or Nicaragua. Soviet foreign policy in the later Leonid Brezhnev era was "less adventurous, energetic, and threatening than conventional Western wisdom proclaims" (Steele, 1983: x).

I am not arguing that the Soviet Union was a passive status quo power, nor am I denying that the Soviets behaved unwisely and inhumanely. In my view the Cold War did involve a real, systemic struggle between rival forms of social organization. But to explain American foreign policy primarily in terms of responses to Soviet action is fundamentally misleading. Policy was shaped in the context of a complex set of political and economic agencies, goals, and conflicts. In the 1970s, for example, a wave of revolutions brought radical regimes to power in a number of third world countries, at a time when U.S. corporate investments and bank loans were mushrooming in semiperipheral areas. In this context the attainment of near parity in strategic forces by the Soviet Union seemed to limit U.S. global leverage. The fervent, almost apocalyptic national security tales of the late 1970s and early 1980s sprang from an America marked by "the subjective traumas of defeat, impotence and public ignominy which had lacerated the U.S. political establishment in the 1970s" (Hobsbawn, 1994: 247). But against the backdrop of economic crisis and third world challenges to American hegemony, the return to Cold War under Carter was also seen by business and political elites as necessary to maintain the international dominance by the United States.

Conclusion: Post-Cold War Quandries

The national security mentality of the Cold War led to distorted stories of the causes of problems in the world and of how the United States should respond to them, based on narratives that exaggerated the idea of a Soviet menace. These national security tales served to bolster a system of power that was subjected to a classic critique by C. Wright Mills, one of the few radical critics of the Cold War in the 1950s. For Mills the American power structure functioned to shrink the democratic public sphere, as public discourse was manipulated by elites and colonized by the market. Among the preconditions of democracy in a modern state were, according to Mills, a public sphere in which real issues were engaged, nationally responsible parties with clear positions, an engaged intelligentsia of genuine independence, and a media of open and genuine communication. These preconditions were being eroded by the "main drift" of the times, not least by the development of a national security state (Mills, 1958: 118–19).

The narrative deformations of the Cold War without a doubt intensified in the 1980s under Reagan, as we are reminded when revelations about Salvadoran death squads or Jonas Savimbi's rampages in Angola reach the news. But they persist when President Bill Clinton's Defense Department recommends a "two wars strategy" and when the president proposes a $25 billion increase in defense spending. They continue when the CIA portrays Haiti's Jean-Bertrand Aristide as an unstable radical, while Russia's Boris Yeltsin is lauded for his commitment to democracy.

Cold War consequences also include a relative neglect of domestic issues by our government, leading to higher child poverty rates, greater inequalities in income distribution, and more urban deterioration than in most other industrial democracies. Yet, as Ronald Steel argues, "A nation prey to drugs, guns, and violence, increasingly stratified by social class, torn by racial tension, and riven by insecurity, will be a weak player on the world stage" (1995: 86). After the Persian Gulf War in 1991, Bush proclaimed, "By God, we've kicked the Vietnam syndrome once and for all." But the end of the Cold War does not seem to have raised American self-confidence. If democracy is to be revitalized, assumptions about what constitutes American security need to be rethought and debated. A critical discussion of the national security tales that gripped America during the Cold War needs to be part of this process.

18

NAFTA Discourse: Tales of Sovereignty, Science, and Adjustment

Philip T. Neisser

To plumb the meaning of the North American Free Trade Agreement (NAFTA) as a political event requires a grasp of various stories of "America" and its position in the world, stories that are told, presumed, implied, and fought about in the various condemnations, justifications, and analyses of the agreement. The faith in "free trade" that supports NAFTA is rooted in a set of stories about postindustrialism, technology, and progress, stories themselves rooted in the tales that helped constitute the Industrial Age. To make a long story short, the United States has been constituted as a nation in part by means of tales that link spirituality, redemption, and virtue with sacrifice, suffering, and material progress. The NAFTA stories represent an adaptation of this discourse in response to a variety of interests and in the face of a new set of stories about "the global economy."

My focus in this chapter is on the tale-telling of NAFTA discourse, rather than the economic impact of NAFTA as a set of rules for trade among the United States, Canada, and Mexico. To focus on the rules for trade is to capitulate too easily to the prepackaged agenda created by the debate itself, as if the choice was simply whether to be "for" or "against" free trade. NAFTA is in many ways unsatisfactory as an agreement—it facilitates an inequitable form of economic growth and shrinks the space people have to speak up concerning the impact of economic change—but to simply be "against" free trade treaties is neither convincing nor practical. What we need is better agreements. To focus on the rules of NAFTA is, moreover, to miss half the action, much of which lies in what has been said by virtue of the fact that the agreement was proposed in the first place. It is almost as if the new rules were proposed in order to create a debate, rather than the other way around.

The discourse surrounding the ratification of NAFTA is especially dependent on, and invoking of, a story of the world more or less taken for granted by the project of social science, in particular of economics as a social science, a story rejected by the postmodernism at work in this essay.

Social science assumes as an axiom that a certain story of our lives must be the single accurate one, and that we should use the process of science to map this story as best we can (despite acknowledged complexity), thus reaching beyond fables to facts. By this view the future is determined by the facts of today, and perhaps by the decisions we make based on the facts. We fail to map our entire future, the story goes, only because there are too many facts, and some are too hard to measure.

This idea of social science is linked to a story about science in general: *Once upon a time we were ignorant, but science has been gradually uncovering the truth, the truth being a thing out there apart from what we think about it.* This tale may help people feel like they are somehow at home in the universe, a universe they can know, but it does not do justice to the fact that knowledge, whether produced through empirically rigorous social science, or in the everyday world of people plumbing each other's statements and behaviors, is a fundamentally political enterprise of representation and creation.

The commitment of social science to replicable empirical studies, the implicit goal being to one day arrive at "laws" of human behavior, must overlook unreflectively held beliefs that cannot be "measured," and it denies the play in life (and the play of power) created by the often realized possibility of reflection upon the previously taken for granted. Such reflection can, in a heartbeat, alter political possibility.

> The discipline [political science] betrays a longing for precisely what must always be missing from politics, a desire to substitute the putative laws of an imaginary social science for the inherent unpredictability and open-endedness of public life. (Dolan and Dumm, 1993: 1)

One way this renegotiability of human life is covered over is by means of a fundamental principle of the discipline of economics, one that holds that humans are self-interested, bargaining creatures. This principle supports a tale assumed to be valid by much of the discourse concerning NAFTA. *Once upon a time human history began, and since then individuals with material interests have compromised or fought over them, telling some stories to each other while they were at it.*

In any conventional economics textbook this story is told by means of the already mentioned assumption that interests are individual and material (or perhaps it is the story that dictates the assumption). By this view, "human wants are virtually unlimited," freedom is "the range of choices available to people," and "equity" is fairness with regard to the satisfaction of universal wants and the universal desire for freedom. Thus "scarcity is the basic economic problem facing all societies" (Byrns and Stone, 1987: 8–9).

This story takes certain interests as given. Some stories are, however, prior to interests. We construct identities under various constraints and partly by means of stories, and it is as such constructed selves that we conclude that this or that is in our interest. What concept of "the national interest" is taken for granted, reasserted, denied, and otherwise at issue in today's free trade storytelling? How is "the inherent unpredictability and open-endedness of public life" denied and therefore blunted in its power by the free trade discourse of sovereignty, science, and adjustment?

Here is President Bill Clinton, defending NAFTA:

> What we are seeing is a period of global stagnation which comes at the end of several years in which global growth did not necessarily mean more jobs or higher incomes in wealthy countries. We are living in a time of great hope where's there's more democracy, more adherence to market economics, when the wonders of technology are providing new areas of economic endeavor and millions of new successes every year in all continents, but where still there is so much frustration for those who cannot figure out how to make these changes friendly to them. (1993: 2199)

Clinton reassures with an update of a familiar tale. *Once upon a time human life was primitive, but market economics, democracy, and technology changed all that. Recently a difficult period came along (postindustrialism), but this is just more progress. We must adjust.*

This is not the only way people make sense of today's situation, but the alternative stories have been effectively marginalized in the NAFTA debate, leaving the mainstream discussion of trade issues to the protectionists, the proponents, and the doubters. The doubters, like the other two groups, largely accept the "scientific" story of markets and freedom, but are concerned about the "side effects" and "dislocations" caused by progress. Many otherwise excellent critics of NAFTA end their statements with counsel of adjustment and compensation, thus cementing the story of the world order as a natural outcome (Blank, 1993: 27, 35; Tobias, 1993: 47). Clinton for example was a doubter, and he and others parlayed their concerns into some "side agreements" that were certainly an improvement over the original treaty. This has, however, only fortified the idea of the economy as a machine independent of politics. Injustice becomes mere "cost," to be balanced against gains, and perhaps compensated for.

This is consistent with the way technology is routinely storied as an independent march of science that creates a given stock of jobs: one not determined by power, but by "efficiency." "Postindustrial" reorganization that is eliminating jobs and weakening the power of laborers is accepted as if it were a natural result of "computerization," just as by the 1920s "the assembly line as an emblem of industrial efficiency became a new 'common sense' " (Aronowitz and DiFazio, 1994: 27). The doubters and protectionists offer no challenge to this view of technology, adding that we must fight somehow to keep "our" jobs. *Once upon a time, "the" jobs were here in the United States, but now "they" are headed elsewhere. We need protection and/or more development to get more jobs.*

I defend here a different tale: *Once upon a time a treaty called NAFTA was imagined because some people needed to find a way to keep telling stories (to themselves and others) of sovereignty and progress, even as (or because) the credibility of such tales is weaker than ever.* NAFTA as an actual economic arrangement can be looked at as a small part of a process, long underway, which is weakening the power of once relatively autonomous wealthy industrialized states. Discussions of NAFTA, however, are typically glaring in their invocation of one of the most basic fables of modernity: that each "nation" charts "its" own way in the world (see chapter 1).

I speak of a story of sovereignty: *Once upon a time "the people" "founded" "the United States" and later others created "Mexico." The things that happen in each country are thus part of the history of that "country." The United States "developed," and now Mexico is "developing."* This idea of national autonomy is crucial to, and cemented by, many assertions of U.S. political life, for example the bedrock assumption, made by most U.S. historiography and political science, that the United States "is" a "democracy" and countries such as Mexico are "struggling" toward the same thing.

Paradoxically, exaggerations of sovereignty persist side by side with exaggerations of the independence of the international economy. *Once upon a time we were on our own but now we are part of a game of international competition. We need to make the rules fair (free trade) because it is the right thing, and also so we can win.* Here is Clinton again:

> what I tried to do . . . was to argue that we needed in America to face the future with confidence, to believe that we can compete and win, not to run away and not to pretend that these global changes had not occurred. (1993: 2200)

Somehow we are both our own masters (sovereign) and also in thrall to a "thing" called the global market. "We" must adjust to "it" (see chapter 19).

NAFTA is, to most economists, a set of steps that takes us a bit closer to "free trade" (Druhe, 1995: 18; Coyne, 1993: 68–73). Totally free trade is considered to be good by definition: it expands the range of voluntary exchange, which is "necessarily advantageous for all . . ." (Riggs and Velk, 1993: 15). This idea, that "markets" are a forum for a series of voluntary exchanges made by independent selves acting in their own interests, lies at the heart of a story oft-invoked more or less tacitly in the NAFTA debate.

Once upon a time rulers and other special interests combined with superstition to severely limit the range of free exchange and so the acquisition of wealth that by definition benefits all. Then a revolution of ideas supported a liberation of entrepreneurial energies. Nonetheless the defenders of free trade have had to continually struggle, against communists, misguided special interests (those, for example, who fight for trade barriers), and paternalistic do-gooders who want to use government to "help" others. These groups cause the overuse of government, which distorts exchanges and so makes the world poorer and more unfair.

This story justifies barriers to democracy in the name of democracy. In the ever-present "now" of partial free trade we must limit the power of people to use government. Popular causes that want the "wrong" things are defined as "special interests" that distort the market. Milton Friedman, for example, tells us to be wary of

> the internal threat coming from men of good intentions and good will who wish to reform us . . . they are anxious to use the power of the state to achieve their ends and confident of their own ability to do so. Yet if they gained the power, they would fail to achieve their immediate aims and, in addition, would produce a collective state from which they would recoil in horror and of which they would be among the first victims. (1962: 201)

This of course is consistent with a classic folktale of U.S. politics: *Once upon a time government was just the right size, but thanks to democracy, political ambition, and foolish ideas, we now have "big government."*

> According to economic theorist James Buchanan, the expansion of government purpose, function, and responsibility is all but inevitable in a democracy: every element of a democratic regime points in that direction. (Greenberg, 1985: 17)

This tale is appealing to many, but the rise of government is better explained as in part a necessary corollary to the dynamics of markets over time, and in part a by-product of much-needed popular resistance to so-called "side effects" of capitalism (Greenberg, 1985). The bulk of government supports markets in one way or another (investment, defense contracts, propping up demand, making social costs like pollution manageable, maintaining confidence, etc.), with a substantial portion also going to unessential supports to mostly well-off constituencies. Since most of those on the gravy train have power by virtue of their market position, even the ugliest side of big government is linked to the success of capitalism. It is not well conceptualized as its opposite.

Thus I point to this counterstory: *Once upon a time economic growth and economic security began to depend more on government subsidy and government regulation.* This tale, never very popular in the United States, was not invoked in the mainstream NAFTA rhetoric, which instead speaks of the battle between "free trade forces" and "special interests." A. R. Riggs and Tom Velk:

> The recent emergence of the United States as the single great power remaining could assist free trade forces. Danger lies, however, in new special interests, operating now on a global level. Protectionists who carry the banner of environmentalism and a list of work-place standards are already presenting tradeoff demands. (1993: 12)

Here with more tale-telling is Remi L. Wrona:

> The doctrine of free trade is in critical condition in the United States today, nearly doctored to death by bad medicine—currency manipulation, trade negotiations and barriers, subsidies and many other harsh political remedies that hinder the function of the body's natural immune system of supply and demand. (1995: 23)

And Andrew Tobias says of NAFTA that "almost everyone knows it's a good thing." This does not, apparently, include Congress or the people—the fact of opposition is "downright zany," says Tobias, because of the misfortune that "a Congressperson who wants to be re-elected follows the polls" (1993: 47).

These quotations exemplify the way NAFTA proponents plug into a story of a titanic struggle between rationality and irrationality, between the natural and the unnatural. The supposed irrationality of democracy must be limited to protect the long-term success of democracy, to be accomplished in part through sending the appropriate message of U.S. "resolve." "Had Clinton failed to best the protectionist forces, other governments would have demanded, in effect, if you can't control your special interests, why should we?" (Thomas, 1993: 30).

Tacitly invoking the story of progress, free trade proponents cast their opponents as less than rational by defining workers' troubles as temporary "dislocation."

> Where we would be today if we had not pursued the development of factory automation even though at the time it created some dislocation of labor? . . . let us give Mexico the opportunity for self-determination. If we believe in democracy, then we must create an economic environment that will allow people to exercise their democratic rights and participate in the economic mainstream that will determine their future and ours. (Wrona, 1995: 26)

The clear implications of the passage in context are that self-determination for the government/country/people (conveniently treated as identical at this moment, but not at others) will flow from free trade, but that such trade requires constraints on self-determination. Through the fiction of sovereignty ("we" pursued automation), and the promise of sovereignty in the future (we have to create the correct environment first), restrictions on democracy are justified. Thus Wrona invokes democracy when defending an agreement that allows laws passed in the United States, Mexico, and Canada "to be overturned in a single decision by a dispute resolution panel consisting of five individuals" (Druhe, 1995: 19). Apparently when it comes to "democracy," "politics" is a problem:

> we have found in this binational panel system [created by the Free Trade Agreement between the United States and Canada] a way of taking the politics out of international trade. This has been extended to the Mexico-Canada-U.S. agreement. . . . Therefore, we will have Canadian activities in Mexico governed by a judicial process with which we are all familiar. (Walker, 1993: 18)

One may well ask: who is the "all" of us familiar with international dispute settlement?

NAFTA discourse gives new postcommunist life to the development tale popular in the 1950s (itself heir to the justificatory tales of colonialism). Michael Elliot, for example, reporting on NAFTA, says that Latin American economies have historically been "inward-looking and protectionist," unlike English-speaking America, where "nations developed that were commercially minded, open to the world and, eventually, democratic" (with Padgett, 1993: 29). Latin America is, however, coming around, says Elliot, because "attitudes" have begun to change (with Padgett, 1993: 30).

The condescending implication (see also Church, 1993: 42) is that we will nudge the "attitudes" of others in the right direction, supposedly by means of helping countries "grow." Michael H. Wilson, Canada's minister of trade in 1993, states that "It is quite clear that as the economic performance of a country improves, so does its record on human rights, and its record on labour standards and environmental standards" (1993: 177). In other words, *once upon a time, people were uncivilized, but. . . .*

Do I need to rebut these stories here? They fall apart, or prove themselves misleading and inadequate, upon examination. For example, while there is a degree of "correlation" of the sort Wilson describes, this does not make development, much less free trade, the cause of human rights improvement. For one thing, some nations can afford environmental standards in part because some other nations cannot (the fable of sovereignty/national autonomy helps block consideration of this idea). Also, whenever human rights records and the rest *have* improved, it is precisely because "special interests" fought for the cause, often in the face of opposition from free market storytellers (and their colleagues who have been making U.S. foreign policy).

And is more free trade always better for all? Are all exchanges voluntary and mutually beneficial if they are not the result of coercion? No. Is a worker's decision to accept a job "voluntary"? In an important sense it often is not. Are the side effects of voluntary exchanges minor enough to keep government "small"? It doesn't seem so (Greenberg, 1985). Powerful critiques of neoclassical economics have been made over and over, at best leaving intact the claim that if we try to do entirely without markets in a large industrial society, there might be benefits, but power is likely to be concentrated in a dangerous way, and markets will persist anyway. Granted. But this is hardly news, and does not translate into a defense of "free trade."

Why does the shaky tale of free trade under attack persist? First of all, one can never prove that perfectly free trade wouldn't in fact solve all the world's problems. No matter what NAFTA appears to have wrought down the road, it can always be said that it "did not go far enough." We have never actually tried "free trade" and, conveniently for some, never can do so.

Second, the free trade fable is appealing because it casts blame for problems on identifiable constituencies—the party in power, do-gooders, etc.—and it appears that they might be held accountable or kept in check. This casts blame in a way that does not demand a great change in most people's lifestyle, and does not challenge many people's already established identification of virtue and freedom with the pursuit of security and affluence.

Third, the invocation of the ideal of free trade makes it endlessly possible to generate support for pro-corporate government policies such as NAFTA.

The free trade debate, then, largely ignores the fact that rather than being an inevitable product of growth and technology, "the particular structure of the world economy . . . emerges out of political negotiations and conflicts among nation-states" (Block, 1990: 17) as well as by virtue of ascendant stories (including the stories that create nation-states). Most people in the world work hard and are poor, in part because of a politically constructed, rhetorically supported structure under which nations compete for investment on investors' terms. The meaning of this discursive structure is covered over by the assumptions of the NAFTA-reinforced tale of sovereignty under duress.

> What most wage workers, farmers, and child raisers need is an adjustment "of" the world order, not an adjustment "to" that order. (Schwartz, 1995: 77–88)

The best NAFTA critics tell a tale more or less like this: *Once upon a time corporate sector workers had more power than they do now, but since then a mostly control- and profit-driven technological and political transformation made the economy more global, in the process deskilling the less educated, rendering capital more mobile, and weakening governments and many laborers.* This account makes excellent sense of the problems people and governments are having around the world, but is apparently threatening to much-needed myths of the sovereignty of one's government and of oneself. It certainly threatens the interests of unhindered capital mobility. NAFTA represents one model of economic integration, a neoliberal business model that removes the barriers to the movement of capital, but leaves workers and governments paying the bill for the dislocation and adjustment costs (Bernard, 1995: 74). The result is "downward harmonization" (Bernard, 1995: 69). "Multinational Corporations have just written themselves a ticket [NAFTA] to go around the world and search out the lowest possible standards" (Bernard, 1995: 71).

> The North American Economic Integration that NAFTA was intended to facilitate is only one aspect of the rapid and momentous historical transformation from a system of national economies toward an integrated global economy. . . . This transformation has had devastating consequences. (Brecher, 1993: 685; see also Brecher, Childs, and Cutler, 1993)

Since this alternative story receives little attention, it has been easy for supporters of NAFTA to lump critics together, as if they were all "protectionist" or "isolationist" (Samuelson, 1993: 28). While opposition to NAFTA includes "the Mexico-bashing bigotry of Pat Buchanan, the populist grandstanding of Ross Perot and the nationalist protectionism of some in the labor movement" (Brecher, 1993: 685), it also includes plenty of others.

> Out of their own experiences and observations, millions of Americans have constructed a new paradigm for understanding the global economy. Poor and working people in large numbers have recognized that NAFTA is not primarily about trade; it is about the ability of capital to move without regard to national borders. (Brecher, 1993: 685)

This recognition needs to find expression in transnational political coalitions like the anti-NAFTA North American Worker-to-Worker Network (Brecher, 1993: 686). Such networks depend on, and can help to spread, counterstories that support alternatives to NAFTA-like accommodations to corporate power.

As alternatives we should consider international workers' rights, codes of conduct for multinationals, debt relief, redistribution, global Keynesianism, and strengthened democracy (Makhijani, 1992). We need an "upward spiral" of growth, where that which goes up is the income of those at the bottom (Brecher, 1993: 687). This may require new ways to reward nonwage work (Makhijani, 1992: 143–44; Block, 1990: 155–89). The latter is all the more crucial as right now political power is pointing technology and production to "the jobless future" (Aronowitz and DiFazio, 1994). We should neither accept this as a given nor assume that such a future has to be at the expense of the "jobless." There is much work to be done besides paid work. Perhaps there are ways to loosen the hinges that connect wage work, survival, and ethical standing in our communities.

The NAFTA debate has marginalized these ideas, leaving us with a trade deal likely to modestly increase growth while exacerbating already egregious inequalities: "unless NAFTA turns out to be much ado about nothing, the agreement will accelerate the labour market changes that are already in evidence" (O'Grady, 1993: 53). Mexico may "catch up" a bit (again the fiction of national autonomy) with the United States and Canada, but inequality in each nation is likely to increase (Dunn, 1993: 89–96; Blank, 1993: 22–35).

The proponents of NAFTA succeeded in part because they participated in an often subtle identification of individual freedom, popular sovereignty, and autonomous national sovereignty. If "one's self-identification as a free individual is bound up with a common belief in the capacity of the state to promote publicly defined purposes" (Connolly, 1991: 198), and if one also accepts "the global economy" as a kind of given to which all must adjust, one is susceptible to the claim that "we" must "tighten our belts," or otherwise "take our medicine," in order to fortify the position of "the nation" and so ourselves. Rather than make "us" stronger, NAFTA discourse, like the NAFTA rules, undermines the partial sort of sovereignty communities can and should have (Bernard, 1995: 69).

Sovereignty should not be conceived of as an absolute mastery that can be entirely justified if properly constructed, but as a necessary, albeit necessarily harmful, power to make do, as a limited power to face specific problems. It needs to be seen as a power constructed by communities that are themselves contestable, that are themselves a form of needed but ambiguous power over the individual participants.

Paradoxically, the very free marketeers who warn us about global competition and tell us we cannot afford to treat our workers "too well" also inflate the idea of national sovereignty. The people of the United States are asked to cede actual sovereignty in order to succeed as a nation in the game of "global competition," as if nations have no one but themselves to thank for their fortunes. Just as an idolization of the Founding Fathers surely at times feeds a sworn and violent opposition to the U.S. government, so an anti-government commitment to free trade can seem a way to preserve the flagging power of the state, and so preserve the sense of the state "as the sovereign center of collective action" (Connolly, 1991; 201). Perhaps, then, Buchanan and Clinton support each other, despite their disagreement about NAFTA. Together they bolster the fantasy, central to modernity, of a human life that is at one with an entirely harmonious, sensible, purposeful order.

Conclusion

In sum, NAFTA, understood as a political event, was party to a discourse that contributes to unjust international and intranational inequalities. The narratives central to this discourse include the tale of social science as a gradual uncovering of the truth, the neoclassical tale of history as the struggle of economic maximizers, the story of postindustrialism as a product of technology and progress to which we must adjust, and the story of national success as linked to victory in the struggle of independent and sovereign nations, each of which charts its own path.

Instead of waiting for sovereignty, as if it will return to us once we "win," we should be doing politics now, locally, nationally, and globally, to make markets bend to the demands of justice, where "justice" is a matter of a democratic debate. This democracy requires multiple and overlapping sovereignties, based on community boundaries that are themselves the subject of discussion, disagreement, and coalition building. Local communities and transnational communities of interest both need a voice in national politics. Such voices could inject into mainstream U.S. political discourse some new ideas about the nature of borders, about what counts as an "American" corporation, and about who counts as part of all those "we" groups always being invoked in politics. Such a turn could transform the political odds, changing the "realities" of the world order to which social science can only accommodate. This is what politics is all about: the transformation of the "unrealistic" into the "realistic" and vice versa, partially by means of storytelling.

19

Is It Global Economics or Neo-Laissez-Faire?

Frances Fox Piven

For more than a century, left-wing political ambitions in Europe and America have rested on the prospect of working-class power. It would be less than honest not to acknowledge that, conceived in this way, the left is foundering. The symptoms are obvious. Unions, the bedrock of working-class power, are on the defensive, and in most advanced capitalist countries they have begun to lose members (Western, 1995). Left parties are in disarray and losing elections. Welfare state protections are under assault in campaigns to make the labor market more "flexible," with the consequence that coverage is being narrowed and expenditures are falling, particularly for the crucial programs that reach the active labor force (Hicks, Misra and Nah Ng 1995). And economic inequalities are growing. In Britain, where the richest 1 percent of the population owns 18 percent of the nation's wealth, fully half the population now lives in households that receive means-tested benefits (Field, 1994, cited in *The Economist* May 20, 1995). In the United States, where wages have been falling steadily, especially for the less skilled, and real poverty is increasing sharply, the richest 1 percent now owns nearly 40 percent of the wealth (Wolff, 1995; Pascale, 1995).

These dismal trends help account for another important development. In all the countries of advanced capitalism, there is a profound discouragement not only about the economic well-being of the working class, but about the possibility of working-class power, now or in the foreseeable future. After a century that witnessed the gradual if uneven expansion of unions, of left parties, and of social democratic policies, a century dominated for the left by a heady belief in labor as the agency of progressive change, the working class seems not to have any future at all. Instead we hope that somehow workers can muster the political muscle just to resist incursions on past gains being pressed by a capitalist class on the move. Even the left parliamentary opposition is reduced to arguing not that it holds the key to a better future, but that it can offer a more intelligent, more efficient, perhaps gentler, administration of the new and inevitable austerities.

Why this impasse? The explanation is a commonplace, quick to spring to the lips of intellectuals and workers alike. The key fact of our historical moment is said to be the globalization of national economies that, together with post-Fordist domestic restructuring, has had shattering consequences for the economic well-being of the working class, and especially for the power of the working class. I don't think this explanation is entirely wrong, but it is deployed so sweepingly as to be misleading. And right or wrong, the explanation itself has become a political force, helping to create the institutional realities it purportedly merely describes.

There are important variations in how economic globalization is characterized. When the argument emerged some two decades ago, the emphasis was on the decentralization of production from older industrial hubs to low-wage countries on the periphery of advanced capitalism. Somewhat later the emphasis shifted from actual plant relocation to the expansion of trade, and the enlarging share of national markets commanded by imports and exports, a development facilitated by new communication and transportation technologies. Either way, the consequences were to pit the organized and better-paid workers of the developed North agains vulnerable workers everywhere. Enlarging circuits of migration that tapped a bottomless reservoir of workers from the South and then from Eastern Europe for labor markets in the metropole had similar consequences (Gallin, 1994). And finally, in its most recent variant, the argument about economic globalism is about the vastly accelerated movement of financial capital, pinning not only workers but entire economies to the wall, and rendering national governments helpless to intervene as, in the words of a *Barron's* columnist, "capital market vigilantes [roam] the globe in search of high returns at relatively low risk" (interview with Gross, 1995).

Whatever the emphasis, all of these arguments lead to a common, and chilling, conclusion. Labor power is, after all, rooted in the fundamental interdependence of capital and labor. The exercise of that power always involves the threat by workers, explicit or not, that they will withhold their contributions to cooperative economic endeavors. Of course, other conditions complicate and obstruct the realization of working-class power—and thus of left possibilities. For one thing, the potential for power has to be recognized; ideology or consciousness is important in this sense because it may obscure or reveal to working people the relations that might yield them power. Workers also typically have to be organized before they can threaten to disrupt economic activity that depends on their collective contributions.

So much seems to me obvious. But there is another important point that bears directly on globalization. The exercise of labor power throughout the history of capitalist markets has always depended on the limited ability of capital to exit or threaten to exit from ongoing economic relationships. Economic globalization, together with domestic restructuring and downsizing made possible by technological change, seems to open unlimited options for capital exit, whether through the relocation of production, or accelerated trade, or through worker replacement, or through capital mobility. And it is simply in the nature of the human condition that workers, tied as they are to place and kin, constrained by their human fear of change, are unlikely to match these options, ever.

This understanding underlies, I think, the widespread discouragement about worker power and left possibility, however defined. Still, I am not entirely convinced, and I will here raise two very large questions.

First, if the real significance of globalization is the opportunities it creates for capital exit, just how new is this? And second, if capital exit is not new, does globalization nevertheless provide such vastly increased exit opportunities relative to the size of the economies of the advanced capitalist nations as to overshadow earlier experience?

As to the first question, I think the answer is clearly "not new at all." The history of power struggles between capital and labor has always necessarily involved efforts to control exit options. Accordingly, capital exerted itself to enlarge employer exit options, or to narrow worker exit options. As early as the fourteenth century, at a time when shackled agricultural workers were only beginning to take advantage of new opportunities resulting from labor scarcity, English landlords tried to limit the exit options of agricultural workers with the Law of Vagrancy (Chambliss, 1964). The strategy was elaborated over the succeeding centuries with laws of settlement, maximum wage laws, the curtailment of outdoor relief, and in the United States, "yellow-dog" employment contracts. Or, at the beginning of the putting-out system, manufacturers shunned the displaced male handloom weavers in favor of more pliant children and women. Or think of the employee lockout which was a tactic regularly used by industrialists in the United States to suppress strike threats. Or the deliberate encouragement of massive immigration and its subsequent deft uses to divide workers along ethnic and racial lines by American industrialists, especially during the industrial takeoff at the turn of the century. Or the massive restructuring of production along Taylorist lines at the end of the nineteenth century with the consequent deskilling of craft workers and the decimation of their unions. Or think of earlier periods of capital flight, which Giovanni Arrighi (1994), following Fernand Braudel, thinks marks not the late twentieth century, but successive epochs of world capitalism. These strategies to block worker exit or enlarge employer exit were often deployed on a vast scale, relative to the scale of the markets in which they were undertaken. And each had devastating consequences on the ability of workers to exercise power in production relations. So, capital exit is not new. Labor has been battered before, but labor power reemerged in new forms shaped by the new conditions.

Is Globalization Increasing?

My second question: Is globalization in fact increasing significantly, relative to vastly increased economic activity? There is reason to wonder. Some years ago, David Gordon argued that much of the economic data that is taken as evidence of the international penetration of the American economy can be understood not as the result of globalization, but as the evidence that we are experiencing the downswing of a long-wave economic cycle (Gordon, 1988, 1996). But I can ask the question in a more commonsense manner. If indeed capital, goods, and labor are circulating the globe with increasing velocity, how can German workers continue to earn—if social benefits are included—nearly twice what workers earn in the United States, or eleven times what workers earn in Thailand? And how can the German economy continue to grow at a brisk rate, with corporate profits soaring? How, if international markets are in command, can there even be much of a German economy? *Business Week*'s Bonn bureau chief answers the question by asserting that Germany is "sleepwalking," but that is merely to elevate convictions about the imperatives of global competition over evidence. And, we might ask more generally, why does there continue to be such large variation among national economies not only in the rewards to labor, but in profit margins as well?

For myself, I remain unsure of the answer to the economic questions about the scale of internationalism, and await clarification. In the meantime, however, I think a good deal of light can be cast on the globalization phenomena if we shift attention away from markets and market determinisms and turn to the politics associated with globalization. Capital exit is clearly not new, and in real terms globalization may not be the main reality. But postindustrial economic changes, including internationalism, have prepared the way for a much more aggressive capitalist-class politics. Put another way, capital is pyramiding the leverage gained by expanded exit opportunities, or perhaps the leverage gained merely by the specter of expanded exit opportunities, in a series of vigorous political campaigns.

Consider the United States, which is surely the singular leader among advanced capitalist countries in the usual measures of labor weakness. American unions have been decimated in just two decades, their membership falling from about thirty-five million to fifteen million. The Democratic Party is fragmented and disorganized, and has veered sharply rightward in its policies and appeals. After more than a decade in which the regulatory and social protection programs of the American welfare state were whittled back, a new round of huge rollbacks are underway. By any measure, the United States has pride of place as the most economically stratified industrial country in the world. And the level of political despair is also rising, taking form in a dangerous scapegoat politics drawing on the race hatred, xenophobia, and peculiar sexual obsessions that American culture provides as fuel for reactionary politics.

All this is undeniable. But while these changes are often read as symptoms of globalization, the United States is far less exposed to international economic currents than Western Europe and most less developed nations. The ratio of imports and exports to gross domestic product stands at 21 percent, unchanged since 1980. Foreign investment in U.S. stocks and bonds has risen, but in 1993 it remained only 6 percent of U.S. stocks, and 14 percent of corporate bonds. And fully 95 percent of investment by Americans remained in domestic stocks or bonds (Samuelson, 1995). True, there is a good deal of capital mobility within the United States, but important interregional movements of industrial production actually began more than a century ago, with the shift of the textile industry from New England to the South. In any case, most plant relocations have been from the old industrial centers of the Northeast and Midwest to the Sun Belt and the new cities. In other words, productive capital has in fact remained within national borders. The importance of this point cannot be overstated. In principle, the national government retains the capacity to regulate the economy.

To understand the paralyzing impact of fears of internationalism in the United States, we have to attend not to the economic data, but to politics, and particularly to the politics of big business. The past two decades have witnessed a business political mobilization of historic scale. For one thing, business organized: near-dormant trade groups were revived and new peak business coalitions were created and honed for political action. Business groups and business money moved into the Republican Party and electoral politics, developing sophisticated campaign techniques and the tight organization that money makes possible. For another, business developed and perfected a political agenda, funding big new national think tanks to do the work that, after the 1960s, universities could not be relied upon to do. And with organization and agenda in formation, business groups mounted a formidable ideological campaign. They launched an argument about the natural and inevitable primacy of markets over politics and the state—no matter that organized business was itself using politics and the state to secure new advantages, and on an unprecedented scale, not least to create some of the very conditions that the ideology described. The argument was, of course, a revival of nineteenth-century laissez-faire, of the theory that market processes reflect the unfolding of the law of supply and demand. If there are social costs as a consequence of the unfettered operation of this species of natural law, if there is suffering, it is because people or places fail to meet the implacable tests of the market. Political interference with natural law only risks calamity. The new end-of-the-twentieth-century narrative twist on nineteenth-century doctrine was that market law now operated on an international scale. Capital and goods now circled the globe in search of local markets where costs were lowest, and profits were highest, and these processes were beyond the reach of politics.

Americans were no doubt more susceptible to this old story than Europeans. For reasons much discussed in the literature on American exceptionalism, features of American culture, especially racism and sectionalism, worked against class consciousness. Moreover this culture coexisted with and in some ways nourished U.S. institutional arrangements that inhibited class politics, including a fragmented and decentralized state structure and widespread disenfranchisement. When worker power did become important in the 1930s, the welfare state programs that emerged were themselves decentralized and fragmented, and heavily marked by racism, with the consequence that welfare state structures continued to nourish the ideological biases that had blunted working-class influence in the first place.

Still, interpretations of the relationship of state and market are complex and shifting. After all, the experience of the Great Depression did shatter laissez-faire convictions. Until very recently, belief in the responsibility of government for popular economic well-being continued to hold sway, even in the United States. Public opinion remains volatile and susceptible to counterarguments, whether mounted by oppositional party leaders, or social movements that have yet to emerge. But ideology does not only reflect experience. It can also be a powerful discursive force in molding the institutions that shape experience. A process like this helps to account for the institutional changes—the dismantling of the Bretton Woods agreement, the creation of the International Monetary Fund—which facilitated international capital mobility, and for the new institutions such as GATT and NAFTA that are encouraging the expansion of trade. In these instances, a hegemonic ideology supporting the necessity and inevitability of the free movement of capital and goods helped to create the institutional conditions that then contributed to making the free movement of capital and goods a reality.

The Contract with America

In parallel fashion, the Republican juggernaut that took power in the United States in 1994, tutored no doubt by business-backed think tanks, undertook a series of changes in American political arrangements that would make the ideology of neo-laissez-faire "true," in the sense that people would come to experience the world in a way that confirms the ideology. The Contract with America proposed to enact new constraints on central government that would indeed make government helpless to regulate markets. Of course, the Contract was many things. It was, for example, propaganda, as suggested by the badly rhetorical titles of its legislative planks: The American Dream Restoration Act; the Personal Responsibility Act; the Common Sense Legal Reform Act. Even the use of the language of contract can be seen as an argument, a symbolic importation of a market idea into political relations between the state and its citizenry. Shielded by this sort of rhetoric, the Contract was also a set of tax and spend measures that would accelerate the redistribution of income and wealth from the poor to the rich.

But I want to direct attention here to another and important feature of this legislative program. Taken as a whole, it would strip the national government of the capacity to do what contemporary governments do—or did—to reduce extremes of inequality, regulate economic instabilities, and curb business excesses. The proposal for a balanced budget amendment to the Constitution is intended to put a brake not only on spending by the national government, but also on its ability to raise taxes. The route of constitutional amendment is extremely cumbersome, and the amendment has temporarily been shelved, but in the meantime, a new House rule requires 60 percent majorities on measures to increase taxes. Other bills impede the federal government's ability to regulate business, by introducing obstructive review procedures or extravagant requirements for compensating private owners for losses due to regulation. Still others discourage citizens from turning to the courts to resolve grievances against corporations. The federal government would also be inhibited from imposing "unfunded mandates" on state or local governments. And finally, the Contract initiated a series of proposals to end federal social welfare entitlement programs, particularly means-tested programs, in favor of federal block grants that the states would run substantially as they pleased. Some of these proposals are now law.

Viewed together, these measures suggest a clear pattern: the decentralized structure of the American state is being reinforced. As the national government is less and less able to do what governments do, responsibilities will devolve to the states, and in some cases, federal funds will be transferred to the states as well. The banner hoisted to explain these changes is that state governments are "closer to the people." The slogan resonates with old arguments of the late-eighteenth-century Anti-Federalists who feared that a remote central government would become an instrument of elites. But in the twentieth century, it is the state governments that are more sensitive to business political pressures simply because states—and localities—are far more vulnerable to the threat of disinvestment. Even in the early part of this century, efforts to pass state worker's compensation laws, for example, were stymied by business threats to move to other states—until, that is, manufacturers themselves, prodded by multiplying damage suits in the courts, decided to back model and modest legislation.

If state governments have always been susceptible to the bribe and threat of business investment and disinvestment, they are far more susceptible now, when capital is increasingly mobile, and when even a single corporate relocation can devastate an entire community. The fact that most movement of American business takes place within the borders of the United States, from Michigan to Tennessee, from Massachusetts to South Carolina, makes the fiscal and regulatory powers of the federal government more important than ever. This is precisely why Republicans are working to cripple those powers. Nor is it the first time that structures have been rearranged to reduce popular influence. In 1787, the authors of the American Constitution contrived to centralize powers granted to the states under the Articles of Confederation because they were alarmed by the surge of radicalism in the state legislatures. They saw debtor relief laws, inflationary currency policies, and resistance to repaying the bonds that had funded the Revolution undermining the influence of the affluent on governance. The solution was the shift of policies crucial to moneyed elites to a newly created central government that, given the primitive communications and transportation of the eighteenth century, would be insulated from postrevolutionary popular agitation.

Now the solution is to shift policies back to the states, the mirror image of the Founding, though ironically the underlying motive for this transformation is similar. The conditions that once prompted centralization now prompt decentralization. Contemporary communications and transportation have brought Washington within reach of democratic publics, while the leverage business gains from capital mobility, as well as from technological change and downsizing, make it a nearly unstoppable force in the state capitals. Populist slogans about "personal responsibility" or "commonsense legal reform" aside, this is the real dynamic underlying the Contract with America.

Conclusion

All of which helps to recall a familiar truth. The realm of politics—of agency, imagination, of demonic and heroic intent, and the stories we tell to justify our intent—all matter in creating the structures that then limit human possibilities.

And which sometimes expand possibilities as well.

References

Acs, Zoltan A., and David B. Audretsch. 1987. "Innovation, Market Structure, and Firm Size." *Review of Economics and Statistics* 69, 4 (November): 567–74.

Adams, James Truslow. 1935. *The Epic of America.* Boston: Little, Brown.

Adler, Mortimer J. 1982. *The Paideia Proposal: An Educational Manifesto.* New York: Macmillan.

Advisory Commission on Intergovernmental Relations. 1977. *Improving Federal Grants Management. The Intergovernmental Grant System: An Assessment and Proposed Policies.* Washington, D.C. (February).

Africa Report. 1976. "Election '76: Jimmy Carter on Africa." 21, 3 (May/June): 18–20.

Albritton, Robert B. 1989. "Impacts of Intergovernmental Financial Incentives on State Welfare Policymaking and Interstate Equity." *Publius* 19 (Spring): 127–41.

Allen, John S. 1989. "Franz Boas's Physical Anthropology: The Critique of Racial Formalism Revisited." *Current Anthropology* 30 (February): 79–83.

Alonso, William, and Paul Starr, eds. 1987. *The Politics of Numbers.* New York: Sage.

Alperovitz, Gar, and Kai Bird. 1993. "Giving Harry Hell." *The Nation* 256, 18 (May 10): 640–42.

Anderson, Benedict. 1983. *Imagined Communities: Reflections on the Origins and Spread of Nationalism.* London: Verso.

Angier, Natalie. 1995. "Disputed Meeting to Ask if Crime Has Genetic Roots." *New York Times* (September 19): C1.

Aronowitz, Stanley. 1994. *Dead Artists, Live Theories and Other Cultural Problems.* New York: Routledge.

Aronowitz, Stanley, and William DiFazio. 1994. *The Jobless Future: Sci-Tech and the Dogma of Work.* Minneapolis: University of Minnesota Press.

Arrighi, Giovanni. 1994. *The Long Twentieth Century.* London: Verso.

Ashley, Richard K. 1989. "Living on Border Lines: Man, Poststructuralism, and War." In James Der Derian and Michael J. Shapiro, eds. *International/Intertextual Relations: Postmodern Readings of World Politics.* Lexington, Mass.: Lexington Books.

Auster, Lawrence. 1990. *The Path to National Suicide: An Essay on Immigration and Multiculturalism.* Monterey, Va.: American Immigration Control Foundation.

Austin, J. L. 1962. *How to Do Things with Words.* Cambridge: Harvard University Press.

Axtell, James. 1981. *The European and the Indian.* New York: Oxford University Press.

Bagnasco, Arnaldo. 1977. *Tre Italie: La Problematica Territoriale Dello Sviluppo Italiano.* Bologna: Il Mulino.

Bal, Mieke. 1988. *Death and Dissymmetry: The Politics of Coherence in the Book of Judges.* Chicago: University of Chicago Press.

Baldwin, Roger N. 1930. "Civil Liberties." In Fred S. Hall, ed. *Social Work Year Book, 1929.* New York: Sage.

Balibar, Etienne. 1991a. "Is There a 'Neo-Racism'?" In Etienne Balibar and Immanuel Wallerstein, eds. *Race, Nation, Class.* Chris Turner, trans. New York: Verso.

———. 1991b. "Racism and Nationalism." In Etienne Balibar and Immanuel Wallerstein, eds.

Ball, George. 1968. *The Discipline of Power.* Boston: Little, Brown.

———. 1977. "Asking for Trouble in South Africa." *The Atlantic Monthly,* (October): 43–51.

Barber, Benjamin R. 1992. *An Aristocracy of Everyone.* New York: Oxford University Press.

———. 1996. *Jihad vs. McWorld: How Globalism and Tribalism Are Reshaping the World.* New York: Ballentine.

Barber, James David. 1972. *Presidential Character.* Englewood Cliffs, N.J.: Prentice-Hall.

Barthes, Roland. 1972. *Mythologies.* New York: Hill and Wang.

Baudrillard, Jean. 1981. *For a Critique of the Political Economy of the Sign.* Charles Levin, trans. St. Louis: Telos.

———. 1983. *Simulations.* New York: Semiotext(e).

———. 1994a. *Simulacra and Simulation.* Sheila Faria Glaser, trans. Ann Arbor: University of Michigan Press.

———. 1994b. *The Illusion of the End.* Chris Turner, trans. Stanford: Stanford University Press.

Baugh, Albert C., and Thomas Cable. 1951. *A History of the English Language,* 4th ed. London: Routledge.

Beard, Charles. 1913. *An Economic Interpretation of the Constitution of the United States.* New York: Macmillan.

Belfrage, Cedric. 1973. *The American Inquisition, 1945–1960: A Profile of the "McCarthy Era".* Indianapolis: Bobbs-Merrill.

Bennett, William. 1993. *The Book of Virtues.* New York: Simon and Schuster.

Bennett, William J., John J. DiIulio Jr., and John P. Walters. 1996. *Body Count: Moral Poverty . . . And How to Win America's War Against Crime and Drugs.* New York: Simon and Schuster.

Berg, Steve. 1995. "Can Congress Really Fix Welfare?" Minneapolis *Star Tribune* (March 26): 10A.

Berlant, Lauren, and Elizabeth Freeman. 1993. "Queer Nationality." In Michael Warner, ed. *Fear of a Queer Planet: Queer Politics and Social Theory.* Minneapolis: University of Minnesota Press.

Bernard, Elaine. 1995. "Free Trade or Free Corporations." In Brenda M. McPhail, ed.

Bernstein, Barton J. 1986. "A Postwar Myth: 500,000 U.S. Lives Saved," *Bulletin of the Atomic Scientists* 42 (June/July): 38–40.

Bernstein, Richard. 1995. *Dictatorship of Virtue: Multiculturalism and the Battle for America's Future.* New York: Knopf.

Best, Joel. 1990. *Threatened Children: Rhetoric and Concern about Child-Victims.* Chicago: University of Chicago Press.

———, ed. 1995. *Images of Issues,* 2nd ed. Hawthorne, N.Y.: Aldine de Gruyter.

Bhabha, Homi. 1992. "A Good Judge of Character: Men, Metaphors, and the Common Culture." In Toni Morrison, ed.

Birch, David L. 1987. *Job Creation in America: How Our Smallest Companies Put the Most People to Work.* New York: Free Press.

Black Scholar, The, ed. 1992. *Court of Appeal.* New York: Ballantine Books.

Blank, Stephen. 1993. "The Emerging Architecture of North America." In A. R. Riggs and Tom Velk, eds.

Blasius, Mark. 1992. "An Ethos of Lesbian and Gay Existence." *Political Theory* 20, 4 (November): 642–71.

Block, Fred. 1990. *Postindustrial Possibilities: A Critique of Economic Discourse.* Berkeley: University of California Press.

Bogdan, Robert, and Margaret Ksander. 1980. "Policy Data as a Social Process." *Human Organization* 39, 4 (Winter): 302–9.

Boorstin, Daniel J. 1953. *The Genius of American Politics.* Chicago: University of Chicago Press.

Bopp, Julie, et al., 1989. *The Sacred Tree.* Twin Lakes, Wisconsin: Lotus Light Publications.

Borneman, John. 1995. "American Anthropology as Foreign Policy." *American Anthropologist* 97: 663–72.

Borstelmann, Thomas. 1993. *Apartheid's Reluctant Uncle: Early Cold War.* London: Oxford University Press.

Boudin, Louis B. 1911. "Government by Judiciary." *Political Science Quarterly* 26: 238–70.

Bower, Lisa. 1994. "Queer Acts and the Politics of 'Direct Access.' " *Law & Society Review* 28(5): 1009–33.

Bowers, C. A. 1993. *Education, Cultural Myths, and the Ecological Crisis: Toward Deep Changes.* Albany: SUNY Press.

———. 1987. *Elements of a Post-Liberal Theory of Education.* New York: Teachers College.

Brameld, Theodore. 1956. *Toward a Reconstructed Philosophy of Education.* New York: Holt, Rinehart & Winston.

Brands, H. W. 1993. *The Devil We Knew: Americans and the Cold War.* New York: Oxford University Press.

Brecher, Jeremy. 1993. "Global Village or Global Pillage?" *The Nation* 257, 19 (December 6): 685–88.

Brecher, Jeremy, John Brown Childs, and Jill Cutler, eds. 1993. *Global Visions: Beyond the New World Order.* Boston: South End.

Brennan, Theresa. 1993. *History After Lacan.* London: Routledge.

Brief of the Pacific Legal Foundation. 1995. Caso and La Fetra, Counsel of Record. *Romer v. Evans,* 94–1039.

Brief of the Attorney General of the State of Colorado. 1995. Gale A. Norton. *Romer v. Evans,* 94–1039.

Brief of Robert Bork. 1995. *Romer v. Evans,* 94–1039.

Brimelow, Peter. 1995. *Alien Nation.* New York: Random House.

Brinkley, Douglas. 1992. *Dean Acheson: The Cold War Years, 1953–1971.* New Haven: Yale University Press.

Brodkin, Evelyn Z. 1986. *The False Promise of Administrative Reform: Implementing Quality Control in Welfare.* Philadelphia: Temple University Press.

Brown, Michael K., ed. 1988. Introduction. In *Remaking the Welfare State: Retrenchment and Social Policy in America and Europe.* Philadelphia: Temple University Press.

Brown, Wendy. 1995. *States of Injury: Power and Freedom in Late Modernity.* Princeton: Princeton University Press.

Buckley, Sandra. 1991. "Penguin in Bondage: A Graphic Tale of Japanese Comic Books." In Constance Penley and Andrew Ross, eds. *Technoculture.* Minneapolis: University of Minnesota Press.

Bulletin of the Department of Education. 1920. "Proceedings of the State Conference on Immigration in Massachusetts Industries." Boston (November 5).

Bumiller, Kristin. 1991. "Fallen Angels: The Representation of Violence Against Women in Legal Culture." In Martha Albertson Fineman and Nancy Sweet Thomadsen, eds. *At the Boundaries of Law.* New York: Routledge.

Burchell, Graham, Colin Gordon and Peter Miller. 1991. *The Foucault Effect: Studies in Governmentality with Two Lectures and an Interview with Michel Foucault.* London: Harvester Wheatsheaf.

Burnham, Walter Dean. 1989. "The Reagan Heritage." In Gerald M. Pomper, ed. *The Election of 1988: Reports and Interpretations.* Chatham, N.J.: Chatham House.

Butler, Judith. 1990. *Gender Trouble: Feminism and the Subversion of Identity.* New York: Routledge.

Byrns, Ralph T., and Gerald W. Stone. 1987. *Economics*, 3rd ed. Glenview, Ill.: Scott, Foresman.

Byroade, Henry. 1953. "The World's Colonies and Ex-Colonies: A Challenge to America." *State Department Bulletin* (November 16): 655–60.

Cajete, Gregory. 1994. *Look to the Mountain: An Ecology of Indigenous Education.* Durango, Colo.: Kivaki.

Caldwell, Dan. 1991. *The Dynamics of Domestic Politics and Arms Control: The SALT II Treaty Ratification Debate.* Columbia: University of South Carolina Press.

Campbell, David. 1992. *Writing Security: United States Foreign Policy and the Politics of Identity.* Minneapolis: University of Minnesota Press.

Carr, E. H. 1962. *What Is History?* New York: Knopf.

Carter, Jimmy. 1977. *Public Papers of the President.* Washington, D.C.: Office of the Federal Reserve, National Archives and Records Service, General Services Administration.

Chambliss, William J. 1964. "On the Law of Vagrancy." *Social Problems* 12(1): 67–77.

Chesterton, Gilbert K. 1922. *What I Saw in America.* New York: Dodd, Mead.

Chicago *Tribune.* 1993. "The New Biology of Violence" (December 19): Section 3, 2.

Choldin, Harvey. 1994. *Looking for the Last Percent: The Controversy Over Census Undercounts.* New Brunswick: Rutgers University Press.

Chomsky, Noam. 1967. "The Responsibility of Intellectuals." *New York Review of Books* (February 23): 16–25.

Church, George J. 1993. "It's Just That Close." *Time* 142 (November 15): 42.

Clarke, Stuart Alan. 1993. " 'Bigger' and 'Booker' and the GOP: Race and E/Racing in the Struggle for Hegemony." In Frederick M. Dolan and Thomas L. Dumm ed.

Clegg, Stewart R. 1989. *Frameworks of Power.* New York: Sage.

Clinton, William. 1992. Acceptance Speech. Democratic National Convention, New York (July 16).

———. 1993. "Remarks at the Wall Street Journal Conference on the Americas in New York City" (October 28). *Weekly Compilation of Presidential Documents*, vol. 29, no. 43 (Monday, November 1), U.S. Government Documents.

———. 1995. State of the Union Address. Washington, D.C. (January 24).

Clough, Michael. 1991. *Free at Last? U.S. Policy Toward Africa and the End of the Cold War.* New York: Council on Foreign Relations.

Coker, Christopher. 1986. *The United States and South Africa, 1968–1985: Constructive Engagement and Its Critics.* Durham: Duke University Press.

Collin, Robert W., and Willa M. Hemmons. 1987. "Equal Protection Problems with Welfare Fraud Prosecution." *Loyola Law Review* 33:1 (Spring): 17–49.

Combs, James. 1993. *The Reagan Range: The Nostalgic Myth in American Politics.* Bowling Green: Bowling Green State University Press.

Conlan, Timothy. 1988. *New Federalism: Intergovernmental Reform from Nixon to Reagan.* Washington, D.C.: Brookings Institution.

Connolly, William E. 1982. "Civic Disaffection and the Democratic Party." *Democracy* 2 (July): 18–27.

———. 1991. *Identity/Difference: Democratic Negotiations of Political Paradox.* Ithaca: Cornell University Press.

Cook, Blanche Wiesen. 1981. *The Declassified Eisenhower: A Divided Legacy of Peace and Political Warfare.* Garden City, N.Y.: Doubleday.

Corn, Joseph J., and Brian Horrigan. 1984. *Yesterday's Tomorrows: Past Visions of the American Future.* New York: Summit.

Corwin, Edward S. 1957. *The President: Office and Powers.* New York: New York University Press.

Cox, Arthur Macy. 1982. *Russian Roulette: The Superpower Game.* New York: Times Books.

Coyne, Andrew. 1993. "Should Free Traders Support NAFTA?" In A. R. Riggs and Tom Velk, eds.

Crary, Jonathan. 1991. *Techniques of the Observer.* Cambridge: MIT Press.

Crenshaw, Kimberley, and Gary Peller. 1992. "Whose Story Is It Anyway?" In Toni Morrison, ed.

———. 1993. "Reel Time/Real Justice." In Robert Gooding-Wilson, ed. *Reading Rodney King/Reading Urban Uprising.* New York: Routledge.

Crittenden, Ann. 1994. "Where Workforce 2000 Went Wrong." *Working Woman* 19 (August): 18.

Crocker, Chester. 1992. *High Noon in Southern Africa: Making Peace in a Rough Neighborhood.* New York: Norton.

Cronin, Thomas E. 1980. *The State of the Presidency.* Boston: Little, Brown.

Cronon, William, George Miles, and Jay Gitlin. 1992. "Becoming West." In *Under an Open Sky: Rethinking America's Western Past.* New York: Norton.

Crystal, Stephen. 1987. "Elder Abuse." *The Public Interest* 88: 56–66.

Cuomo, Mario. 1995. *Reason To Believe.* New York: Simon and Schuster.

Curry, Richard O. 1988. *Freedom at Risk: Secrecy, Censorship, and Repression in the 1980s.* Philadelphia: Temple University Press.

Danaher, Kevin. 1985. *The Political Economy of U.S. Policy Toward South Africa.* Boulder, Colo: Westview.

Danforth, John C. 1994. *Resurrection: The Confirmation of Clarence Thomas.* New York: Viking.

Danziger, Sheldon, and Peter Gottschalk. 1995. *America Unequal.* Cambridge: Harvard University Press.

Davie, Michael. 1967. *LBJ: A Foreign Observer's Viewpoint.* New York: Ballantine Books.

de Man, Paul. 1986. "The Resistance to Theory." In *The Resistance to Theory.* Minneapolis: University of Minnesota Press.

Delgado, Richard. 1989. "Storytelling for Oppositionists and Others: A Plea for Narrative." *Michigan Law Review* 87 (August): 2411–41.

Deng Ming-Dao. 1992. *365 Tao: Daily Meditations.* San Francisco: HarperCollins.

Derrida, Jacques. 1977. *Of Grammatology.* Baltimore: Johns Hopkins University Press.

———. 1981. *Dissemination.* Barbara Johnson, trans. Chicago: University of Chicago Press.

———. 1982. "White Mythology: Metaphor in the Text of Philosophy." In *Margins of Philosophy.* Alan Bass, trans. Chicago: University of Chicago Press.

———. 1986. "Declarations of Independence." *New Political Science* 15: 10–17.

———. 1988. *Limited, Inc.* Evanston: Northwestern University Press.

———. 1994. *Specters of Marx: The State of the Debt, the Work of Mourning & the New International.* Peggy Kamuf, trans., Bernd Magnus and Stephen Cullenberg, introduction. New York: Routledge.

Deutsch, Richard. 1980. "Reagan's African Perspectives." *Africa Report* (July–August): 4–7.

Dewey, John. 1916. *Democracy and Education.* New York: Macmillan.

Diamante, Thomas, Charles L. Reid, and Leo Giglio. 1995. "Making the Right Training Move." *HRMagazine* 40 (March): 60–65.

DiIulio, John J. 1994. "The Question of Black Crime," *The Public Interest,* 117, Fall: 3–32.

DiIulio Jr., John J., and Donald F. Kettl. 1995. *Fine Print: The Contract with America, Devolution, and the Administrative Realities of American Federalism.* Washington, D.C.: Brookings Institution.

Dobrzynski, Judith H. 1995. "Some Action, Little Talk." *New York Times* (April 20): D1.

Dolan, Frederick, and Thomas Dumm, eds. 1993. *Rhetorical Republic: Governing Representations in American Politics.* Amherst: The University of Massachusetts Press.

Donahue, John D. 1989. *The Privatization Decision: Public Ends, Private Means.* New York: Basic Books.

Dosi, Giovanni. 1988. "Sources, Procedures, and Microeconomic Effects of Innovation." *Journal of Economic Literature* 26, 3 (September): 1120–71.

Douglas, Mary. 1992. *Risk and Blame: Essays in Cultural Theory.* New York: Routledge.

Druhe, Virginia. 1995. "A View of NAFTA's Problems." In Brenda M. McPhail, ed.

Dumm, Thomas L. 1996. *Michel Foucault and the Politics of Freedom.* Thousand Oaks, Calif.: Sage.

Dunn Jr., Robert M. 1993. "Winners and Losers from NAFTA." In A. R. Riggs and Tom Velk, eds.

Duster, Troy. 1990. *Backdoor to Eugenics.* New York: Routledge.

Dye, Thomas R. 1990. "The Policy Consequences of Intergovernmental Competition." *Cato Journal* 10 (Spring/Summer): 59–73.

Dyer, Richard. 1988. "White." *Screen* 29(4): 44–64.

Dyson, Esther. 1995. "Friend and Foe: The Wired Interview." *Wired* (August): 106–12.

Edelman, Murray. 1988. *Constructing the Political Spectacle.* Chicago: University of Chicago Press.

Edelman, Peter, and David Satcher. 1993. "Violence Prevention as a Public Health Priority." *Health Affairs* 12 (1993): 123–25.

Efron, Edith. 1992. "Native Son: Why a Black Supreme Court Nominee Has No Rights White Men Need Respect." *Reason* (February 1): 28.

El-Khawas, Mohamed A., and Barry Cohen, eds. 1976. *The Kissinger Study of Southern Africa: National Security Study Memorandum 39.* Westport, Conn.: Lawrence Hill.

Elmer-Dewitt, Philip. 1995. "On a Screen Near You: Cyberporn." *Time* 93 (July): 38–45.

Elliot, Michael, with Tim Padgett. 1993. "Yanquis, Come Here." *Newsweek* 122 (November 15): 29.

Ely, John Hart. 1980. *Democracy and Distrust: A Theory of Judicial Review.* Cambridge: Harvard University Press.

Ethelbrick, Paula L. 1995. "The Law and the Lesbian and Gay Community." In Paula S. Rothenberg, ed. *Race, Class, and Gender in the United States: An Integrated Study,* 3rd ed. New York: St. Martin's.

Evangelista, Matthew. 1982–83. "Stalin's Postwar Army Reappraised." *International Security* 7 (Winter): 110–38.

Ewen, Stuart. 1976. *Captains of Consciousness: Advertising and the Social Roots of the Consumer Culture.* New York: McGraw-Hill.

Faludi, Susan. 1991. *Backlash: The Undeclared War Against American Women.* New York: Crown.

Fanon, Franz. 1967 (1952). *Black Skin, White Masks.* New York: Grove.

Fatton, Robert. 1984. "The Reagan Foreign Policy Toward South Africa: The Ideology of a New Cold War." *African Studies Review* 27, 1 (March): 57–58.

Ferguson, Andrew. 1994. "Chasing Rainbows." *Washingtonian* 29 (April): 35–42.

Field, Frank. 1994. *Making Welfare Work.* London: Institute for Community Studies.

Financial Mail. 1976. "U.S. President-Elect, Jimmy Carter" (November 3): 1.

Fiske, Edward B. 1987. "With Old Values and New Titles, Civics Courses Make a Comeback." *New York Times* (June 7): 1.

Fiske, John. 1989. *Understanding Popular Culture.* Boston: Unwin Hyman.

———. 1993. *Power Plays, Power Works.* London: Verso.

Fix, Michael, and Jeffrey S. Passel. 1993. "Immigrants and Welfare: New Myths, New Realities." Testimony before the U.S. House of Representatives, Committee on Ways and Means, Subcommittee on Human Resources (November 15). Washington, D.C.: Urban Institute.

Forbath, William E. 1991. *Law and the Shaping of the American Labor Movement.* Cambridge: Harvard University Press.

Forester, John. 1993. *Critical Theory, Public Policy, and Planning Practice.* Albany: SUNY Press.

Fortin, A. J. 1995. "AIDS, Surveillance, and Public Policy" *Research in Law and Policy Studies* 4: 173.

Foucault, Michel 1973. *The Order of Things: An Archaeology of Knowledge.* New York: Vintage.

———. 1977. *Discipline and Punish: The Birth of the Prison.* Alan Sheridan, trans. New York: Pantheon.

———. 1983. "The Subject and Power." In Herbert L. Dreyfus and Paul Rabinow, eds. *Michel Foucault: Beyond Structuralism and Hermeneutics*, 2nd ed. Chicago: University of Chicago Press.

———. 1984a. "The Order of Discourse." Ian McLeod, trans. In Michael J. Shapiro, ed. *Language and Politics*. New York: New York University Press.

———. 1984b. "What Is an Author?" *The Foucault Reader*. Paul Rabinow, ed. New York: Pantheon Books.

———. 1986. "Of Other Spaces." *Diacritics* 16 (Fall): 22–27.

———. 1991. "Governmentality." In Graham Burchell et al., eds.

France, Alan W. 1988. "Misogyny and Appropriation in Richard Wright's *Native Son*." *Modern Fiction Studies* 34, 3 (Autumn): 413–23.

Frankfurter, Felix, and N. Greene. 1930. *The Labor Injunction*. New York: Macmillan.

Franklin, Bruce H. 1993. *M.I.A. or Mythmaking in America: How and Why Belief in Live POWs Has Possessed a Nation*. New Brunswick: Rutgers University Press.

Fraser, Nancy. 1990. "Struggle Over Needs: Outline of a Socialist-Feminist Critical Theory of Late-Capitalist Political Culture." In Linda Gordon, ed.

Fraser, Nancy, and Linda Gordon. 1994. "A Genealogy of Dependency: Tracing a Keyword of the U.S. Welfare State." *Signs: Journal of Women in Culture and Society* 19, 2 (Winter): 309–36.

Freedman, Estelle. 1992. "The Manipulation of History at the Clarence Thomas Hearings." *Journal of Higher Education* (January 8): B2–B3.

Freire, Paulo. 1973. *Pedagogy of the Oppressed*. Myra Bergman Ramos, trans. New York: Seabury.

Friedman, Milton. 1962. *Capitalism and Freedom*. Chicago and London: University of Chicago Press.

Fullerton, Howard N. 1989. "New Labor Force Projections, Spanning 1988 to 2000." *Monthly Labor Review* 112 (November): 3–11.

Funiciello, Theresa. 1990. "The Poverty Industry: Do Governments and Charities Create the Poor?" *Ms.* (November/December): 33–40.

Gallin, Dan. 1994. "Inside the New World Order: Drawing the Battle Lines." *New Politics* 5(1).

Gallup Report. 1989. "Reagan Job Approval Rating the Highest Since Franklin Roosevelt" (January): 3.

Galston, William A. 1987. *One Year to Go: Citizen Attitudes in Iowa and New Hampshire*. Washington, D.C.: Roosevelt Center for American Studies.

Gamson, Joshua. 1995. "Must Identity Movements Self-Destruct? A Queer Dilemma." *Social Problems* 42: 390–407.

Gans, Herbert J. 1995. *The War Against the Poor: The Underclass and Antipoverty Policy*. New York: Basic Books.

Gardiner, John A., and Theodore R. Lyman. 1984. *The Fraud Control Game: State Responses to Fraud and Abuse in AFDC and Medicaid Programs*. Washington, D.C.: U.S. Department of Justice, National Institute of Justice.

Gavora, Jessica. 1996. "Maryland's Prison of Last Resort." Washington *Post* (August 25): C8.

Gaynor, Patricia E., and Rickey C. Kirkpatrick. 1994. *Introduction to Time-Series and Forecasting in Business and Economics*. New York: McGraw-Hill.

Geertz, Clifford. 1973. "Ideology as a Cultural System." In *The Interpretation of Cultures.* New York: Basic Books.

Gilbert, Neil. 1994. "Miscounting Social Ills." *Society* 31 (March): 18–26.

Gilder, George. 1984. *The Spirit of Enterprise.* New York: Basic Books.

Gillespie, Ed, and Bob Schellhas, eds. 1994. *Contract with America: The Bold Plan by Rep. Newt Gingrich, Rep. Dick Armey and the House Republicans to Change the Nation.* New York: Random House.

Gilson, Nancy. 1997. "Against the Grain: Black Conservatives and Jewish Neo-Cons." In Z. P. Franklin, ed. *Blacks and Jews in American History.* Carbondale: University of Illinois Press.

Goldberg, Suzanne. 1994. "Gay Rights Through the Looking Glass: Politics, Morality and the Trial of Colorado's Amendment 2." *Fordham Urban Law Journal* 21: 1057–82.

Goldman, Eric F. 1969. *The Tragedy of Lyndon Johnson.* New York: Knopf.

Goldstein, Robert Justin. 1978. *Political Repression in Modern America.* Cambridge, Mass.: Schenkman.

Gordon, Colin. 1991. "Governmental Rationality: An Introduction." In Graham Burchell et al., eds.

Gordon, David. 1988. "The Global Economy: New Edifice or Crumbling Foundation?" *New Left Review* 168 (March/April): 24–65.

———. 1996. *Fat and Mean.* New York: Free Press.

Gordon, Linda, ed. 1990. *Women, the State, and Welfare.* Madison: University of Wisconsin Press.

———. 1994. *Pitied But Not Entitled: Single Mothers and the History of Welfare.* New York: Free Press.

Gramsci, Antonio. 1971. *Selections from the Prison Notebooks.* Q. Hoare and G. Nowell Smith, eds. and trans. New York: International Publishers.

Green, Mark, and Gail McColl. 1987. *Reagan's Reign of Error: The Instant Nostalgia Edition.* New York: Pantheon.

Greenberg, Edward S. 1985. *Capitalism and the American Political Ideal.* Armonk, N.Y.: Sharpe.

Gross, William H. 1995. Interview, "Back in the Soup." *Barron's* (June 19): 24–28.

Gusfield, Joseph. 1984. *The Culture of Public Problems: Drinking-Driving and the Symbolic Order.* Chicago: University of Chicago Press.

Habermas, Jurgen. 1973. *Legitimation Crisis.* Thomas McCarthy, trans. Boston: Beacon Press.

———. 1989. *The Theory of Communicative Action.* Volume 2. Thomas McCarthy, trans. Boston: Beacon.

Hall, Jacquelyn Dowd. 1983. " 'The Mind That Burns in Each Body': Women, Rape, and Racial Violence." In Ann Snitow, Christine Stansell, and Sharon Thompson, eds. *Power of Desire: The Politics of Sexuality.* New York: Monthly Review.

Hall, Stuart. 1986. "On Postmodernism and Articulation: An Interview with Stuart Hall." In Lawrence Grossberg, ed. *Journal of Communication Inquiry* 10, 2 (Summer) 45–62.

Hanauer, Amy. 1994. Personal Communication. Office of Wisconsin State Senator Gwendolynne Moore (September 27).

Handler, Joel F. 1991. "Letter to the Editor." *New York Times* (July 23): A20.

Handler, Joel F., and Yeheskel Hasenfeld. 1991. *The Moral Construction of Poverty: Welfare Reform in America.* Newbury Park, Calif.: Sage.

Hanson, Russell L., and John T. Hartman. 1994. "Do Welfare Magnets Attract?" Madison: Institute for Research on Poverty, University of Wisconsin-Madison, Discussion Paper #1028–94.

Harrison, Bennett. 1994. *Lean and Mean: The Changing Landscape of Corporate Power in the Age of Flexibility.* New York: Basic Books.

Harrison, Bennett, and Barry Bluestone. 1988. *The Great U-Turn: Corporate Restructuring and the Polarizing of America.* New York: Basic Books.

Hartz, Louis. 1955. *The Liberal Tradition in America.* New York: Harcourt Brace.

Hawkesworth, M. E. 1988. *Theoretical Issues in Policy Analysis.* Albany: SUNY Press.

Hayles, N. Katherine. 1993. "Virtual Bodies and Flickering Signifiers." *October* 66: 69–91.

Hennessy, Rosemary. 1994. "Queer Theory, Left Politics." *Rethinking Marxism* 7: 85–111.

Hensley, Thomas R., and James C. Rhoads. 1989. "Studying the Studies: An Assessment of Judicial Politics Research in Four Major Political Science Journals, 1960–1987." *Law, Politics, and Judicial Process Section Newsletter* 6: 1.

Hersh, Seymour. 1983. *The Price of Power: Kissinger in the Nixon White House.* New York: Summit Books.

Hicks, Alexander, Joya Misra, and Tang Nah Ng. 1995. "The Programatic Emergence of the Social Security State." *American Sociological Review* 60, 3 (June): 329–49.

Higginbotham Jr., A. Leon. 1992. "An Open Letter to Justice Clarence Thomas From a Federal Judicial Colleague." In Toni Morrison, ed.

Higham, John. 1955. *Strangers in the Land.* New Brunswick: Rutgers University Press.

Hilgartner, Stephen, and Charles L. Bosk. 1988. "The Rise and Fall of Social Problems." *American Journal of Sociology* 94: 53–78.

Hirsch Jr., E. D. 1987. *Cultural Literacy: What Every American Needs to Know.* Boston: Houghton Mifflin.

Hoagland, Doug. 1991. "We're Losing Good Minds." Fresno *Bee* (March 3): A1, A8.

Hobbes, Thomas. 1968 (1651). *Leviathan.* C. B. Macpherson, ed. and introduction. Baltimore: Penguin.

Hobsbawn, Eric. 1994. *The Age of Extremes: A History of the World, 1914–1991.* New York: Pantheon.

Hochschild, Jennifer L. 1995. *Facing Up to the American Dream: Race, Class, and the Soul of the Nation.* Princeton: Princeton University Press.

Hoff, Joan. 1991. *Law, Gender and Injustice: A Legal History of U.S. Women.* New York: New York University Press.

Holstein, James A., and Gale Miller, eds. 1993. *Reconsidering Social Constructionism.* Hawthorne, N.Y.: Aldine de Gruyter.

Honig, Bonnie. 1991. "Declarations of Independence: Arendt and Derrida on the Problem of Founding a Republic." *American Political Science Review* 85, 1 (March): 97–113.

House Republicans. 1995. *Restoring the Dream.* Stephen Moore, ed. New York: Times Books.

Hubbard, Ruth, and Elijah Wald. 1993. *Exploding the Gene Myth: How Genetic Information Is Produced and Manipulated by Scientists, Physicians, Employers, Insurance Companies, Educators, and Law Enforcers.* Boston: Beacon Press.

Hughes, Mark Alan. 1996. "The Welfare Dustbowl." *The Honolulu Advertiser* (October 20): B1.
Hughes, Emmet John. 1973. *The Living Presidency.* New York: Coward McCann and Geoghegan.
Hull, Richard W. 1990. *American Enterprise in South Africa: Historical Dimensions of Engagement and Disengagement.* New York: New York University Press.
Hunt, Lynn. 1993a. "Introduction: Obscenity and the Origins of Modernity, 1500–1800." In Lynn Hunt, ed. *The Invention of Pornography: Obscenity and the Origins of Modernity, 1500–1800.* New York: Zone Books.
———. 1993b. "Pornography and the French Revolution." In Lynn Hunt, ed.
Hunt, Michael N. 1987. *Ideology and U.S. Foreign Policy.* New Haven: Yale University Press.
In These Times. 1995. "Flawed Exhibit Hands Right a Victory" (20 February): 2.
Ingersoll, Robert. 1892. Speech. *Truth-Seekers* (February 28).
Jackson-Leslie, Llenda. 1992. "Tom, Buck and Sambo or How Clarence Thomas Got to the Supreme Court." In The Black Scholar, ed.
Jameson, Fredric. 1981. *The Political Unconscious: Narrative as a Socially Symbolic Act.* Ithaca: Cornell University Press.
Jamieson, David, and Julie O'Mara. 1991. *Managing Workforce 2000.* San Francisco: Jossey-Bass.
Jencks, Christopher. 1994. *The Homeless.* Cambridge: Harvard University Press.
Jennings, Francis. 1984. *The Ambiguous Iroquois Empire.* New York: Norton.
Johnson, Barbara. 1988. "The Re(a)d and the Black." In Harold Bloom, ed. *Richard Wright's* Native Son. New York: Chelsea House.
Johnston, William B., and Arnold E. Packer. 1987. *Workforce 2000: Work and Workers for the Twenty-first Century.* Indianapolis: Hudson Institute.
Jordan, June. 1992. "Can I Get a Witness?" In The Black Scholar, ed.
Joyce, Joyce Ann. 1986. *Richard Wright's Art of Tragedy.* Iowa City: University of Iowa Press.
Judd, Dennis R., and Todd Swanstrom. 1994. *City Politics: Private Power and Public Policy.* New York: HarperCollins.
Kahne, Joseph. 1996. *Reframing Educational Policy.* New York: Teachers College.
Kairys, David. 1982. "Freedom of Speech." In David Kairys, ed. *The Politics of Law: A Progressive Critique.* New York: Pantheon.
———. 1993. *With Liberty and Justice for Some: A Critique of the Conservative Supreme Court.* New York: New Press.
Karplus, Walter J. 1992. *The Heavens Are Falling: The Scientific Prediction of Catastrophes in Our Time.* New York: Plenum.
Keane, John. 1984. *Public Life and Late Capitalism: Toward a Socialist Theory of Democracy.* Cambridge: Cambridge University Press.
Kelley, MaryEllen R. 1993. "Organizational Resources and the Industrial Environment: The Importance of Firm Size and Inter-Firm Linkages to the Adoption of Advanced Manufacturing Technology." *International Journal of Technology Management* 8.
Kelley, MaryEllen R., and Harvey Brooks. 1991. "External Learning Opportunities and the Diffusion of Process Innovations to Small Firms: The Case of Programmable Automation." *Technological Forecasting and Social Change* 39 (April): 103–25.

Kelman, Mark. 1991. "Reasonable Evidence of Reasonableness." *Critical Inquiry* 17 (Summer): 798–817.

Kilpatrick, William Heard. 1921. *The Project Method.* New York: Teachers College.

King Jr., Martin Luther. 1963. "I Have A Dream." Address at the Lincoln Memorial (August 28).

Kitsuse, John I., and Aaron Cicourel. 1963. "A Note on the Use of Official Statistics." *Social Problems* 11: 131–39.

Koenig, Louis W. 1986. *The Chief Executive.* San Diego: Harcourt Brace Jovanovich.

Kofsky, Frank. 1993. *Harry S. Truman and the War Scare of 1948.* New York: St. Martin's.

Kolbert, Elizabeth. 1995. "The Vocabulary of Votes: Frank Luntz." *New York Times Magazine* (March 26): 46–49.

Krishnamutri, Jiddu. 1953. *Education and the Significance of Life.* New York: Harper.

Kurth-Schai, Ruthanne. 1992. "Ecology and Equity: Toward the Rational Reenchantment of Schools and Society." *Educational Theory* 42, 2: 147–63.

Kusnet, David. 1992. *Speaking American: How the Democrats Can Win in the Nineties.* New York: Thunder's Mouth.

Lane, Robert. 1962. *Politcal Ideology: Why Common Man Believes What He Does.* New York: Free Press.

Larson, Erik. 1994. "A False Crisis: How Workplace Violence Became a Hot Issue." *Wall Street Journal* (October 13): A1, A10.

Latour, Bruno. 1986. "The Powers of Association." In John Law, ed. *Power, Action, and Belief: A New Sociology of Knowledge?* New York: Routledge.

———. 1993. *We Have Never Been Modern.* Cambridge: Harvard University Press.

Leffler, Melvyn P. 1984. "The American Conception of National Security and the Beginnings of the Cold War, 1945–48." *American Historical Review* 89, 2 (April): 346–81.

———. 1992. *A Preponderance of Power: National Security, the Truman Administration, and the Cold War.* Stanford: Stanford University Press.

Lewis, Anthony. 1993. "Secrecy and Cynicism." *New York Times* (27 December): A17.

Lewontin, Richard C., Steven Rose, and Leon J. Kamin. 1984. *Not in Our Genes: Biology, Ideology, and Human Nature.* New York: Panethon.

Linfield, Michael. 1990. *Freedom Under Fire: U.S. Civil Liberties in Times of War.* Boston: South End.

Lipsky, Michael. 1984. "Bureaucratic Disentitlement in Social Welfare Programs." *Social Service Review* 58:1 (March): 3–27.

Litvan, Laura M. 1994. "Casting a Wider Employment Net." *Nation's Business* (December): 49–51.

Lodge, Tom. 1983. *Black Politics in South Africa Since 1945.* New York: Longman.

Los Angeles *Times.* 1993. "Fear Clouds Search for Violence's Genetic Roots." (December 30): 1.

Loury, Glenn C. 1994. "Listen to the Black Community." *The Public Interest* 117 (Fall) 19: 35.

Lowi, Theodore J. 1969. *The End of Liberalism.* New York: Norton.

———. 1985. "Foreward." In Raymond Seidelman. *Disenchanted Realists: Political Science and the American Crisis, 1884–1984.* Albany: SUNY Press.

———. 1992. "The State in Political Science: How We Become What We Study." *American Political Science Review* 86: 1–7.

Lubiano, Wahneema. 1992. "Black Ladies, Welfare Queens, and State Minstrels: Ideological War by Narrative Means." In Toni Morrison, ed.

Luhmann, Niklas. 1990. *Political Theory in the Welfare State.* Berlin: Walter de Gruyter.

Luker, Kristin. 1984. *Abortion and the Politics of Motherhood.* Berkeley: University of California Press.

Lyotard, Jean-Francois. 1984. *The Postmodern Condition: A Report on Knowledge.* Minneapolis: University of Minnesota Press.

MacDonald, Andrew. 1980. *The Turner Diaries,* 2nd ed. Washington, D.C.: National Alliance.

Magnet, Myron. 1993. *The Dream and the Nightmare: The Sixties' Legacy to the Underclass.* New York: Morrow.

Makhijani, Arjun. 1992. *From Global Capitalism to Economic Justice: An Inquiry into the Elimination of Systemic Poverty, Violence and Environmental Destruction in the World Economy.* New York: Apex.

———. 1994. "Energy Enters Guilty Plea." *Bulletin of the Atomic Scientists* 50 (March–April): 18–29.

Malcolm, Andrew H. 1987. "What Five Families Did After Losing the Farm." *New York Times* (February 4): A1.

Marcosson, Samuel. 1995. "The 'Special Rights' Canard in the Debate Over Lesbian and Gay Civil Rights." *Notre Dame Journal of Law, Ethics & Public Policy* 9: 137–183.

Marshall, Eliot. 1993. "NIH Told to Reconsider Crime Meeting." *Science* 262 (October 1): 23–24.

Marx, Karl. 1972. "The Eighteenth Brumaire of Louis Bonaparte." In Robert C. Tucker, ed. *The Marx-Engels Reader,* 2nd ed. New York: Norton.

Matusow, Allen J. 1984. *The Unraveling of America: A History of Liberalism in the 1960's.* New York: Harper Torchbooks.

Mayer, Jane, and Jill Abramson. 1994. *Strange Justice: The Selling of Clarence Thomas.* Boston: Houghton Mifflin.

McCann, Michael. 1994. *Rights at Work: Pay Equity Reform and the Politics of Legal Mobilization.* Chicago: University of Chicago Press.

McCann, Michael W., and Gerald L. Houseman. 1989. *Judging the Constitution: Critical Essays on Judicial Lawmaking.* Glenview, Ill.: Scott, Foresman.

McCarthy, Michael. 1983. *Dark Continent: Africa as Seen by Americans.* Westport, Conn.: Greenwood.

McClure, Kirstie. 1993. "On the Subject of Rights: Pluralism, Plurality and Political Identity." In Chantal Mouffe, ed. *Dimensions of Radical Democracy: Pluralism, Citizenship, Community.* New York: Verso.

McKinley, Edward H. 1974. *The Lure of Africa: American Interests in Tropical Africa, 1919–1939.* Indianapolis: Bobbs-Merrill.

McPhail, Brenda M., ed. 1995. *NAFTA NOW! The Changing Political Economy of North America.* Lanham, Md.: University Press of America.

Melucci, Alberto. 1989. *Nomads of the Present.* Philadelphia: Temple University Press.

Mencken, H. L. 1943. *The American Language.* New York: Knopf.

Mestel, Rosie. 1994. "What Triggers the Violence Within?" *The New Scientist* (February 26): 26–34.

Metz, Steven. 1986. "The Anti-Apartheid Movement and the Populist Instinct in American Politics." *Political Science Quarterly* 101(3): 379–395.

Miller, John C. 1951. *Crisis in Freedom: The Alien and Sedition Acts.* Boston: Little, Brown.

Miller, Ron. 1992. *What Are Schools For? Holistic Education in American Culture.* Brandon, Vt.: Holistic Education Press.

Mills, C. Wright. 1958. *The Causes of World War III.* New York: Simon and Schuster.

Milwaukee County Welfare Rights Organization. 1972. *Welfare Mothers Speak Out: We Ain't Gonna Shuffle Anymore.* New York: Norton.

Minter, William. 1986. *King Solomon's Mines Revisited: Western Interests and the Burdened History of Southern Africa.* New York: Basic Books.

———. 1994. *Apartheid's Contras: An Inquiry into the Roots of War in Angola and Mozambique.* London: Zed Press.

Mishel, Lawrence, and Ruy A. Teixeira. 1991. *The Myth of the Coming Labor Shortage: Jobs, Skills, and Incomes of America's Workforce 2000.* Washington, D.C.: Economic Policy Institute.

Mitchell, W. J. T. 1994. *Picture Theory.* Chicago: University of Chicago Press.

Moffitt, Robert. 1992. "Incentive Effects of the U.S. Welfare System: A Review." *Journal of Economic Literature* 30 (March): 34–36.

Mohanty, Chandra Talpade. 1991. "Cartographies of Struggle: Third World Feminism and the Politics of Feminism." In Chandra Talpade Mohanty, Ann Russo, and Lourdes Torres, eds. *Third World Women and the Politics of Feminism.* Bloomington: Indiana University Press.

Mootry, Maria K. 1984. "Bitches, Whores and Women Haters: Archetypes and Typologies in the Art of Richard Wright." In Richard Macksey and Frank E. Moorer, eds. *Richard Wright: A Collection of Critical Essays.* Englewood Cliffs, N.J.: Prentice-Hall.

Morone, James A. 1990. *The Democratic Wish: Popular Participation and the Limits of American Government.* New York: Basic Books.

Morris, Roger. 1977. *Uncertain Greatness: Henry Kissinger and American Foreign Policy.* New York: Harper and Row.

Morrison, Toni. 1992. "Introduction: Friday on the Potomac." In Toni Morrison, ed. *Race-ing Justice, En-gendering Power: Essays on Anita Hill, Clarence Thomas, and the Construction of Social Reality.* New York: Pantheon Books.

Moynihan, Daniel P. 1969. *Maximum Feasible Misunderstanding: Community Action in the War on Poverty.* New York: Free Press.

Murphy, Paul L. 1979. *World War I and the Origin of Civil Liberties in the United States.* New York: Norton.

Murray, Charles. 1984. *Losing Ground: American Social Policy 1950–1980.* New York: Basic Books.

Myers, Anthony J. 1968. "U.S. and South Africa: The Ties, the Differences." *U.S. News and World Report* 64 (April 22): 96–99.

Narayan, Uma. 1988. "Working Together Across Difference: Some Considerations on Emotion and Political Practice." *Hypatia* 3, 2: 31–47.

Nation Institute, The. 1991. "Clarence Thomas: Career, Writings and Decisions," (September 5): 1–35.

National Association of Secondary School Principals. 1996. *Bulletin* (April).

National Health Policy Forum. 1997. *Joblessness, the Urban Underclass, and Welfare Reform, Highlights of a Discussion with William Juius Wilson, Ph.D., September 20, 1996.* Washington, D.C.: George Washington University.

National Institutes of Health. 1994. *Report of the Panel on NIH Research on Antisocial, Aggressive, and Violence-related Behaviors and Their Consequences.* Bethesda, Md.: NIH, April.

National Opinion Research Center. 1991. Poll (February–April).

National Research Council. 1994. *Understanding and Preventing Violence,* vol. II: Biobehavioral Influences. Washington, D.C.: National Academy Press.

Nelkin, Dorothy. 1995. "Biology Is Not Destiny" *New York Times*: A27.

Neustadt, Richard E. 1960. *Presidential Power.* New York: John Wiley.

New Republic, The. 1996. "White Lies, Black Lives: Rethinking Race and Crime" (Special Issue, January 1).

New York Times. 1992. "Young Black Men" (May 7): A26.

———. 1993. "For Black Women, Space Isn't the Frontier" (March 3): B13.

———. 1994. "In Their Own Words: The Republican Promises" (November 9): A12.

———. 1995. "Race Certainly Has a Biological Reality" (November 4): A22.

———. 1996. "After Decade, Juvenile Crime Begins to Drop" (August 9): A1.

Newman, Kathleen. 1993. *Declining Fortunes: The Withering of the American Dream.* New York: Basic Books.

Nixon, Richard M. 1960. Acceptance Speech, Republican National Convention, Chicago (July 28).

———. Acceptance Speech. Candidate for President. *Vital Speeches of the Day.* XXXIV (September 1): 674–77.

———. 1971. State of the Union Message. *Vital Speeches of the Day.* XXXVII (February 1): 226–30.

Nixon, Rob. 1994. *Homelands, Harlem and Hollywood: South African Culture and the World Beyond.* New York: Routledge.

Noer, Thomas J. 1985. *Cold War and Black Liberation: The United States and Black Liberation in Africa, 1948–1968.* Columbia: University of Missouri Press.

Norton, Anne. 1993. *Republic of Signs: Liberal Theory and American Popular Culture.* Chicago: University of Chicago Press.

Nye Jr., Joseph S. 1990. *Bound to Lead: The Changing Nature of American Power.* New York: Basic Books.

O'Brien, David. 1993. *Storm Center: The Supreme Court in American Politics,* 3rd ed. New York: Norton.

O'Donnell, L., S. Cohen, and A. Hausman. 1990. *The Evaluation of Community-based Violence Prevention Programs. Background paper prepared for the Forum on Youth Violence in Minority Communities: Setting the Agenda for Prevention.* Newton, Mass.: Educational Development Center.

OECD. 1985. "Employment in Small and Large Firms: Where Have the Jobs Come From?" *Employment Outlook.* Chapter 4.

Offe, Claus. 1985. *Disorganized Capitalism: Contemporary Transformations of Work and Politics.* Cambridge: MIT Press.

Office of National Drug Control Policy, The White House. 1994. *National Drug Control Strategy: Reclaiming Our Communities from Drugs and Violence.* Washington, D.C.: The White House.

O'Grady, John. 1993. "The Social Side of NAFTA: Labour Adjustment, Income Distribution, and Labour Standards." In A. R. Riggs and Tom Velk, eds.

Ollman, Bertell. 1990. Introduction. In Bertell Ollman and Jonathan Birnbaum, eds. *The United States Constitution: 200 Years of Anti-Federalist, Abolitionist, Feminist, Muckraking, Progressive, and Especially Socialist Criticism.* New York: New York University Press.

———. 1993. "The Ideal of Academic Freedom as the Ideology of Academic Repression, American Style." In *Dialectical Investigations.* New York: Routledge.

Orren, Karen. 1995. "The Primacy of Labor in American Constitutional Development." *American Political Science Review* 89: 377–88.

Osborne, David E., and Ted Gaebler. 1992. *Reinventing Government: How the Entrepreneurial Spirit Is Transforming the Public Sector.* New York: Penguin.

Ottaway, David, and Walter Pincus. 1985. "MX Vulnerability 'No Longer An Issue.' " *Manchester Guardian Weekly* (17 March).

Pascale, Celine-Marie. 1995. "Normalizing Poverty." *Z Magazine* (June): 38.

Pateman, Carole. 1988. *The Sexual Contract.* Stanford: Stanford University Press.

———. 1989. *The Disorder of Women.* Stanford: Stanford University Press.

Patton, Cindy. 1993. "Tremble, Hetero Swine!" In Michael Warner, ed. *Fear of a Queer Planet: Queer Politics and Social Theory.* Minneapolis: University of Minnesota Press.

———. 1995. "Refiguring Social Space." In Linda Nichlolson and Steven Seidman, eds. *Social Postmodernism: Beyond Identity Politics.* Cambridge: Cambridge University Press.

Paulos, John Allen. 1988. *Innumeracy.* New York: Hill and Wang.

Peterson, Paul E. 1995. *The Price of Federalism.* Washinghton, D.C.: Brookings Institution.

Peterson, Paul, and Mark C. Rom. 1990. *Welfare Magnets: A New Case for a National Standard.* Washington D.C.: Brookings Institution.

Peschek, Joseph. 1993. "Raymond Williams: Culture, Politics, and Democracy." *New Political Science* 27: 17–30.

Pinckney, Darryl. 1995. "Promissory Notes." *New York Review* (April 6): 41–46.

Piore, Michael J., and Charles F. Sabel. 1984. *The Second Industrial Divide: Possibilities for Prosperity.* New York: Basic Books.

Piven, Frances Fox. 1990. "Ideology and the State: Women, Power, and the Welfare State," in Linda Gordon, ed.

Piven, Frances Fox, and Richard A. Cloward. 1979. *Poor People's Movements: Why They Succeed and How They Fail.* New York: Vintage Books.

———. 1982. *The New Class War: Reagan's Attack on the Welfare State and Its Consequences.* New York: Pantheon Books.

———. 1993. *Regulating the Poor: The Functions of Public Welfare,* updated edition. New York: Vintage Books.

Plato. 1961. "The Republic II." *The Collected Dialogues.* Edith Hamilton and Hunting Carins, eds. Princeton: Princeton University Press.

Powell, Colin L., with Joseph E. Persico. 1995. *My American Journey.* New York: Random House.

Prothrow-Stith, Deborah, with Michaele Weissman. 1991. *Deadly Consequences: How Violence Is Destroying Our Teenage Population and a Plan to Begin Solving the Problem.* New York: HarperPerennial.

Providence *Journal.* 1989. "Best Lines Slung from Tongues in '88" (January 3): B4.

Public Culture. 1994. "The Black Public Sphere" 7.

Rabban, David M. 1981. "The First Amendment in Its Forgotten Years." *Yale Law Journal* 90: 514–595.

Randall, Clarence. 1963. "South Africa Needs Time." *Atlantic* 211 (May): 78–80.

Ranney, David C. 1994. "Labor and an Emerging Supranational Corporate Agenda," *Economic Development Quarterly* 8, 1: 83–91.

Reagan, Ronald. 1981. *Public Papers of the President.* Washington, D.C.: Office of the Federal Reserve, National Archives and Records Service, General Services Administration.

———. 1987. Remarks on arrival at West Lafayette, Ind. (April 9).

Reddy, William M. 1992. "Postmodernism and the Public Sphere: Implications for an Historical Ethnography." *Cultural Anthropology* 7, 2 (May): 134–68.

Reich, Robert B. 1992. *The Work of Nations: Preparing Ourselves for 21st Century Capitalism.* New York: Vintage Books.

Rein, Martin, and Donald Schon. 1994. *Frame Reflection: Toward the Resolution of Intractable Policy Controversies.* New York: Basic Books.

Reiss Jr., Albert J., and Jeffrey A. Roth, eds. 1993. *Understanding and Preventing Violence.* Washington, D.C.: National Academy Press.

Reiss Jr., Albert J., Klaus A. Miczek, and Jeffrey A. Roth, eds. 1994. *Understanding and Preventing Violence, Volume II: Behavioral Influences.* Washington, D.C.: National Academy Press.

Remnick, David. 1995. "Negative Capability." *The New Yorker* (December): 40–44.

Reston, James. 1978. "A Republican Manifesto." *New York Times* (May 5).

Ricci, David M. 1984. *The Tragedy of Political Science: Politics, Scholarship, Democracy.* New Haven: Yale University Press.

Ridgeway, James. 1994. "This Is Not Only a Test." *Village Voice* (January 5–11): 15–16.

Riggs, A. R., and Tom Velk, eds. 1993. *Beyond NAFTA: An Economic, Political and Sociological Perspective.* Vancouver, British Columbia: Fraser Institute.

Roe, Emery. 1994. *Narrative Policy Analysis.* Durham: Duke University Press.

Roelofs, Joan. 1992. "Foundations and Political Science." *New Political Science.* 23: 328.

Rogin, Michael. 1987. *Ronald Reagan, the Movie and Other Episodes in Political Demonology.* Berkeley: University of California Press.

Rohrer, Judy. 1996. "Is It Right to Focus on 'Rights'?" *Harvard Gay and Lesbian Review* 3(1): 1, 56–58.

"Ronald Reagan and David Brinkley: A Farewell Interview." 1988. ABC News broadcast (December 22).

Roosevelt, Theodore. 1889. *The Winning of the West.* New York: Putnam's.

Roper, William. 1991. "The Prevention of Minority Youth Violence Must Begin Despite Risks and Imperfect Understanding." *Public Health Reports* 106 (May–June): 229–31.

Roper Organization. 1938. Survey (November).

———. 1984. Survey.

———. 1987. For the *Wall Street Journal,* mid-October 1986. Reported in *The Polling Report* (February 23): 1.

Rose, Nikolas. 1990. *Governing the Soul: The Shaping of the Private Self.* London: Routledge.

———. 1991. "Governing by Numbers: Figuring Out Democracy." *Accounting, Organizations and Society* 16:7: 673–92.

Rose, Nikolas, and Peter Miller. 1992. "Political Power Beyond the State: Problematics of Government." *British Journal of Sociology* 43:2 (June): 173–205.

Rosen, Jeffrey. 1995. "The War on Immigrants." *The New Republic* 212 (January 30): 22–26.

Rosenberg, Emily S. 1993. "Commentary: The Cold War and the Discourse of National Security." *Diplomatic History* 17, 2 (Spring): 277–84.

Ross, Edward Alsworth. 1914. *The Old World in the New.* New York: Century.

Ross, William G. 1994. *A Muted Fury: Populists, Progressives, and Labor Unions Confront the Courts, 1890–1937.* Princeton: Princeton University Press.

Rossignol, Marie-Jeanne. 1995. "Early Isolationism Revisted: Neutrality and Beyond in the 1790's." *Journal of American Studies* 29: 215–27.

Rossiter, Clinton. 1960. *The American Presidency.* New York: New American Library.

Rousseau, Jean-Jacques. 1911. *Emile.* New York: Everyman Library.

Rubin, Lillian B. 1972. *Busing and Backlash: White Against White in an Urban School District.* Berkeley: University of California Press.

Russell, Bertrand. 1926. *Education and the Good Life.* New York: Boni & Liveright.

Sales Jr., William W. 1992. "Comments on the Controversy Surrounding the Nomination and Confirmation of Judge Clarence Thomas to the Supreme Court." In The Black Scholar, ed.

Samuelson, Robert J. 1993. "The Isolationist Illusion." *Newsweek* 122 (November 22): 28.

———. 1995. "Global Mythmaking." *Newsweek* 124 (May 8): 55.

Sandel, Michael J. 1996. *Democracy's Discontents: America in Search of a Political Philosophy.* Cambridge: Harvard University Press.

Sanders, Jerry. 1983a. *Empire at Bay: Containment Strategies and American Politics at the Crossroads.* New York: World Policy Institute.

———. 1983b. *Peddlers of Crisis: The Committee on the Present Danger and the Politics of Containment.* Boston: South End Press.

Sandroff, Ronni. 1990. "Why It Won't Be Business as Usual." *Working Woman* 15 (January): 58–62.

Schacter, Jane. 1994. "The Gay Civil Rights Debate in the States: Decoding the Discourse of Equivalents." *Harvard Civil Rights—Civil Liberties Law Review* 29: 283–317.

Schmitt, Eric. 1996. "English as Official Language Wins Backing of House Panel." *New York Times* (July 25): A11.

Schneider, Keith. 1993. "1950 Note Warns About Radiation Test." *New York Times* (December 28): A8.

Schram, Ryan. 1995. "Smoking Cultures." Proposal to the National Endowment for the Humanities.

Schram, Sanford F. 1995. *Words of Welfare: The Poverty of Social Science and the Social Science of Poverty.* Minneapolis: University of Minnesota Press.

———. 1997. "Welfare Cuts to Hit Legal Immigrants the Hardest." *The Honolulu Advertiser* (January 19): B1.

Schram, Sanford F., and Gary Krueger. 1994. " 'Welfare Magnets' and Benefit Decline: Symbolic Problems and Substantive Consequences." *Publius* 24, 4 (December): 44–67.

Schuck, Peter H. 1995. "The Message of 187: Facing up to Illegal Immigration." *The American Prospect* 21 (Spring): 85–92.

Schwartz, Mildred A. 1995. "NAFTA: Where Are We Going." In Brenda M. McPhail, ed.

Scott, James C. 1990. *Domination and the Arts of Resistance: Hidden Transcripts.* New Haven: Yale University Press.

Seidelman, Raymond. 1985. *Disenchanted Realists: Political Science and the American Crisis, 1884–1984.* Albany: SUNY Press.

Selzer, Mark. 1992. *Bodies and Machines.* New York: Routledge.

Sengenberger, Werner, Gary W. Loveman, and Michael J. Piore. 1990. *The Re-Emergence of Small Enterprises: Industrial Restructuring in Industrialized Countries.* Geneva, Switzerland: International Institute for Labour Studies.

Shapiro, Michael J. 1988. *The Politics of Representation: Writing Practices in Biography, Photography, and Policy Analysis.* Madison: University of Wisconsin Press.

———. 1993. *Reading "Adam Smith": Desire, History and Value.* London: Sage.

———. 1995. "The Ethics of Encounter: Unreading/Unmapping the Imperium." Paper presented at the Annual Meeting of the International Studies Association. Chicago, Illinois (February).

Shapiro, Michael J., and Hayward R. Alker, eds. 1996. *Challenging Boundaries: Global Flows, Territorial Identities.* Minneapolis: University of Minnesota Press.

Shepherd, George. 1977. *Anti-Apartheid: Transnational Conflict and Western Policy in the Liberation of South Africa.* Westport, Conn.: Greenwood Press.

Shor, Ira. 1992. *Empowering Education: Critical Teaching for Social Change.* Chicago: University of Chicago Press.

Skolberg, Kai. 1994. "Tales of Change: Public Administration Reform and Narrative Mode." *Organization Science* 5, 2: 219–38.

Skowronek, Stephen. 1993. *The Politics Presidents Make: Leadership from John Adams to George Bush.* Cambridge: Harvard University Press.

Smith, Gaddis. 1986. *Morality, Reason, and Power: American Diplomacy in the Carter Years.* New York: Hill and Wang.

Smith, J. Allen. 1907. *The Spirit of American Government: Its Origins, Influence, and Relation to Democracy.* New York: Macmillan.

Smith, Rogers M. 1988. "Political Jurisprudence, the New Institutionalism, and the Future of Public Law." *American Political Science Review* 82: 89–108.

Sollors, Werner. 1986. *Beyond Ethnicity: Consent and Descent in American Culture.* New York: Oxford University Press.

Spector, Malcolm, and John I. Kitsuse. 1977. *Constructing Social Problems.* Menlo Park, Calif: Cummings.

Spring, Joel. 1994. *The American School 1642–1993.* New York: McGraw-Hill.

Stack, Carol B. 1996. *Call to Home: African-Americans Reclaim the Rural South.* New York: Basic Books.

———. 1974. *All Our Kin: Strategies for Survival in a Black Community.* New York: Harper & Row.

Staniland, Martin. 1983–84. "Africa, the American Intelligentsia and the Shadow of Vietnam." *Political Science Quarterly* 98 (Winter): 595–616.

———. 1991. *American Intellectuals and African Nationalists,* 1955–1970. New Haven: Yale University Press.

Statistical Abstract of the United States 1994. 1994. Washington, D.C.: U.S. Bureau of the Census.

Steel, Ronald. 1995. "The Domestic Core of Foreign Policy." *The Atlantic Monthly* 275, 6 (June): 84–92.

Steele, Jonathan. 1983. *Soviet Power: The Kremlin's Foreign Policy Brezhnev to Andropov.* New York: Simon and Schuster.

Stepan, Nancy, and Sander L. Gilman. 1993. "Appropriating the Idioms of Science: The Rejection of Scientific Racism." In Sandra Harding, ed., *The 'Racial' Economy of Science: Toward a Democratic Future.* Bloomington: Indiana University Press.

Stevenson, Richard W. 1995. "Researchers See Gene Link to Violence But Are Wary." *New York Times* (February 19): 29.

Stone, Allucquère Rosanne. 1991. "Will the Real Body Please Stand Up?: Boundary Stories about Virtual Cultures." In Michael Benedikt, ed. *Cyberspace: First Steps.* Cambridge: MIT Press.

———. 1995. *The War of Desire and Technology at the End of the Mechanical Age.* Cambridge: MIT Press.

Stone, Deborah. 1988. *Policy Paradox and Political Reason.* Boston: HarperCollins.

———. 1997. *Policy Paradox: The Art of Political Decision-Making.* New York: Norton.

Swidorski, Carl. 1994. "Corporations and the Law: Historical Lessons for Contemporary Practice." *New Political Science* 28/29: 167–209.

———. 1995. "Constituting the Modern State: The Supreme Court, Labor Law, and the Contradictions of Legitimation." In David S. Caudill and Steven J. Gold, eds. *Radical Philosophy of Law.* Atlantic Highlands, N.J.: Humanities Press.

Swoboda, Frank. 1990. "Students of Labor Force Projections Have Been Working Without a 'Net.' " *Washington Post* (November 6): A17.

Tanner, Michael, Stephen Moore, and David Hartman. 1995. "The Work vs. Welfare Trade-Off: An Analysis of the Total Level of Welfare Benefits by State." Policy Report No. 240 (September 19). Washington, D.C.: Cato Institute.

Tardiff, K., P. M. Marzuk, A. C. Leon, C. S. Hirsch, M. Stajic, L. Portera, and N. Hartwell. 1995. "A Profile of Homicides on the Streets and in the Homes of New York City." *Public Health Reports* 110 (January–February): 13–17

Tedford, Thomas L. 1985. *Freedom of Speech in the United States.* New York: McGraw-Hill.

Thach Jr., Charles C. 1923. *The Creation of the Presidency, 1775–1789.* Baltimore: Johns Hopkins University Press.

Thomas, Clarence. 1989. "The Higher Law Background of the Privileges and Immunities of the Fourteenth Amendment." *Harvard Law Journal of Law and Public Policy* 12: 63–70.

Thomas, Rich. 1993. "NAFTA: More Winners Than Losers." *Newsweek* 122 (November 29): 30.

Thompson, E. P. 1980. "The State of the Nation." In *Writing By Candlelight.* London: Merlin Press.

Tobias, Andrew. 1993. "Why NAFTA Is Good Medicine." *Time* 142 (November 15): 47.

Tolday, Stewart, and E. M. Beck. 1995. *A Festival of Violence.* Chicago: University of Illinois Press.

Tolley Jr., Howard. 1990–91. "Interest Group Litigation to Enforce Human Rights." *Political Science Quarterly* 105, 4 (Winter): 617–38.

Tulis, Jeffrey. 1987. *The Rhetorical Presidency*. Princeton: Princeton University Press.

Turner, Bryan. 1984. *The Body & Society: Explorations in Social Theory*. Oxford: Basil Blackwell.

Turner, Stansfield. 1985. *Secrecy and Democracy: The CIA in Transition*. Boston: Houghton Mifflin.

U.S. Bureau of the Census. 1989. "Technology Usage in U.S. Manufacturing Industries: New Evidence from the Survey of Manufacturing Technology," paper CES 91–7.

U.S. Civil Service. 1981. *Survey* (March 5–18).

U.S. Congress, Committee on Foreign Affairs. 1977. Hearings before the Subcommittee on African Affairs. *Ambassador Young's African Trip*. 95th Congress, 1st Session (June 6): 6–7.

U.S. Congress, Office of Technology Assessment. 1994. *Technologies for Understanding and Preventing Substance Abuse and Addiction*. OTA-EHR-597-S (September).

U.S. Department of Labor. 1987. *Workforce 2000: Executive Summary*.

U.S. House of Representatives. 1989a. *Hearing on Workforce 2000 and on H.R. 2235, Committee on Education and Labor*. June 15.

———. 1989b. *Hearing on H.R. 2235, Workforce 2000 Employment Readiness Act of 1989, Committee on Education and Labor*. November 3.

U.S. House of Representatives, Committee on Ways and Means. 1993, 1994. *The Green Book*. Washington, D.C.: U.S. Government Printing Office.

U.S. Senate, Judiciary Committee. 1991. *Hearings before the Committee on the Judiciary on the Nomination of Judge Clarence Thomas to be Associate Justice of the Supreme Court of the United States* (September 20–October 13), vols. 1–4.

U.S. Senate, Committee on the Judiciary. 1993. *Children and Gun Violence*. Senate Hearing 102–1067 (June 9 and September 13).

Urofsky, Melvin I. 1988. *A March of Liberty: A Constitutional History of the United States*. New York: Knopf.

Van Gelder, Lindsey. 1985. "The Strange Case of the Electronic Lover." *Ms.* (October): 94–104.

Veblen, Thorstein. 1953. *The Theory of the Leisure Class*. C. Wright Mills, introduction. New York: New American Library.

Vieira, Sergio, William G. Martin, and Immanuel Wallerstein, eds. 1992. *How Fast the Wind: Southern Africa, 1975–2000*. Trenton, N.J.: Africa World Press.

Wald, Priscilla. 1995. *Constituting Americans: Cultural Anxiety and Narrative Form*. Durham: Duke University Press.

Walker, J. Samuel. 1990. "The Decision to Use the Bomb: A Historiographical Update." *Diplomatic History* 14, 1 (Winter): 97–114.

Walker, Michael A. 1993. "Free Trade and the Future of North America." In A. R. Riggs and Tom Velk, eds.

Warner, Michael. 1992. "The Mass Public and the Mass Subject." In Craig Calhoun, ed. *Habermas and the Public Sphere*. Cambridge: MIT Press.

Washburn, Wilcombe E., ed. 1964. *The Indian and the White Man*. New York: New York University Press.

Weatherford, Jack. 1988. *Indian Givers*. New York: Fawcett/Columbine.

Weeks, Jeffrey. 1995. *Invented Moralities: Sexual Values in an Age of Uncertainty*. New York: Columbia University Press.

Weiler, Kathleen. 1988. *Women Teaching for Change: Gender, Class and Power.* New York: Bergen & Garvey.

Western, Bruce. 1995. "Union Decline in Eighteen Advanced Capitalist Countries." *American Sociological Review* 60, 2 (April): 179–201.

White, Hayden. 1979. "Michel Foucault." In John Sturrock, ed. *Structuralism and Since: From Levi Strauss to Derrida.* New York: Oxford University Press.

———. 1980. "The Value of Narrativity in the Representation of Reality." *Critical Inquiry* 7 (Autumn): 5–28.

White, John Kenneth. 1990. *The New Politics of Old Values.* Hanover, N.H.: University Press of New England.

White, Lucie. 1990. "Subordination, Rhetorical Survival Skills, and Sunday Shoes: Notes on the Hearing of Mrs. G." *Buffalo Law Review* 38:1 (Winter): 1–58.

Wiesel, David, and Buck Brown. 1989. "The Hyping of Small-Firm Job Growth," *Business Week* (November 8): 20.

Williams, Juan. 1987. "A Question of Fairness." *Atlantic Monthly* (February): 74.

Williams, Lena. 1992. "Companies Capitalizing on Worker Diversity." *New York Times* (December 15): A1, D20.

Williams, Patricia. 1991. *The Alchemy of Race and Rights.* Cambridge: Harvard University Press.

Williams, Raymond. 1977. *Marxism and Literature.* New York: Oxford University Press.

———. 1989. *Resources of Hope.* London. Verso.

Wills, Garry. 1978. *Inventing America.* New York: Vintage Books.

———. 1981. *Reagan's America: Innocents at Home.* Garden City, N.Y.: Doubleday.

———. 1995. "Thomas' Confirmation: The True Story." *New York Review* (February 2): 36–43.

Wilson, James Q. 1967. "A Guide to Reagan Country: The Political Culture of Southern California." *Commentary* (May): 37–45.

Wilson, James Q., and Richard Herrnstein. 1985. *Crime and Human Nature.* New York: Simon and Schuster.

Wilson, Michael H. 1993. "NAFTA's History and Future Prospects." In A. R. Riggs and Tom Velk, eds.

Wirthlin, Richard B. 1981. "Final Report of the Initial Actions Project" (January 29).

———. 1988. Interview. Washington, D.C. (November 22).

Wiseman, Michael. 1993. "Welfare Reform in the States: The Bush Legacy." *Focus* 15 (Spring): 18–36.

Wodiczko, Krzysztof. 1995. *Art public, art critique: textes, propos et documents.* Paris: Ecole Nationale Superior des Beaux-Arts.

Wolff, Edward N. 1995. "How the Pie Is Sliced: America's Growing Concentration of Wealth." *The American Prospect* 22 (Summer): 58–64.

Wolin, Sheldon. 1987. "Democracy and the Welfare State: The Political and Theoretical Connections Between *Staatsrason and Wohlfahrtsstaatsraon.*" *Political Theory* 15, 4 (November): 467–500.

Wolpert, Julian. 1993. *Patterns of Generosity in America.* New York: Twentieth Century Fund Press.

Wright, Richard. 1991 (1940). *Native Son.* New York: Harper.

Wrona, Remi L. 1995. "The NAFTA Dilemma." In Brenda M. McPhail, ed.

Yergin, Daniel. 1977. *Shattered Peace: The Origins of the Cold War and the National Security State.* Boston: Houghton Mifflin.

Zizek, Slavoj. 1989. *The Sublime Object of Ideology*. London: Verso.

———. 1994. "The Spectre of Ideology." In *Mapping Ideology*. New York: Verso.

———. 1995. "Between Fiction and Fantasy." *Cardozo Law Review* 16: 1511–32.

Cases Cited

Adarand v. Pena, No. 93-1841 U.S. (1995).

Anderson v. Green, 1995 WL 68473 (U. S.), (February 22, 1995).

Bowers v. Hardwick, 478 U.S. 186 (1986).

Brown v. Board of Education, 347 U.S. 483 (1954).

Evans v. Romer, 854 P.2d 1270 (Colo. 1993).

Evans v. Romer, 882 P.2d 1335 (Colo. 1994).

Hague v. CIO, 307 U.S. 496 (1939).

Hudson v. McMillan, 503 U.S. 1 (1992).

Lochner v. New York, 198 U.S. 45 (1905).

RAV v. St. Paul, 505 U.S. 377 (1992).

Romer v. Evans, 94-1039 (United States Supreme Court, May, 20,1996).

Shapiro v. Thompson 394 U.S. 618 (1969).

Shaw v. Reno, 509 U.S. 630 (1993).

United States v. Carolene Products Co., 304 U.S. 144 (1938).

United States v. X-Citement Video, No. 93-723 U.S. (1995).

Index

About the Contributors:

Joel Best, chair and professor of sociology at the University of Southern Illinois-Carbondale, and editor of Social Problems, teaches courses in social problems and social movements.

Barbara Cruikshank, assistant professor of political science at the University of Massachusetts at Amherst, teaches courses in political theory and political economy.

Donald R. Culverson, assistant professor of political science at the University of Houston, teaches courses in political economy and U.S. politics.

R. Scott Daniels, received his Ph.D. in political science from the University of Hawai'i at Manoa in 1996; he is currently research specialist with the University of Hawai'i Research Corporation.

Charles R. Green, professor of political science at Macalester College, St. Paul, Minnesota, teaches courses in public policy and political theory.

Gerard Fergerson, assistant professor of public policy and history at the Wagner School of Public Policy at New York University, teaches courses in public policy and social history.

Jonathan Goldberg-Hiller, assistant professor at the University of Hawai'i at Manoa, teaches courses in public policy, constitutional law, and political theory.

Joseph Kling, associate professor of government at St. Lawrence University, in Canton New York, teaches courses in U.S. politics, political economy, and urban politics.

Gary Krueger, associate professor of economics at Macalester College, teaches courses in econometrics and comparative economic systems.

Ruthanne Kurth-Schai, associate professor of education at Macalester College, teaches courses in education and public policy.

Philip T. Neisser, associate professor of politics at State University of New York College at Potsdam, teaches courses in political theory and political economy.

Lawrence Nitz, associate professor of political science at the University of Hawai'i at Manoa, teaches courses in research methods and public policy.

Joseph Peschek, chair and associate professor of political science at Hamline University, St. Paul, Minnesota, teaches courses in political theory and political economy.

Frances Fox Piven, distinguished professor of political science at the Graduate Center of the City University of New York, teaches courses in political economy and public policy.

Miriam B. Rosenthal, doctoral candidate in political science at the University of Hawai'i at Manoa, is writing a dissertation in the American Dream.

Phillip H. Sandro, director of the Higher Education Consortium of Universities of the Twin Cities, teaches courses in political economy, public policy, and urban politics.

Sanford F. Schram, visiting professor of social work at Bryn Mawr College of Social Work and Social Research, teaches courses in public policy, political economy, and political theory.

Michael J. Shapiro, professor of political science at University of Hawai'i at Manoa, teaches courses in political theory.

Carl Swidorski, professor of political science at College of St. Rose, Albany, New York, teaches courses in political theory, U.S. politics, and constitutional law.

Leslie J. Vaughan, visiting assistant professor of political science at the University of Minnesota-Duluth, teaches courses in political theory, U.S. politics, and constitutional law.

John Kenneth White, professor of politics at Catholic University of America, Washington, D.C., he teaches courses in U.S. politics, the presidency, and political parties.